YOUR CHOICE OF
A-LEVELS

Mary Munro and
Alan Jamieson

The essential guide
to A-level subjects
and examinations

CRAC

Hobsons Cambridge

Acknowledgements
The editors and publishers are most grateful to the subject contributors who provided articles and a great deal of advice, and to the secretaries and examination officers of the Examination Boards.

CRAC publications are published under exclusive licence and royalty agreements by Hobsons Limited. The Careers Research and Advisory Centre is an independent non-profit-making body.

P355/d10rq/C/HE
ISBN: 0 86021 739 6

Published 1981 by Hobsons Limited,
Bateman Street, Cambridge CB2 1LZ
Reprinted 1982, 1983
Second Edition, 1985

Contents

Section 1
Courses and methods

Introduction: choosing your A-levels

What do you want to know about A-levels?

When you begin to think about your choice of advanced level subjects you need a lot of advice and information to help you. You need to know, for example, which subjects go well together at A-level, which subjects you need for this or that career, which subjects you need to get a place at university or college, and so on.

There may be other questions, too, puzzling you. What is really involved in studying, say, economics at A-level? What is the content of physics, art, design, geology? Is A-level geography like ordinary level geography, only harder and with more field trips? How much is A-level French different from — and harder than — O-level or CSE French? Is it true you can get up to A-level standard in Spanish in two years from scratch? Is A-level art just painting all day?

Then there are the subjects you may never have come across before. Do you know what's involved in studying sociology, psychology, general studies, engineering science and history of art? What do they involve, and how can you find out what you will be doing if you choose to take an A-level course in one of these subjects?

Some people know the answers

In order to help you find out the answers to some of these questions, experienced teachers and lecturers have been asked to write short chapters about their own subjects. They explain what the A-level courses cover, and describe what goes on both inside the classroom and outside it. They write about homework, fieldwork, laboratory and workshop teaching. They tell you about practicals, projects, syllabuses.

Most of the writers are also experienced examiners. Some are chief or senior examiners for one of the eight Examination Boards which set and mark A-level examinations, so they know exactly how students' examination work is assessed. Finally, they are people who have devoted most of their working lives to their subjects because they are deeply interested in them, and they hope that you will be, too.

Ask your teachers

It is important to realise that these subject chapters give only one person's view of the subject. The staff at your school, sixth-form college or further education college may have other ideas. The book is not intended to be used instead of talking to your teachers, attending open days or open evenings, or going to talks and discussions about the various subjects and what they lead to. You should do all of these things. *Your choice of A-levels* is a starting point. You should use the book as a beginning, helping you to find out about these subjects, so that you can add to your knowledge by talking to teachers at your local centres.

Making your choice

You will find over 45 different subjects in this book. But it is very unlikely that you will have a free choice of all of them. School sixth forms are restricted in the number of subjects they can offer, and although in sixth-form colleges and further education colleges the choice is generally wider than in schools, there will not be a total choice. Financial restrictions of one kind or another have slowed down the expansion of courses. You may be faced with making a decision between the choice of A-levels at your local school or college, or travelling some distance to another college to study an unusual subject.

A glance at the league table of the numbers of student entries for the various subjects shows that the vast majority of students take subjects whose names are familiar to you from O-level and CSE: maths, physics, English, history, geography. But don't forget that these subjects are very different at A-level from O-level and CSE courses. It is important to find out what these subjects will be like at A-level and not just assume they will be a continuation of O-level.

There may be other factors. For example, the methods and the quality of teaching a certain subject at your present school may mean that you have dismissed the idea of studying it for A-level. Think again. Give the subject a fair chance. It may come alive for you at A-level, or with a different teacher.

For new and unfamiliar subjects it is most important to find out what is involved. Don't just go for the novelty value of a subject; instead, make sure your interest is based on a realistic picture of what the subject is all about.

Careers, jobs and higher education

Another vitally important consideration when choosing your A-levels is where they are going to lead you afterwards. In each chapter you will find information about the careers which could be open to you after taking these A-level courses. There is also a lot of information and advice about further courses at universities, polytechnics and colleges.

We hope, therefore, that this book will help you with your

choice of A-levels. Remember that it is only a starting point. You should read more about these subjects and talk to people — teachers, lecturers, employers and friends — about them. *Your choice of A-levels* won't give you all the answers, but it will help you to ask the right questions of yourself and of other people.

Chapter 2

Entry totals for A-level subjects

In the summer term, 1983, there were over 600,000 A-level entries for examinations taken in schools and colleges and other A-level centres in the United Kingdom. The table below shows the total numbers of 'home' entries by academic subject for the eight Examination Boards in England and Wales. In Appendix D you will find a table showing which examination boards offer the various subjects.

Entry total for A-level subjects, summer 1983
(The 1980 position is shown in parentheses.)

1 Mathematics	89,630		(1)
	approx 73,574 candidates		
	11% SMP & 1.7% MEI		
2 English literature	67,030		(2)
3 Physics	56,678 (16% Nuffield)		(3)
4 Chemistry	46,378 (15% Nuffield)		(4)
5 General studies	46,017		(8)
6 Biology	43,805 (6% Nuffield)		(6)
7 History	40,871		(7)
8 Economics	40,082		(5)
9 Geography	36,544		(9)
10 French	25,779		(10)
11 Art	25,137		(11)
12 Sociology	18,183		(12)
13 Government and politics	10,191		(14)
14 German	9,365		(13)
15 Computer science	6,777		(24)
16 Law	6,033		(15)
17 Religious studies	5,933		(16)
18 Home economics	5,657		(18)
19 Accounting	4,984		(17)
20 Music	4,767		(19)
21 Geology	4,177		(20)
22 Psychology	3,228		(26)
23 Technical drawing	3,159		(21)
24 Spanish	2,962		(23)
25 Business studies	2,869		(30)
26 Economic history	2,696		(22)
27 Latin	2,357		(25)
28 Human biology	2,162		(33)
29 History of art	2,105		(27)
30 Statistics	2,055		(28)

31 Craft, design and technology	1,878		(38)
32 Theatre studies	1,561		
33 Social biology	1,368		(36)
34 Communication studies	1,232		(43)
35 Ancient history	1,175	(52% JACT)	(34)
36 Crafts	1,131		(32)
37 Classical civilisation	1,074	(50% JACT)	(35)
38 Italian	739		(37)
39 Zoology	702		(31)
40 Physical science	683	(78% Nuffield)	(29)
41 Electronics	679		
42 Environmental science	631		(48)
43 Welsh	566		(41)
44 Photography	507		(45)
45 Engineering science	452		(40)
46 Greek	471		(42)
47 Woodwork	344		(47)
48 Russian	308		(46)
49 Building	304		(49)
50 Physics and mathematics	281		
51 Botany	246		(44)
52 Metalwork	234		(50)
53 Surveying	231		
54 Ceramics	117		(56)
55 Archaeology	62		(58)
56 Logic	48		(55)
57 Embroidery	48		(39)
58 Horticulture	21		(57)
59 Chinese	20		(53)

Chapter 3

A-level courses

Length of courses

A-level courses usually last for two academic years, with exams taken after six terms of full-time study. Older students sometimes take intensive one-year courses, reaching the exam after only a year of study. Others, who may only be able to attend part-time classes, take one subject at a time over several years. But for the majority of students, A-levels follow on immediately after O-level, and most students usually study two or three (occasionally four) subjects.

If you aim to go on to university after A-levels, you should attempt three subjects. Some A-level centres encourage all students to start with three subjects, with the option of dropping one at the end of the first year. Other schools and colleges prefer students who are not going to university to concentrate on two subjects, and to take more O-levels, OA-levels or other courses at the same time. For older students who have had a break from study and who wish to take A-levels as preparation for a university course, two subjects would be sufficient, especially if they are trying to complete the course in one year.

The vast majority of students take A-levels during June, although the AEB and Cambridge Boards also offer a limited range of the most common subjects in November, and the London Board also runs examinations in January.

Building on your O-levels

Before deciding about A-levels, it is very important to make sure that you have an adequate background of O-level and CSE passes to build on.

A-level study is of a much more intensive academic nature than O-level study and involves more reading and essay-writing, the acquisition of more detailed knowledge, and a more analytical approach to the subject. So, if you only just scraped through O-level, you may find your A-level course very hard going indeed. Some schools and sixth-form colleges insist on a fixed entry requirement of four or five O-levels or CSE grade 1 passes; others have no restrictions. But no centre would advise a 16-year-old with the barest minimum of O-levels to go on to A-levels, unless there were very unusual circumstances.

The range of O-level subjects is also important. It is very useful but not essential to have passes in English language, mathematics and a science subject, and also a modern foreign language. These provide a good broad base which will keep

17

open a wide range of career and further course options. Even if you could scrape passes in one or two A-levels without adequate O-levels behind you, you would not be able to make much use of them afterwards. Entry requirements for most courses of higher education and for most careers are firmly in terms of A-level and O-level passes, with a minimum of five different subjects usually required. For adults or mature students these requirements are less rigid, but for them it could also be a mistake to try to move too quickly into advanced studies without adequate background preparation.

If you are not sure about going on for A-levels, discuss it with your teachers. It may be wiser to think of other courses or career plans, or even spending an extra year consolidating O-level studies. You could, for example, study another science subject, take an entirely new subject, or sit O-levels in subjects you took originally at CSE, before you go on to the next stage.

Choosing arts or science subjects

When choosing A-level subjects, most people concentrate on either arts and humanities, or science subjects. However, mixed A-levels are becoming much more common. The reason for specialisation is usually because of future career plans. On the science side, many degree courses require at least two science A-levels. Therefore, by taking three sciences, students have a much greater choice for science careers at the end of an A-level course. For example, the most common combinations of science subjects are maths, physics and chemistry, and physics, chemistry and biology. Both open up a wide range of scientific careers and courses. The combination of maths, physics and history, although broad in educational terms, actually narrows the choice of scientific careers by eliminating all those which require chemistry. To take a more extreme example, suppose you chose one science subject (chemistry), one arts subject (history) and one social science subject (sociology), you would certainly study a broad range of subjects. But this combination could be too narrow in the sciences to enable you to make use of the science subject in a scientific career. Mathematics or biology are often taken with two arts and social science subjects, and these can be very useful groupings as long as the mathematics student has quite decided against going on to study engineering or sciences in higher education, and the biology student does not hope to study biology beyond A-level without chemistry to support it.

On the arts and humanities side, English, economics,

history, French and geography are popular subjects and can be grouped or combined in any format. Students wishing to go on to study languages in further or higher education should usually take two modern languages at A-level although this is not essential. A foreign language is useful but not essential for people interested in going on to study history or English after A-level. In general, there is more flexibility on the arts side, because very few courses have strong vocational implications, and students are encouraged to follow their interests. It is important to note that many degree courses and careers accept students who have studied any subjects at A-level so long as they have shown reasonable success in doing so. It is possible, therefore, to experiment and to choose unusual subjects in combination with familiar ones, but make sure you fully explore the implications of doing so for further courses or careers.

In general, therefore, you should choose at least two but preferably three science subjects if you wish to have the option of entering a scientific, medical or technical career. Arts subjects lead towards careers in administration, financial services, sales, social services and creative fields. Students with mixed A-levels or with arts A-levels and with maths and at least one other science O-level, can find openings in semi-technical fields such as architecture, surveying, nursing, other careers related to medicine, and industrial management, production management, purchasing and marketing.

Balancing interests and career options

If you were choosing your A-levels on purely logical grounds in terms of the width of opportunities, taking maths, physics and chemistry would undoubtedly leave open the widest range of options. Many of the non-scientific professions such as accountancy, journalism, librarianship and business management also welcome students with science A-levels. However, if everyone did A-levels in only these subjects it would be a very dull world indeed! For students with no interest in science subjects, it would be unwise to select these as A-levels. There is a wide range of careers open to people with arts, humanities and social science qualifications, and this includes some quite technical careers in industry and business. In arriving at the right choice of A-levels, you are trying to balance four important factors:

- your academic interests
- your personal abilities, aptitudes and skills

- the width of career choice
- subjects available in your school, college, or A-level centre.

Number of A-levels

It is one of the more regrettable things about our present system of education that choice of A-levels has to be made early in your school career and on a base of two or three subjects. Some schools offer the chance to do four A-levels, but this is usually three familiar or grouped subjects, plus an extra or linked subject such as general studies, further maths, or art. For example, to take maths, physics, chemistry and biology, or history, English, French and German would be a very heavy programme, and is not recommended.

Most people who are accepted on university courses have studied three subjects to A-level. Those accepted with two are usually mature students, or those who are special cases, for example when unusual circumstances make it impossible to take three subjects. With increased competition for places in universities, many more people going on to degree courses in polytechnics have also studied three A-levels. However for many careers and most courses in polytechnics and colleges of higher education, two A-levels is a sufficient entry qualification and some students are better advised to concentrate on two subjects at A-level, and make up their timetable with non-A-level subjects or courses. Studying only one A-level is not likely to be useful although you can in theory get into some courses, such as higher diplomas at polytechnics or colleges, with one A-level pass. Although entry to these diploma courses specifies only one A-level pass, in practice many of the courses (particularly on the technical side) require the student to have studied another subject to A-level, even if an exam pass has not been obtained. There are some students in sixth forms and colleges who attempt one A-level with other subjects at O-level, or with vocational studies such as secretarial subjects. You should realise, however, that there are few courses or careers for which only one A-level is a required entry, and two A-level passes open up many more possibilities.

Subject combinations and new subjects

There are several very traditional subject combinations. Among them are maths, physics and chemistry, and physics, chemistry and biology. On the arts side English, history and French is a very popular grouping, as is geography, history and economics. These traditional combinations have the advantage of keeping open very wide ranges of options, and are all well-known and respected academic subjects. But, increasingly, students are now offered a much wider choice, not only in different combinations of well-known school subjects, but also in the possibility of starting a new subject at A-level. Among these are the history of art, ancient history, psychology, computer sciences, communication studies, and others. The idea of a fresh subject can be very appealing but it is important to find out what is involved and not choose a subject simply because it is new. You must look at the career implications as well as the content of the course, and make sure it is going to suit you better than the traditional school subjects you already know something about.

You will see from the table of subject entries that over 85% of the A-level examinations taken each year are in very familiar traditional school subjects such as maths, physics, English, chemistry, biology, history, geography, French, and art. You will also see that economics and sociology are the most popular of the newer subjects. General studies also comes high on the list as it is a traditional A-level for students sitting the A-level examinations of the JMB. It is often taken as a fourth A-level (see section on general studies).

Getting more popular every year are accounting, law, computer science, government and politics, history of art and theatre studies. But these are still taken by relatively few people. None of these newer subjects are likely to be made entry requirements for either jobs or degree or other courses in higher education. Employers and admissions staff know they are only offered in a few centres and so if they are not available to you do not be too disappointed. If you are interested in the subject, you will be able to apply for a course in higher education even if you have not studied it at A-level.

The availability at A-level of subjects such as those above and others such as business studies, geology, environmental sciences, building, and philosophy which have previously only been available at degree level can lead to some confusion. Students rather naturally suppose that they would have to take A-level in, for example, geology or business studies in order to get on to a degree course in that subject. But this is not the case and these 'new' subjects are never required for entry. In fact in many cases the traditional school subjects may be preferable for the reasons given in the section above as they leave open a wider range of choice and keep more options open. If degree or other courses have named specific subjects as entry requirements, these will only be traditional school subjects. Quite a number of courses and careers will accept students who have taken any A-level subjects, and 'new' subjects will be acceptable for these, but the options open to you if you take at least some familiar subjects in your A-levels are wider.

So if you are keen on a 'new' subject and it is available in your A-level centre, a compromise may be best: thus a new subject could be mixed with more traditional subjects. Taking three *new* subjects could seriously narrow the range of future careers or courses, particularly if your range of O-levels is rather narrow too. If you have a particular career in mind or a range of careers, check the likely requirements first. If you are interested in going on to university or polytechnic you should check the entrance requirements of the courses you would like to have as possibilities. A vocational-sounding A-level may not necessarily be an advantage, particularly if it is taken instead of a basic subject such as maths or physics, English or French. On the other hand it could be to your advantage if taken with those basic subjects.

If you want to study a very unusual subject you will have to wait until you get to higher education where you could take on anything from acoustics to Zulu!

A-level examinations

The examinations for A-levels are set by eight different Examination Boards for England and Wales (you will find the addresses in Appendix C). In Scotland, the Scottish Certificate of Education Examination Board sets exams at 'Ordinary' and 'Higher' grades which are different from O- and A-levels. Some Scottish schools and colleges also enter students for English Boards' A-level examinations. Not all Examination Boards offer all the subjects and syllabuses listed in this book. A full list of subjects and Boards is in Appendix D. Local education authority schools and colleges usually enter pupils for the examinations of the Board in their region, and most public schools have traditionally taken exams of the Oxford and Cambridge Board. The Associated Examining Board (AEB) is the only Board to be independent of university control, and it has traditionally designed special syllabuses to suit the colleges of further education. These traditions are nowadays breaking down and schools and colleges are selecting courses which best suit their staff and facilities. The Examination Boards often co-operate with each other in designing new syllabuses, particularly experimental projects such as SMP

(School Mathematics Project) mathematics, Nuffield sciences and the classics syllabus of JACT (Joint Association of Classics Teachers). In the past, so many different syllabuses have grown up that there is now considerable pressure for the Boards to make their syllabuses more alike and to cover a basic common core in each subject. This process has now begun and will start to affect some of the A-level syllabuses in two or three years' time.

How examinations are set and marked

For each subject of each Examination Board, the syllabuses are prepared by specialists, many of whom are subject teachers at university, college or school level. The examination questions are set by a team of senior examiners working with a chief examiner, and a marking scheme is agreed. The other examiners who mark the scripts are recruited on a part-time basis mainly from the teaching profession (both active and retired!). These examiners meet the senior examiners to agree on the marking scheme and procedures. During the marking process, several sample marked scripts from each examiner are re-checked by the senior examiner to ensure that there are equal standards throughout the team.

Students are given a mark for each question and each script, and these are added together with other marks for oral work, for example, in a language exam, or projects, where the syllabuses permit it. The distribution of marks of all entrants is then checked by the senior examiners, and grades of A,B,C,D,E,O and F are awarded. A,B,C,D and E are pass grades, and O is equivalent to an O-level pass grade C or above. F is an outright fail.

The problem of setting the borderlines or divisions between grades is given to a panel of experienced examiners. Guidance for the setting of the borderlines is taken from the full range of students' marks and from records of previous years' decisions. The accuracy and fairness of these divisions is tested by a panel of examiners who re-examine a broad sample of students' scripts lying across these dividing lines. When they are satisfied, the grades are then finally established.

When the results are published, usually in mid-August for the June exams, the student's school or college can appeal to the Examination Board for a re-marking if they feel the result is inaccurate. In practice, very few of these appeals lead to re-grades, and schools and colleges are reluctant to appeal except where there is a very strong case.

Illness and other problems

If the student is unwell immediately before or during the exam, this can be taken into account by the examiners. A doctor's letter should be sent to the Board at the time of the examination and not when the results come out! Students with special problems, such as broken wrists, dyslexia or physical handicaps should appeal for special consideration. Extra time may be allowed, or a scribe (writer) or amanuensis can be provided. These arrangements should be made well in advance by the exam centre or the school. Entries for the June examination have to be made by the middle of February and by the end of September for the November or January exams. Late entries are possible but may involve an extra fee.

Special papers

Students who are very strong academically can also enter for a Special or S paper in their A-level subjects. This will involve doing an extra exam in the subject. The exam is designed to test a deeper understanding of the subject than the A-level papers. The questions are normally within the syllabus of the A-level paper but of a more searching type. They are designed to test a candidate's intellectual grasp and capacity to think about the subject. Candidates for Special papers usually have extra classes in the subject, normally in the second year of an A-level course. Attainment is by 1 (distinction) or 2 (merit) grades, or unclassified for those who fail to qualify for an award.

Some schools are more geared to entering students for Special papers than others. These papers are not essential qualifications for entry purposes to any university. However some Oxford and Cambridge colleges may give a student who is known to be taking S papers an offer of a place, which is conditional on passing both A-level and S paper. If your school or college does not offer the opportunity to take these papers you will not be at any disadvantage. The vast majority of students are better advised to concentrate their efforts on achieving the best grades they can on A-level subjects. S papers do have a useful role for very bright students who enjoy the stimulus of undertaking more testing and additional work.

OA level

Boards also offer many subjects at OA or AO level. These Alternative Ordinary or Ordinary Alternative exams are at a level between O- and A-levels, and are based on A-level syllabuses. They are usually designed as one-year courses.

A-level grades required by universities and polytechnics
In 1983, approximately 157,000 UK students applied for university places, and approximately 70,000 were successful. The grades required varied considerably from one university to another and from one subject to another. Students seeking entry to some universities will find that they need to have A or B grades in all of their A-levels. Other universities or departments accept students to some courses with D or E grades. However, selection is not by grades alone. Other factors such as your school or college reports, your educational background, health, O-level grades, and interview, if there is one, all have a bearing.

As a general guide, the average grades of students getting places on arts or humanities courses at universities are approximately two Bs and one C (B,B,C). The average grades for science departments are around three Cs (or B,C,D). Some popular subjects such as medicine, law and veterinary science demand very much higher grades, such as A,A,B. Other subjects such as maths, physics or classics, which have far fewer applicants, ask students for high grades because of the nature of the subject. It is also probable that students who expect to get lower grades may be advised to apply for an alternative subject.

The popularity of subjects, and therefore the A-level grades sought for these subjects, varies from year to year. In the past few years, vocational courses such as medicine, law, accountancy and business studies have increased in popularity, whereas languages and social sciences have become less popular. Recently, too, applications to courses in electronics, electronic engineering and computer sciences have increased substantially.

Polytechnics, colleges of higher education and further education colleges
The entry grades for polytechnic degree courses are on the whole lower than university, but again there are variations between subjects and between polytechnics. The pressure on places for different subjects at universities is reflected in the applications to polytechnics. For example, it may be possible for someone with three C grades at A-level to be offered a polytechnic place for a popular subject such as law and a university place for a less popular subject such as economics.

At colleges of higher education the pressure is very much less, and except for a few very popular courses students can usually get a place with a minimum of two A-level passes (plus three suitable O-level passes in other subjects).

For higher diploma courses at polytechnics and further education colleges where the formal entrance requirements are one A-level pass, with supporting O-levels, there is a wide range of standards. Some students on these courses may have two or three A-level passes at much higher than minimum grades. The vocational courses they wish to study will normally not be offered at a university. For specialist courses at polytechnics or colleges of music, drama and art, the actual grades at A-level play a very much smaller part in the selection procedure. Other factors such as art-folios, coursework and auditions are of major importance.

Entry to careers

For people going into jobs after A-levels and aiming for further qualifications by part-time study, two A-level passes are extremely useful. Entry as a student to various professional bodies such as the Association of Certified Accountants, the Royal Institution of Chartered Surveyors, and the Chartered Insurance Institute requires two A-level passes or the equivalent BTEC (Business and Technician Education Council) qualification. For a wide range of professional and semi-professional careers, two A-levels and supporting O-levels are minimum qualifications even for people starting at 18 or 19. For students with only one A-level pass, the choice is not so wide and they may have to start lower down the career ladder, or choose a field of work where there is not such a strong tradition of examination qualifications, and where selection and progress depend more on personal qualities and other skills.

Entry qualifications to the medical profession and related careers also go up and up each year. Now, almost all para-medical (such as physiotherapy, speech therapy, dietetics etc) courses, with the exception of nursing, require at least two good A-level passes in addition to a wide range of O-levels including maths and science subjects. Full details of each career area and its entry qualifications can be obtained from some of the books recommended at the end of this book, or from your local careers office or school careers library. *Jobs and Careers After A-levels*[1] is a useful guide for those going into work after

[1] *Published by CRAC.*

A-levels and gives career profiles for 42 A-level leavers in a wide range of jobs.

A-levels: what are the alternatives?

Before you get down to the serious consideration of which A-levels to study, it is worth making sure you are really aiming in the right direction. Earlier, we considered the wisdom of proceeding too quickly to A-levels before fully consolidating O-level studies, but for the 16-year-old who wishes to stay in education there are other alternatives. Your local further education college will be able to offer a range of certificate and diploma courses for the qualifications of BTEC (Business and Technician Education Council). These are one-, two-, and three-year courses which are rather broader in scope than A-levels and usually have a vocational orientation. For example, you could take a two-year BTEC national diploma course in sciences, engineering, catering, building and construction, business studies or in computer studies. Your local further education college may also offer vocational courses such as catering, nursery nursing or secretarial studies. These may be a more sensible choice than A-levels for some students.

You shouldn't think that further full-time study for its own sake is bound to be a career advantage. Many employers prefer to take on 16-year-olds with O-level passes (usually maths and English), and are much less keen to take on an 18-year-old with poor or failed A-levels. Students who are unlikely to be successful at A-levels or those who genuinely prefer part-time study might be better to try to get onto a good training scheme and try to increase their qualifications by day-release courses. The Youth Training Scheme has increased opportunities for 16-year-olds to do this, and many employers are still keen to recruit well-qualified fifth-year leavers.

In fields such as engineering where there is a strong tradition of training technicians by means of apprenticeships, it may be wiser to try for one of these at 16 and to continue studying by day-release for a BTEC certificate. On the other hand, you may feel you would be capable of succeeding both at A-levels *and* later on a degree or higher diploma course. The main entry points to careers in engineering are at O-level and at graduate or higher diploma level. A-level students are usually only recruited in order to be sponsored on degree or diploma courses. In some career areas there is not a strong tradition of recruiting A-level students, and this should be borne in mind when considering your future career.

Fuller details of all the alternative courses available to 16-year-olds are explained in other books published by CRAC[2]. Many local education authorities also publish booklets giving information about courses available in the schools and colleges in their area. You should also ask your local college of further education for a prospectus of courses both full-time and part-time.

Summary

When choosing your A-levels, the most important thing for you to remember is to try to balance your interests with career and further course implications. How this is done will vary from one person to another, but a wise strategy is to try to keep open as many likely options as possible. This does not mean choosing three unappealing subjects in order to leave open options of careers which are of no interest! A sensible balance should be your aim. When in doubt, it always seems preferable to go for a subject you are really keen on. Your interest and enthusiasm are likely to lead to success and a high grade, and that in itself is good for future courses, employment prospects, and also for you!

It is also worth noting that although universities in general have apparently fairly rigid requirements in terms of A-level subjects, there is almost always one university, polytechnic or college somewhere which will offer you a course you want to do even if you have taken subjects other than those usually required. For instance, it is possible to enter a course in engineering without A-level physics; to take a degree in English without A-level English, a degree in biology without A-level chemistry. However this does not mean you shouldn't consider your A-level subjects very seriously. If you are in the situation described above, your choice is very limited and you will have to make up your lack of knowledge very quickly once you get on to your higher education course.

[2]*Decisions at 15/16+*, *Your Choice at 17+* and *Beyond School* (all CRAC publications).

Chapter 4

Places to study, timetabling, teaching and learning methods

A-level centres

A-level courses are available in school sixth forms, sixth-form colleges, further education centres, and tertiary colleges (colleges which offer a full range of courses, full-and part-time, for 16- to 19-year-olds and adults). Some students also study for A-levels by correspondence course or at private tutorial centres and a few do so entirely on their own. Many students will have some choice of where they wish to take their A-level course, although for others there won't be any choice. This will depend on the facilities available to you locally.

Where there is an opportunity to change place of study at 16, some students are attracted to the idea of going to a sixth-form college or a further education college. They feel this new environment will give them an adult status, away from the regulations, uniform, organisation and responsibilities which they associate with school.

Other students prefer to stay on in their own well-known, familiar environment with teachers they have had and liked in the past. Here, at school, they can enjoy the more independent and individualistic atmosphere of the sixth form. Although there may be more choice of subjects at a further education centre or other type of sixth-form college, it is very important to consider the social differences too. Make sure you get the right facts about your local college and the students who go there. Do not rely on local stories and rumours. Don't forget, too, that it can be very time-consuming and of doubtful value to travel long distances each day in order to study an unusual subject not available at a school nearer home. Other considerations such as facilities for sport, art, music and drama, and other extra activities outside the A-level course will be relevant to the choice of centres.

Most A-level centres publish booklets and hold open days or open evenings. At these times prospective students and their parents can see round the college, meet the staff, and talk about the courses and subjects offered. This is an opportunity which you are well advised to make use of, both to get an idea of the atmosphere in the sixth form or further education centre and also to take the opportunity to discuss your choice of subject with the specialist teachers who will teach you if you choose that course.

Timetabling

On most full-time two-year A-level courses, students have five or six hours on the timetable per subject. Some centres work on a 40-minute period timetable; other centres have double 40-minute periods. This can mean the equivalent of seven or eight single periods per subject. Further education colleges and some schools operate on an hourly timetable, and classes usually consist of one-hour blocks. It is very common to have double periods for subjects such as physics, chemistry and biology, where a lot of practical work is involved, and for subjects such as art, music, and craft, design and technology.

A-level centres (schools, sixth-form colleges or colleges of further education) try to organise their timetables to allow students a maximum choice of subjects. However, this is not always easy, particularly with a small sixth form, so you may find that the three subjects you are interested in are offered but cannot be combined together because of timetable clashes. Subjects are often divided into blocks and students can choose one subject from each of three or four blocks. The blocks are designed to facilitate the most popular and common subject combinations and it is usually only unusual combinations which cause problems. There are considerable differences in methods of timetabling and you can only find out about these from the individual centres.

Spare time
If you are studying three A-levels, these will take up about three-quarters of your timetable time in the sixth form or sixth-form college. During the rest of the time, you may well have the opportunity to study for extra O-levels, OA levels (eg additional mathematics) or perhaps do another subject such as general studies for A-level, or alternatively take a programme covering a wide variety of other activities, as well as private study periods. A full general studies programme could aim towards taking general studies at A-level, described fully in a later chapter, or 'general studies' could be a term used for a programme covering things as diverse as study skills, computing, art, music, woodwork, metalwork, careers education, work experience and community work. Students sometimes have a choice of several activities and you may wish to use the time to follow up hobby interests, or start a new subject, or join sports clubs and societies. Alternatively, you may prefer to do something practical as a relief from the bookwork of the rest of your A-level programme. You may also be able to spend some time on work experience (say on a half a day a week basis) if your school runs such a programme. This can help you with career plans at the end of your course.

When considering your activities outside A-levels, remember that both potential employers and university admissions tutors pay a good deal of attention to what students do with their spare time. A-level grades give only an indication of a student's academic abilities. Hobbies, interests and other activities give an indication of other qualities such as the ability to organise things, and to get on with other people. These wider interests help employers and admissions tutors to judge if you will be capable of coping with a position of responsibility in a job or with student life. Therefore, make full use of opportunities outside the A-level course. You will find there is a bonus: you will develop your interests and enjoy yourself.

For adults doing an A-level crash course, these extra opportunities will not be so easily available, nor will they be a very high priority. Crammers or tutorial centres also prune extra activities down to the barest minimum in order to devote the maximum resources to the A-level subjects. But for both these groups who are presumably taking A-levels with the particular purpose of gaining entry to higher education, it is important to remember that for them, too, admission staff are interested in the 'whole student' and not just in academic grades attained at A-level.

Teaching and learning methods
Teaching methods vary from subject to subject and from school to college. For science subjects, most of the timetabled periods of study are spent in laboratories, with a mixture of taught lessons, practical assignments and experiments. Similarly, craft and art subjects are taught in specialist rooms, studios, workshops and labs.

On the arts side, teaching is mainly in small groups, and is a mixture of lectures and talks, and discussions based on reading assignments or essays. These can take place anywhere — in classrooms, lecture rooms, in the library or in specialist tutorial rooms. Modern languages at A-level are primarily concerned with the study of literature, so access to a language laboratory although desirable is not essential.

When you move from O-level to A-level, you move to a higher level of work. This brings with it more personal responsibilities. Your teachers will expect you to show evidence of an academic attitude to work. This means you will be expected to read more widely than at O-level, to work on your own without supervision, to make full use of school and public libraries, to discuss ideas with students on the same course, and all without detailed supervision by the teacher. In science, maths and lab or workshop subjects, you will be expected to work outside formal timetabled periods, and to complete tasks which you started but didn't finish in class time.

Using the time to advantage

Each subject has its own methods of study. You will find detailed descriptions of teaching techniques and what students have to know and do in each subject section of this book. On the arts side, most courses require extensive reading. You must expect to go beyond the textbooks, to read biographies and specialised books, and consult the academic journals (under the supervision of the teacher) relevant to the subject. You will be taught how to write well-constructed essays and reports. You will be given lots of practice in discussing topics which arise out of your reading and essay work. Some of the best teaching at A-level is where the teacher or tutor leads a discussion on some aspect of literature, or on a knotty historical problem, or on a business or economics subject which is presently in the news. In this way, you will be taught how to argue logically and lucidly, using the facts and your knowledge of books to present a case, or your opinion.

In science, you will be introduced to the methods of scientific inquiry, learning how to make observations, how to set up experiments, how to observe carefully, and how to record your findings. There will be, too, a lot of textbook-reading in science as there is in the arts subjects, but you should expect to go beyond the basic textbook into wider sources of knowledge, reading topic books, articles in scientific magazines such as *New Scientist* and watching television programmes such as *Horizon* on BBC. You will also be encouraged to develop related skills in, for example, computing and statistics.

On your own

As you can see, whatever subject you are studying, you must expect to work for a lot of the time on your own. Your teachers will give you book-lists, essay questions, assignments, project outlines, design briefs and so on. They will take you on field trips, to libraries and museums, to law-courts, manufacturing and business companies and universities. But you will be expected to show personal responsibility in following up the suggestions and the leads which teachers give you. You should extend the formal, timetabled work by arranging your own trips and excursions, by exploring libraries, by finding out about lectures given locally at universities and colleges which might extend your knowledge, and perhaps by joining a local society concerned with a subject near to your A-level work.

Chapter 5

Money and jobs

Counting the cost

For anyone considering staying on in education for a full-time A-level course, the financial side is very important. If you attend a local education authority school or sixth-form college, you will not have to pay fees. Students in further education centres in their own county (provided they are under 19) do not pay fees for full-time courses, books or equipment or for transport costs, and are in much the same situation as school pupils. LEAs also pay the cost of the examination fees and travel. Free lunches are available for low-income families in the same way as at a school.

For older students in further education colleges and for those at private schools or colleges, tuition fees and other expenses will have to be met by the students and their families. The current cost of a one-year full-time A-level course in a local further education college can be obtained from your local college, or from the local education authority. You will probably find part-time study is a lot cheaper than full-time, but you will not get so much teaching. Examination fees are about £9-10 per subject. Other expenses incurred will include travel, living expenses, books and stationery. For some students who have to attend field trips, or provide calculators or laboratory coats, there will be some additional expenses.

Grants and maintenance allowances

It is extremely difficult to get a grant for A-level courses. The only financial assistance towards living expenses available for students in the 16-19 age range is maintenance allowance for low-income families, available through the educational welfare office of the local education authority. These allowances are worked out on a sliding scale depending on net family income. Local education authorities have been under some pressure recently to increase these allowances and the range of families who would benefit, and some authorities have responded more generously than others. When a young person stays on in full-time education after 16, the family will continue to receive child benefit until the end of the A-level or equivalent course. The only organisations to sponsor A-level students are the armed services. Another way of increasing income during this period is by taking a Saturday or evening job. Many students seem to manage a part-time job (where and when they can get them) at least in the first year of their A-level course, without adverse effects on their studies.

For the older student who wishes to return to full-time

education, the financial obstacles can be considerable. These students are faced with not only paying the fees and other expenses, but also having to manage without an income during the one-year or nine-month crash course. For this reason, many older students go to part-time or evening classes, or study by means of a correspondence course, while at the same time they continue in their job. If they achieve their objective of a place on a degree or diploma course at university, polytechnic or college, the financial side then becomes easier. Grants are available for higher education (indeed they are mandatory, enforced by law), provided the student fulfils the residential qualification and has not previously had a grant for this level of course. Details of grants and maintenance allowances can be obtained from your local education authority or through your present school. Information on fees, both full-time and part-time, can be obtained from your further education college.

Going on

Another factor to remember is that at the end of the first year of a two-year A-level course, you should start to have some ideas about further or higher education, or about getting a job. You should therefore, in your first year of A-level work, think about and find out about career and educational opportunities after 18. You should take advantage of any opportunities to visit local industry and other places of employment. Careers conventions are also ways of meeting people in careers areas which interest you, or you may be able to visit a local practitioner of an individual career. You should try to get an appointment to discuss your plans with your careers officer, and talk to the careers teacher, other teachers, your parents, employers and friends.

If you feel completely baffled about what to do next, you may be able to complete a careers interest questionnaire. This will involve answering questions about which activities and subjects you enjoy and which you would or would not like to be part of any future job. The results of the questionnaire should help to narrow down your choice of careers to three or four areas. You should then concentrate on finding out more about what is involved and the job opportunities in them.

If you are interested in going on to higher education, you should consult the school's careers library, send away for prospectuses, read CRAC's *Degree Course Guides*, and *Your Choice of Degree and Diploma*, and take any opportunity you can to visit a university or polytechnic. If you are hoping to go into a job after A-level, you also have a lot to do. To make the best of A-levels in a career requires as much, if not more, preparation and planning as doing a degree course. Read CRAC's *Jobs and Careers after A-levels*. Don't just sit back hoping something will come up because it may well not do so. Be positive! Use the careers library and discuss your interests and ideas with your careers teacher and careers officer. The careers officer will know a lot about local job opportunities and be able to put you in touch with likely employers. If there are unlikely to be any suitable openings in your area, or if you would like to work away from home, the careers officer's contacts will help here too. CRAC's *The Job Book* should be available in your careers library and it will give you an idea of some of the training schemes for A-level entrants run by large national employers. Your careers officer should be able to give you a list of local firms who employ A-level leavers in specialist areas such as accountancy, banking, computing, laboratory work etc. University, polytechnic and job applications take place in the first two terms of the second year of your A-level course. This should leave you free to concentrate on the A-level examinations in the summer term. Your future is too important just to leave to chance, so make time to work on this also during your A-level course.

Section 2
Subject Choice

Chapter 6

Mathematics and sciences

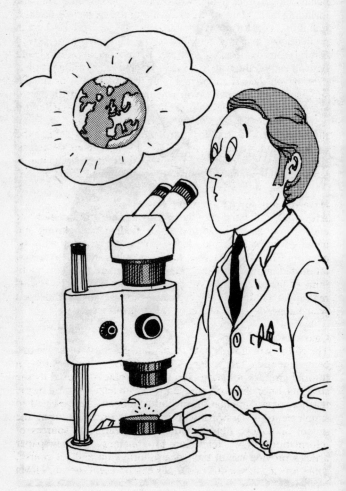

Biology (including human biology, botany and zoology)
by Mary Peach

What is A-level biology about?

A-level biology is concerned with the origins, structure and behaviour of the living world, both plants and animals, including man. Many of the problems of today, such as disease, pollution, conservation, the growth and control of human populations, and food supplies in the Third World are given careful consideration. The study of biology at A-level and beyond can be the way to a satisfying and worthwhile job, but even if you do not follow a career in a biological or related subject, it can also give you a lifelong interest in the world around you. It enables you to make the most of your leisure activities, whether they be the study and enjoyment of living things around you, walking, gardening, or simply watching the excellent natural history and medical programmes on television. Biology is so much a part of daily life that extended knowledge can only enhance your understanding and appreciation.

Have you any special interests?

Are you interested in the lifestyle and preservation of endangered species? Do you enjoy finding, recognising and naming wild animals and plants? Are you concerned with the environment? Do you care about people's health? Are you interested in pets and farm animals? If you are then you might think of taking biology as one of your A-level subjects. It adds real understanding to subjects such as these, and will deepen your knowledge and awareness of your interests.

Course of study

The course will include both theory and practical work, the one complementing the other. Theory lessons may be run in tutorial groups, involving discussion of topics prepared by the students, or on a more formal pattern with lectures given by the teacher, or a combination of both. Students are expected to supplement all classwork with background reading, using the school or college library and public libraries as sources of information. Many television programmes and newspaper articles provide useful biological information and, of course, some articles in scientific journals can be useful to an A-level biologist.

A proper understanding of mathematical concepts is required so that biological data can be interpreted correctly. Histograms, scatter diagrams and graphs using linear and logarithmic scales are widely used to interpret experimental data. In most schools and colleges you are expected to plan your own working time at home. You are given essays to write, which may be broad in character or may be more specifically geared to examination questions and, also, topics to prepare for class discussion.

Some Examination Boards set a special topic as part of the examination. The Oxford Local Examination Board is one of these: the range of topics includes industrial biology, public health and hygiene. The Joint Matriculation Board includes topics such as micro-organisms, birds, insects and crop production and protection.

Practical work
Practical work is carried out both in the laboratory and in the field. Some laboratory work will involve the use of a microscope for studying sections of plant and animal tissues, small whole organisms and parts of organisms. Simple dissection technique is used in the display and examination of the internal organisation of a mammal, usually a mouse or rat. Devising and carrying out experiments, and presenting and discussing results, form an important aspect of practical work in the laboratory. Fieldwork may consist of identifying and sampling plant and animal populations, of studying some of the factors that affect them, such as temperature, soil type, rate of water flow and of how natural communities may change over periods of time. Visits to field centres, although not essential, are desirable as they reinforce the importance of fieldwork to a biologist and the importance of ecology to us all. Some Boards (Cambridge, Oxford and Cambridge) offer optional experimental projects as part of the examination. A successful project could result in the awarding of a higher final grade to the candidate.

Is O-level biology necessary?
As biology has a technical vocabulary of its own, it obviously helps if the subject has been taken at O-level. However, if you are prepared to make the extra effort required in the early stages and read all you can, you should have no difficulty with A-level, even without an O-level pass in biology. On the other hand it is usually required that both chemistry and mathematics

are studied to at least an O-level standard. Some knowledge of physics is also an asset. Without some of this background knowledge, parts of an A-level biology course would prove very difficult to understand.

A-level syllabuses

The syllabuses of the various Examinations Boards have a common basic content, only varying from each other in minor ways. Your A-level biology course will therefore not really be affected by the Examination Board for which your school or college enters candidates.

The subject areas covered by all Boards include cell structure, both at microscopic and electron-microscope levels, and the organisation of plants and animals, that is, the ways in which their bodies are constructed.

The life processes, such as respiration, excretion, and control mechanisms of plants and animals form an important part of the common syllabus content. The study of populations and of environments, of reproduction and inheritance, and of evolution are also common to all syllabuses. In the Nuffield biology syllabus great emphasis is laid upon devising, carrying out experiments and analysing critically the results of such experiments. Only schools which are interested in this approach and which have sufficient laboratory space, ample resources and skilled laboratory assistance can effectively follow this syllabus.

Thus you study not only the technical and detailed structure of living organisms, but you are also able to consider their place in and their effect on the world in which we live today.

Examinations

The examination usually consists of two, sometimes three, theory papers and a practical component. Practical work is either assessed throughout the A-level course, that is, by continuous assessment (JMB) or is tested as a practical examination taken at the completion of the course together with the relevant theory papers (Oxford Local, Oxford and Cambridge, Welsh, and Cambridge). The practical grade awarded by the London Board is made up of a practical examination component and a teacher's assessment component, based on the student's practical work during the whole course. Where there is no practical examination, questions may be set in the theory papers which test experimental procedure. The style of theory papers depends on the requirements of the Examination Board. In one type of paper, candidates are required to select a set number of examination questions, in which the orderly presentation of facts in clear English is essential. Another type of paper consists of many compulsory short-answer questions, which may require the manipulation of data, interpretation of diagrams and selection of relevant facts. A further variation may involve both these types of question in separate sections of the same paper.

Scripts are marked by a panel of examiners composed of experienced teachers from schools, universities and higher education establishments. Marking schemes are drawn up before the examination is taken and are then amended, where necessary, after samples of candidates' scripts have been scrutinised by the examiners. The scripts are then placed in appropriate groupings and grades awarded accordingly. Where a separate practical examination is taken this is normally given a separate grading, eg a B grade overall and a C grade in practical will be shown as BC.

Subject combinations

Biology is very often taken with physics and chemistry at A-level. This is a very useful combination for most biology careers and for entry to further courses at university and polytechnic. Degree courses in biology, biochemistry, medicine, veterinary science, horticulture and agriculture all require A-level in chemistry for entry. Many of the ancillary medical professions such as dietetics, pharmacy and ophthalmic optics require one or both of these subjects. Biology could also be combined with other sciences such as physics and/or maths, but care must be taken to ensure the combination is sensible for the range of careers the student may be interested in. As biology becomes more biochemical, anyone intending to study a biologically-related subject after A-levels should include chemistry in his or her choice.

Biology could also be combined with arts subjects which can be very suitable for many of the paramedical careers mentioned below, for diploma level courses in horticulture and agriculture, and for a wider general education no matter which career is envisaged.

Careers

An A-level in biology can lead on to a wide variety of careers. Obviously it is very useful for entrance to a medical, dental or veterinary school, but there are many other professions concerned with the care of the sick such as nursing, physiotherapy, dietetics, speech therapy, occupational therapy, chiropody, osteopathy, radiography and pharmacy for which A-level biology is welcomed. Any one of these provides a career that gives the satisfaction of increasing the human health, happiness and social well-being of others. If you wish to care for people and have the necessary temperament then one of these might suit you.

For graduates in biochemistry, horticulture and agriculture (who would have studied A-level biology) there are openings in industries concerned with fertilisers, chemicals and seeds, with feeding-stuffs, and with various associations such as the Milk Marketing Board, National Dairy Council etc.

Biology graduates have more difficulty in finding work directly related to the subject of their degree course. Figures for 1982 leavers from universities showed that less than 20% were able to do so immediately. Others found jobs with employers who recruit graduates of any discipline, or took further training for research, teaching, nursing or other specialist areas. Those who have interests and/or skills in genetic engineering could have good prospects in the new and developing industries concerned with biotechnology.

For biologists who wish to train as laboratory technicians, posts are available in government and hospital laboratories, school, university and polytechnic laboratories, industry research associations, such as those for brewing, baking, wool, etc and in water authorities, etc. In most of these posts, opportunities exist for both training and studying for higher qualifications with good prospects of promotion. Here again interest and knowledge of chemistry is also essential.

Finally, it should be said that the study of biology can be regarded as a good background for a range of careers not directly concerned with the subject. The training of biologists, involving as it does some writing, the handling of data and problem-solving, taken together with a background interest in conservation, medical and other important concerns, means that these students are useful employees for a wide range of possible jobs.

Human biology

A syllabus in A-level human biology is offered by the Associated Examining Board and is essentially the study of mammalian structure and physiology. The emphasis throughout is on man; thus, in the section on man's environment, stress is laid on how man affects his environment and how the environment affects man. This section also includes parasites of man such as fleas, athlete's foot fungus and viral infections together with the body's defence mechanisms, antibodies and immunity.

Human biology provides a useful subject for careers in nursing and the ancillary medical services — physiotherapy, speech therapy etc — but is narrower than full biology and less suitable for those interested in plants and animals.

Botany and zoology as separate A-level subjects

It is possible to take separate A-levels in botany and zoology. The A-level botany and zoology syllabuses require the study of a wide range of groups in much greater detail than is possible for A-level biology.

A-level botany provides a good basis for a degree course in pure botany, horticulture or agriculture.

A-level zoology may be substituted for biology as an entrance requirement for some medical and veterinary schools, and also provides a good basis for a degree course in pure zoology or agriculture. However it is preferable to take biology and chemistry rather than botany and zoology with no chemistry if university entrance is required.

Building construction
by Jack Sanderson

Building is an activity which impinges on many aspects of our society. We use buildings for living, working, studying – even examining; the basic terminology is part of our everyday vocabulary. Building involves the integration of technology, management, environmental studies, physics, law and communication to produce a structure which will satisfy many criteria.

The scope of the A-level examination

Building construction is offered as an A-level subject by only one Board, the AEB. It is an extension of O-level studies, developing into more complex buildings such as industrial, commercial and public buildings in addition to domestic buildings. Some students who are studying in Further and Higher Education could enter directly for an A-level and indeed many entries are from the Further Education sector. In practice, the A-level course tends to incorporate some revision of O-level work by providing questions at a greater depth. A student who has already studied the subject at O-level should have more time to concentrate on new ideas and concepts.

Syllabus

The syllabus is broken down into a number of areas of study, representing the functional parts of buildings such as walls, roofs, doors and windows; the environmental and physical services, heating, lighting, water supply etc; the properties and uses of the materials for building; legal requirements for health and safety; the performance of the whole structure in terms of stability, weather resistance and fire protection, and the identification of defects and their rectification.

The examination

This takes the form of two written papers, each of three hours' duration and each contributing 50% of the total marks. Paper 1 is predominantly graphical, requiring formal drawings and sketches. Paper 2 consists mainly of questions requiring descriptive answers, often including an essay question. In each paper, attempting four questions from six is usual.

Coursework and teaching methods

In view of the nature of the subject and the many 'visual aids' available, visits to sites and works in course of progress, practical workshop experience, evaluating the performance of occupied buildings, and assessing manufacturers' presentations and display form an important part of the course. Classroom activity is mainly devoted to discussion and developing and practising techniques for efficient communication of information in graphical and written form.

Further courses

About ten per cent of the working population of this country is involved in the construction industry either directly or indirectly through the professions or as suppliers. An A-level pass is not an essential subject for a degree or diploma in the area of construction, but it would be useful. It would also be valuable to have an A-level pass in maths and physics or a BTEC diploma in construction. It is also worth considering the number of professions in which a knowledge of building is useful, including financial investment in property, surveying, environmental health, social services and housing management. In the past, some educational and professional institutions did not accept building construction as an academic entry requirement. This situation is changing, and if applying for a course it would be wise to check with the admissions tutor or institution secretariat as to their policy on this subject.

However you will have studied an interesting and stimulating subject – and hopefully will be a better-informed house-owner one day.

Chemistry
by John Raffan

What is chemistry?
Chemistry is all around us. In some form it has been part of human activity for thousands of years, since our early ancestors found methods for extracting metals from rocks and converting juices into medicines. Through such techniques and attempts by alchemists to discover the 'elixir of life' and the 'philosopher's stone', practical skills and chemical knowledge grew. Slowly, with much argument, theories appeared which began to make sense of the flood of information, and today chemistry is providing us with an ever deeper understanding of the nature of matter in all its forms.

Most chemistry involves change. We try to find how substances can be broken down into simpler parts, how the parts may be rearranged and joined to give new materials. We look at the way substances affect each other, how reactions and properties are affected by energy — heat, light and electricity — and how all of this may be interpreted in terms of the tiny building blocks of nature — molecules, atoms, ions and electrons.

As in all sciences, chemistry depends on people asking questions. How and why do substances behave the way they do under different conditions? Are there patterns in the way changes occur? Are we able to predict the future behaviour of substances from our present knowledge? Can we make use of our knowledge to help in the fight against disease and hunger, to improve people's lives at home and work, to make our industries safer, cleaner, more efficient and profitable? Can we learn not to misuse our knowledge and let chemistry help us avoid waste and pollution of the environment?

Chemistry alone does not answer these questions but, as a central science, it is linked directly to physics and biology and also to the medical sciences, earth sciences, metallurgy and other technologies. It can share and borrow ideas and techniques for its aims of unlocking the secrets of nature, and making imaginative and practical use of the discoveries.

Qualifications

If you are thinking of taking chemistry to A-level, you will already have experience of the subject. By now you are familiar with some of the techniques used to explore and rearrange matter and you know some of the theories. Your knowledge and vocabulary contain a store of chemical facts and technical terms; you probably can say what a catalyst is, for example. Perhaps you are about to take the O-level examination in chemistry. This is the ideal preparation and qualification for entry to an A-level course and you should be capable of a grade C or better. A good grade in physical science, or other form of integrated science, is usually acceptable but you may have to do some extra study at times, as present A-level syllabuses are based on the foundation of O-level chemistry.

You should ask for advice at your school, college or A-level centre about the qualifications which are suitable for entry to A-level chemistry. For example there are local variations in whether or not a qualification in CSE chemistry, or which grades in the joint 16+ examinations, are acceptable. Some centres allow students to start the A-level course in September but expect them to take the O-level examination in December.

What will you find when you go from O-level to A-level? Obviously, there is much more time available for the subject. Classes are likely to be quite small — rarely more than 15 in chemistry. With the smaller classes and more time available most teachers like to encourage pupils to take greater responsibility for their own learning.

Syllabuses

In the past, chemistry syllabuses and examinations were criticised for demanding too much memorising of facts. Fortunately, the Examination Boards have been reducing the factual content of their syllabuses in order to encourage understanding of principles and the processes of investigation. However, as in most advanced studies, anyone who wants to succeed in A-level chemistry examinations must be prepared for a certain amount of memory work. Chemistry at A-level is not a soft option. Its rewards and pleasures are many, but really only available to people prepared to put in the necessary effort.

When you look at an A-level chemistry syllabus you may find it is divided into sections. As any subject becomes larger, parts of it start to have identities of their own and science, for example, has long been divided into the areas we know as chemistry, physics, biology etc. At the university level, as chemistry grew, it was found convenient to divide it too, so that chemists could concentrate on their specialist interests. The areas of physical, organic and inorganic chemistry appeared. There are other divisions for particular applications of chemistry. You may hear of *analytical chemistry* (detecting and measuring chemicals, usually in very small quantities); *radiochemistry* (production and use of radioactive isotopes); *polymer chemistry* (production and study of very long molecules), and so on. However, the physical, organic and inorganic divisions are still the most obvious and several of the A-level syllabuses show signs of these divisions.

In physical chemistry, for example, we look at how particles such as atoms and ions are held together in molecules and crystals, and how we explore these structures. We measure and interpret the energy changes in chemical reactions. We find how fast and how far reactions can go under different conditions (of great importance in the production of chemicals on which the nation's economy depends).

Organic chemistry is most simply explained as the chemistry of compounds containing the element carbon. When we realise that the whole of our biology depends on carbon compounds — we are carbon compound people (our food, medicines, fuels and textiles are almost all carbon compounds) — it is not difficult to see why society devotes huge resources of time and money to the study and application of organic chemistry.

Inorganic chemistry too has provided us with a vast wealth of new materials as it is the study of all the other elements (metals, hydrogen, sulphur etc) and their compounds. At A-level we use the organising help of the periodic table to look at the patterns of behaviour of some groups of elements, rather than study many individual elements in detail.

The Nuffield A-level chemistry course, developed by teachers funded by the Nuffield foundation, has been particularly influential in encouraging a more unified approach. Nuffield is the only published example of a fully developed A-level chemistry course, with its own examination, and is based on seven main themes:

● particular chemical changes in materials

- patterns in the chemical behaviour of materials
- structure of atoms, molecules and crystals
- rates of reaction
- equilibrium in chemical systems
- energy changes accompanying chemical changes
- applications — industrial, medical, economic and other social aspects of chemistry.

These are the themes which link the topics in the course. The topics themselves have different titles, such as periodicity, structure and bonding, and carbon chemistry and appear as chapters in the student books.

The syllabuses of other Boards are usually shown as a series of topics, also under headings such as periodicity etc, sometimes within the main divisions of physical, organic or inorganic chemistry.

Options

Another development at A-level by some Boards puts part of the syllabus into optional studies. In the Nuffield scheme, about 90% of the time available is spent on the 'core course' (topics like those mentioned above) and the remaining 10% is given to the study of an aspect of applied chemistry. The published Nuffield 'special studies' are: biochemistry, chemical engineering, food science, metals as materials, chemistry and the environment, surface chemistry, mineral process chemistry. Teachers, possibly in negotiation with their students, choose one of these or can develop a special study of their own.

The Cambridge Board syllabus and Joint Matriculation Board syllabus 'A' have an 80% core and two options of 10% each, chosen from eight titles (Cambridge) and ten titles (JMB). Other Boards may well follow this trend as the optional studies are usually very popular with teachers and pupils.

Practical work

Anyone who wants to take chemistry at A-level should have some liking for, and ability at, practical work. Chemistry is an experimental science. The theories grew out of information gathered in laboratories and are only used for as long as they explain practical observations. Theory and practical work flow into each other and ideally most of your work in A-level chemistry should be based in a lab. In practice this may not always be possible, as schools must sometimes ration their laboratory time. However you will have more time in a lab than before A-level and you may be able to work on your own or with only one partner.

The range of possible practical work is enormous, with greater depths and interest than in earlier years. You may be asked to prepare pure samples of some rather odd organic compounds or analyse precisely the quantity of chlorine in swimming-pool water. You will build models of crystals and molecules and plan your own investigations into topics such as metal corrosion or plastics or enzymes. It will all help you to understand and apply your growing knowledge and make you more skilful in handling chemicals and equipment. If you are fortunate enough to be in a school or college which encourages visits to industry and field-trips you may find your practical work is linked to industrial applications of chemistry.

Teaching style

How you experience the more theoretical and descriptive parts of the course will depend largely on the style used by your teachers. They may encourage a lot of discussion, both in full class and small groups; they may give occasional lectures. Many teachers use worksheets to guide both practical work and discussion, or ask their pupils to read a variety of textbooks and write their own notes on a topic. You will probably have a book of chemical data and be encouraged to use it in interpretation of observations, looking for patterns and solving problems. Some teachers use all of these techniques but, most important of all, they want pupils to take an active interest in their own learning.

As microcomputers have become more widely available, chemistry teachers are finding how useful they are in extending the range of laboratory and classroom activities. Chemical data is easily stored on cassette or disk; your results from practical investigations may be processed quickly and displayed by the computer in numerical or graphical form. Computer simulations of chemical processes and programs which both inform and ask questions on, for example, chromatography or spectra or energy changes, are all powerful aids to teaching and learning.

Work outside class: books

At the A-level stage you will have an amount of free time during the day. Not everyone wants to use this for study but it does give an opportunity, with the library and other resources nearby, to do the independent work which is necessary. You will have to write up accounts of your experiments (there is often little time for this during the official practical sessions), follow up recommended readings, plan projects, revise for tests, do set problems and write essays. You will probably find that much of this becomes homework and many teachers feel it is reasonable to expect A-level candidates to spend at least five hours per week on each subject, outside the time in class. Apart from your own investigations, you may be encouraged to find inspiration and information from a variety of sources. Many schools and colleges purchase or hire films, computer programs, video and audio recordings but the main source of help (apart from teachers) will probably still be books.

There is a large selection of excellent textbooks for A-level chemistry. Many deal with one area of the traditional divisions, physical, organic or inorganic; some now adopt the unified approach. The Nuffield chemistry scheme is supported by student books which guide pupils through the course, asking questions, advising on experiments and giving some background information. They are not like normal textbooks as the answers to their questions are supposed to come from your own investigations and wider reading.

A good chemistry department will either have its own library or see that the school library is well stocked with a variety of textbooks, general readers and perhaps magazines such as *New Scientist* and *Scientific American*. How much you read around the subject will, of course, depend on your depth of interest but sensible extra reading is always an aid to success.

Mathematical needs
Many people thinking of taking A-level sciences are concerned about the amount of mathematics required. Some of the Boards state quite clearly in their syllabuses which mathematical topics are necessary and we can use one of these as our guide. It says: 'While it is not necessary for a candidate to have a knowledge of mathematics beyond that of O-level of the traditional or a project syllabus, it would be to the candidate's advantage to be familiar with the following topics . . .' It then gives details of some mathematical topics under the following headings:

● indices
● logarithms
● formulae (eg quadratic and simultaneous equations)
● graphical methods

• gradient at a point, rates of change, simple differentiation and integration.

Often schools and colleges organise lessons for people who feel that their mathematical skills are inadequate. Your willingness to use mathematics in chemistry is essential.

Examinations

Eventually comes the time of the examinations. The style and number of the written papers varies between Boards but most use the same types of questions. The whole or part of one paper may consist of objective (multiple-choice type) questions. There are questions requiring short answers (brief calculations, drawings, one word or a few sentences). There is usually a paper with essay or free-response questions, looking for longer answers. In this you may be expected to quote examples and use information from a book of chemical data. Some questions may allow you to show that you have read widely around the subject and can discuss the problems of the applications of chemistry in society. Other questions may be entirely based on calculations. At least in the longer-answer paper you have a choice of questions (from two to six to be answered out of nine to twelve, depending on the Board). Usually all questions must be answered on the objective and short-answer papers.

In the overall planning of their questions some Boards tell us how the marks are divided between the various abilities. For example the Joint Matriculation Board (JMB) gives, in the written papers:

Knowledge: 40%
Comprehension and application: 50%
Evaluation and investigation: 10%.

There is one mark for each objective question. In the short answer paper the marks are often shown beside the question and this helps candidates to know how much to write.

Assessment of practical work

There are different methods used for the assessment of practical abilities. Most Boards set a practical examination. Candidates have about three hours to complete three problems based on physical, organic and inorganic chemistry. Most marks are awarded for the accuracy of measurements and observations, the rest for the interpretations and conclusions.

Some Boards (Cambridge, JMB, Oxford and Cambridge, and London including Nuffield) provide schemes for the internal assessment of practical work. This means assessments made throughout the course by the teachers. The main advantage is that candidates are judged on a variety of practical skills, as part of their normal work, on more than one occasion. The skills assessed are in observation, manipulation, interpretation and planning. Teachers are also asked, in the JMB and London schemes, to assess student attitudes to practical work. Marks are given for all of these and the total percentages are sent to the Board for moderation. This is a process of comparison and adjustment used to make allowance for different standards of marking from different teachers. Obviously the internal assessment must be made as fair to candidates in its marking as the normal external examination.

Using your A-level chemistry

When the great day comes and you are awarded your A-level in chemistry you will find it a useful qualification in many fields.

You may want to study a subject or begin training for a career for which an A-level chemistry qualification is either essential or most desirable. Entry to most medical, dental, veterinary, various biological sciences, material sciences and pharmacy departments requires A-level chemistry. It is useful, though perhaps not so essential, for entry to physics, engineering, earth sciences, environmental sciences and agriculture.

You may want to study chemistry further at a university or other institute of higher education. After gaining a degree, your knowledge and skills will be in great demand, even in times of national economic difficulty. Industries need people trained in chemistry for research, development and production. The public services employ chemists in important analytical work for the detection of crime and in consumer protection by ensuring the safety of food, drink and all goods sold to the public. Chemists monitor pollution and advise on methods of keeping air and water as clean as possible. They are essential to the Health Service in aiding the clinical diagnosis of ailments and ensuring the purity of drugs and medicines. As you probably already realise, large numbers of chemists teach the subject in schools, colleges and universities.

Increasingly chemists are also finding jobs not strictly related to chemistry, where their qualities of scientific thinking are appreciated, in marketing, management, accountancy and law.

For those going into work after A-levels, chemistry is useful for many types of laboratory work in research institutes, industrial laboratories with companies producing chemicals, agrochemicals, food, drink and pharmaceuticals, and also in hospital chemical laboratories. Further qualifications appropriate to these fields can be taken through day-release courses at a nearby college or polytechnic. Chemistry is also useful for other paramedical training courses including nursing, dietetics, and environmental health, and for such diverse activities as photographic processing, beauty therapy and picture restoration.

A-level chemistry could be one of your wisest investments.

Computer science
by Alan Mills

Introduction
The last few years have seen an explosive growth in the use of computers in the business world and in administration. The range of jobs for which computers are used has increased enormously and many commonplace products such as washing machines, cookers and cars may now contain a small computer or microprocessor.

Academic studies have kept pace with this growth and in many instances have provided the stimulus for it. This is reflected by the number of Examination Boards now offering computer science as an A-level subject and by the opportunities for continuing its study in further and higher education. There are also many career opportunities both within computing itself and in areas in which the computer is used.

What is computer science?
Computer science consists of a study of two related areas:

i   The computer system itself: what does it consist of? How does it work? How is it organised to function as a unit?
ii The applications of computers. What can they actually do? How do we use them and why? What are computers currently used for and what implications are there for the future?

In order to get a feel for the subject it is necessary to consider these two areas more closely.

Computer hardware

A computer system consists of *hardware* and *software*. The hardware is that part of the computer system which can be seen and touched, and conceptually looks like:

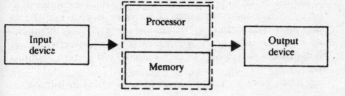

An input device may be a computer terminal (keyboard plus screen) or a punched-card reader. It may also be a device to recognise the human voice or perhaps give the position of a train on a piece of track. An input device, then, presents information to the computer about the real world whether it be the rate of pay of an employee, the population of London in 1850 or the temperature of a deep fat fryer!

The processor processes this information in some way which has already been specified by a computer programmer. The instructions which tell the processor what to do form the program and are to be held in the memory together with any necessary data. There are many different types of memory (eg core store, read-only memory, silicon chip technology, magnetic tape, floppy discs etc) and in addition processors also vary widely in construction and the way in which they function (called computer architecture).

An output device enables the computer to communicate with the outside world. Such a device may be a printer, a television screen (perhaps in colour) or a graph plotter. It could also be a device which talks (speech synthesis) or it may give control signals to a lift, telling the lift where to stop next.

This then is the computer hardware which exists in a variety of forms depending upon the use to which the computer is to be put.

Computer software

However, there is much more to the use of a computer than an understanding of the hardware.

Firstly, it is necessary to know how data such as numbers and text are represented within the computer using the binary system. It is then necessary to consider the methods of storing collections of data, such as student records, within the computer's memory and also how this data, now in the form of a file, may be processed.

The processing of data, and indeed the control of the computer hardware itself, is carried out by sets of instructions collectively known as software. Indeed the computer hardware cannot function without software. The software consists of programs (sets of instructions) which tell the computer how to perform the required tasks (eg produce pay slips from the number of hours worked, rate of pay etc, or perhaps simulate the effect on wildlife of a reduction in woodland); such programs are called *applications software*. In addition there is also *systems software* which enables the computer to perform applications software. The systems software does such things as translate programs written in a language convenient for programmers (eg BASIC, COBOL) into a language which the computer understands (a binary code). Further, the computer may perform many different tasks simultaneously. Another function of the systems software is to schedule these tasks in an efficient order.

This is still not the end of the story. The techniques of systems analysis and design together with general problem-solving principles must be understood in order to avoid designing a computer system which sends customers bills for £0.00! Finally, a suitable programming language is necessary in order to be able to write the computer programs.

The use of home computers

With more and more households acquiring microcomputers, it is reasonable for prospective students of computer science without access to a computer at home to wonder whether they will be disadvantaged. Clearly they will be at some disadvantage but not seriously so. A home computer may assist in the study of computer hardware, but since the typical microcomputer system found in the home lacks the sophistication of its larger brothers, the minis and mainframes, a study of its architecture and systems software alone is insufficient. Similarly the typical home computer costing £200–£300 does not support the range of applications which is necessary for an A-level candidate to study. Further, one hears quite often of students who have embarked upon their A-level project using their own machine only to discover later that its limitations lead them to lose valuable time in transferring to the school or college computer.

Applying and using the computer

Ultimately, computers exist to solve problems and are used in ever-widening areas. Thus a large component of computer science is studying the application of computers to many diverse areas. These areas include the following:

i Technical processing which includes scientific calculations (eg solving sets of equations), and also techniques such as simulation where the computer can be used to evaluate alternative courses of action in, say, the economy or traffic control.

ii Control processing where the computer is used to control, for example, a washing machine or a machine tool.

iii Operational processing which includes commercial data processing and is where systems such as payroll, stock control, sales recording are handled by computer.

iv Information processing where the computer is used to analyse information such as sales analyses, census returns, results of experiments etc, in order to answer a question or assist in decision-making.

In addition, it is necessary for a student of computer science to realise the implications of computerisation for society, in particular in areas such as employment and privacy.

The A-level syllabuses

A-level computer science is offered by most of the Examination Boards including AEB, Cambridge, JMB, London, Oxford and WJEC. The relationship between A-level and O-level varies from Board to Board; thus AEB A-level 'does not assume previous knowledge of computing', whilst for the JMB examination it is assumed 'that candidates have a knowledge of the topics of the Ordinary level syllabus'. However an O-level pass would not normally be a prerequisite for entry on to an A-level course.

A knowledge of physics is not required as computer science involves an understanding only of the control and function of the various hardware components and not of complicated electronics.

Computer science is often thought to be a mathematical subject and whilst this was true in the early 1970s it is no longer the case. The current approach is typified by the latest revision to the syllabus made by the AEB, for examinations from 1986 onwards, which removed the few remaining mathematical topics. The Oxford Board is unusual in retaining topics of a mathematical nature, as well as requiring more than a superficial knowledge of analogue computers.

Broadly, the philosophy of A-level computer science is to develop an understanding of the fundamental principles of computer systems, problem solving and the processing of information, by a theoretical and practical consideration of the computer and its applications.

Examinations

Computing is necessarily a practical subject and this is emphasised by all the Boards and reflected in the examinations. For all the Boards, the examination is in two parts:

- two unseen examination papers of three hours each
- one project completed by the candidate in his/her own time.

The project carries 20% of the overall marks (Oxford: 25%).

A candidate has therefore an opportunity to obtain a flying start before the examinations commence by completing a good project. In addition it is sensible to relate the project to some important aspects of the syllabus in order to gain a better understanding of these topics. Computer games, whilst normally acceptable, do not benefit the candidate as much as, say, a commercially oriented project, a simulation program, or an exercise in systems software.

Practical work

In addition to the theoretical aspects of the syllabus which will normally occupy the student for three hours a week over the two-year period, an equal amount of practical work is necessary. This will take the form of computer programming preferably using two or more programming languages and ideally with some experience of operating a small computer. Depending upon the application areas being studied, the practical work may involve a case study of a particular computing system or application. Case studies are also a popular method of introducing topics during the course. In the second year the bulk of this practical time (and an hour or two more) would be devoted to the project. In order to maintain interest in the project it could be related to the student's favourite subject — maybe a topic from another A-level course, or a problem concerned with a hobby.

Computing, being a relatively new subject, is still changing rapidly and it is necessary to read around the subject. Useful information can be obtained from the computer press including *Computer Weekly, Computing* and the many periodicals devoted to microcomputers.

Subject combinations at A-level
Computer science is often combined with mathematics and statistics at A-level, but it can also be combined with many other subjects. Anyone interested in the engineering aspects of computers would be advised to study mathematics and physics as well. Those interested in business applications might take economics or business studies, or other arts or social science subjects.

The relevance of computer science for higher education
A-level computer science provides an excellent foundation for further study at higher diploma or BSc level, but is not a requirement for entry to computing courses in higher and further education. Some degree or diploma courses which combine mathematics, statistics and computing require A-level mathematics. Others concerned more with business applications and data processing will accept any A-level subjects at suitable grades for entry. Applications to these courses have increased markedly in the last few years as career prospects increase.

Computer studies is also an essential part of many other courses in both further and higher education ranging from accountancy to building, nursing to librarianship. Studying computing at A-level will enable the relevance of computing to these specialist areas to be better understood and provide a sound basis for future specialism.

Careers
For people leaving school or college after A-levels, a pass in computer science is useful in applying for jobs as a trainee computer programmer or computer operator. However, many firms now recruit HND or Higher Diploma (BTEC) or BSc students for computer programming and A-level students may have to start as operators. Computer science is valuable for almost every job. The study of computer applications gives an insight into the functioning of commerce and industry, and the techniques of problem-solving, together with systems analysis and design, improve the analytical abilities of the student. There is a wide range of careers for people with some knowledge and expertise in computing.

Some careers such as accountancy have already been mentioned. Others are within the whole field of economics — banking, building societies, business companies, industry and so on. Statisticians, mathematicians and actuaries, as well as economists, need to know about computers. There are opportunities in the services (RAF, Army, Navy, Royal Marines), in work study, air traffic control, the Civil Service, the hospital service, and in engineering, printing and many other technical careers.

For those wanting to study computer science at degree or diploma level, an A-level in the subject is useful but by no means essential. Many university degree courses in computer sciences require A-level mathematics for entry, but there are a wide range of computer studies courses at degree and diploma levels which do not. Someone wishing to work in the hardware side of computing would also need to study mathematics and physics or engineering science at A-level.

Electronics
by Michael Brimicombe

Although electronics is a relatively young subject for schools to offer at A-level, it is growing rapidly. The usefulness and relevance of a study of electronics is obvious: advances in electronics have been responsible for the explosive growth in the fields of computing and communication which are now taking place. Furthermore, the hardware of electronics (ie integrated circuits) is so cheap and easy to obtain that schools can teach the subject with the help of real, up-to-date components. Furthermore, a student who has a qualification in electronics need not be too dismayed about his future employment prospects!

There are two possible courses of study of electronics at A-level. The syllabuses are offered by the AEB and the Cambridge Board. The Cambridge course has only recently become available and differs in several important respects from the AEB course which has been available since 1975. Both courses assume that students start off with no previous knowledge or experience of electronics, either as a separate O-level or as part of, say, physics or technology O-level. Neither of the courses assume that students are necessarily studying physics and maths at A-level, so the overlap between electronics and physics or maths is very small.

The systems approach

Both the AEB and Cambridge courses have adopted a systems approach to electronics. This means that they are concerned with the behaviour and function of an electronic device, and how that behaviour is modified when the device is linked to another device. Neither course is concerned with the physics behind the device ie how it works. The systems approach treats an electronic component such as a logic gate or a transistor as a 'black box' with a number of leads going into it and coming out of it. The behaviour, in electronic terms, of the 'black box' is completely understood once you know how its output signals are related to its input signals. If you are just interested in using the 'black box', then its contents (ie exactly how it is made) are largely irrelevant.

A systems approach to electronics is necessary for two reasons. Firstly, any useful electronic circuit, however large or small, may be considered as an assembly of mutually interacting systems. In turn, each of those systems can be treated as a number of smaller systems linked to each other. Ultimately, there are a small number of basic system components (such as resistors, transistors, logic gates and flip-flops) which can be used to assemble other electronic systems. Once you understand the function and behaviour of each of those basic components and understand how that behaviour is changed when basic components are linked together, you can understand the behaviour of any complex system assembled from those components. Secondly, although there are only a limited number of basic components, the technology used to build them changes all the time. By concentrating on the function of a component (which does not change) and ignoring the physics of why it works (which changes constantly) you ensure that your electronics skills cannot become out of date. Today's technology will soon be in tomorrow's dustbin, so there is no point in learning about what makes an electronic component work if that knowledge is going to be out of date soon. The systems approach teaches you the aspects of electronics which are not going to become redundant, without affecting your ability to design and understand complex electronic systems which are useful today.

The two syllabuses

There is one main difference between the AEB and the Cambridge course. The AEB course aims to teach 'systems', with electronics as the main example; hence its title 'electronics systems'. The Cambridge course (called 'electronics') uses the systems approach to explain electronics. So, as part of the AEB course you would study a number of non-electronic systems such as biological ones, thermal ones and mechanical ones. The electronic systems met in this course serve to illustrate the general nature of systems, and are a particularly convenient and economical way of studying complex systems. The Cambridge course, on the other hand, concentrates exclusively on the analysis and design of electronic circuits.

AEB course

This is split up into four parts, system components (an introduction to the properties of the basic electronic components), processing, feedback and communication. The section on processing is concerned with decision-making and the storage and retrieval of information, and uses examples from computing as well as human problem-solving and mechanical systems. Feedback is a technique used in systems to ensure that the behaviour of the outputs is accurately controlled by the signals fed into the inputs; a portion of the output signal is fed back into the input of a system, fundamentally altering the behaviour of the whole system in the process. The final section on communication looks at the ways in which information can be coded and transmitted. It takes a detailed look at the human ear and eye, and covers radio and television receivers.

Cambridge course

The Cambridge syllabus identifies a number of ideas and techniques which are central to electronics. These are system synthesis (see above), electrical circuit theory, energy transfer, AC theory, feedback, information transfer, Boolean algebra and transducers. The systems which are studied fall into two broad, but distinct categories. There are analogue systems, such as amplifiers, radio transmitters and receivers, signal generators and oscillators. Then there are digital systems, such as counters, computers and logic systems.

Practical work

In order to learn about electronics you must (effectively) spend a lot of time at the bench, assembling and exploring circuits. Both courses require that students spend about six weeks of course-time on two projects or investigations chosen by the student. These carry 20% of the marks for the A-level examination, reflecting the importance of practical work for the subject. A wide variety of practical work is available, from simply assembling circuits to verify their behaviour, to assembling circuits of your own design to perform particular functions. The Cambridge course expects students to do some programming of microprocessors in machine code, whereas the AEB course requires the student to learn a bit about programming in BASIC.

After A-level
A student who has an A-level qualification in electronics should experience little difficulty in obtaining a job in the electronics construction and service industry; few teenagers come on to the jobs market with much experience of electronics, and the rapid growth of the industry means that their employment prospects are good. Those going into trainee technician jobs could go on to obtain Higher BTEC qualifications in electronics, by part-time study.

There is a wide variety of electronics-based courses offered by universities and polytechnics, ranging from computer science to electronic engineering. However, universities and polytechnics usually insist on passes at physics and maths A-level as the criterion for entry. Most institutions are willing to accept an electronics A-level as a 'third A-level', supporting what they regard as the students' other principal A-level subjects.

So if you are considering carrying on your study of electronics after A-level, you should also do maths and physics A-levels. Since electronics can be a 'stand-alone' A-level, there is no reason why you have to take maths and physics with it if you do not wish to study electronics further. The AEB course, which covers topics outside electronics, has a particular appeal for non-scientists and both courses would be a useful background for people seeking a career in technical marketing, computer sales and maintenance, work study, computing and a range of 'semi' technical careers. Both courses can be used as fourth A-levels by students studying science and maths.

Engineering science
by Deryk Kelly

What is engineering science?
Engineering science courses at A-level are basically physics courses with an engineering application. Most A-level physics

students go on to study and/or work in engineering, applied science or industrial management in some form or other. Engineering science gives experience of some of the skills demanded in these careers, in addition to the scientific skills which are the concern of all A-level physical science courses.

Engineering is concerned with producing the materials, goods and services needed by society. Science is a major resource for engineering, and engineering is the major user of science. Many students find the application of physics in society more interesting than physics itself; engineering science brings the study of the two together. But design and production decisions are not made on scientific criteria alone, and the effects of limitations of time, money and the available expertise are looked at in a number of ways. Very often, of course, science lags behind need, and decisions have to be made in the absence of firm scientific data. In such situations the engineer might conduct experiments, call on experience and intuition, and proceed to a number of trial solutions to the problem.

Engineering science gives students the opportunity, in a small way, to experience such problems themselves. They have to carry out experiments which they themselves have designed in answer to some scientific problem. An example might be the physical properties of some comparatively new material or the behaviour of a particular structure under stress. They are also encouraged to undertake an engineering project of their own choice. In engineering science, then, there is scope for a lot of individual initiative and decision-making.

If you are interested in the ways in which science is used in society, and if you like tackling practical problems, engineering science has much to offer you. If, on the other hand, your prime or sole interest is in physics and in the analysis of theoretical problems you might be better advised to study one of the range of physics A-level courses.

Engineering science courses available to schools and colleges
The Associated Examining Board (AEB), the Joint Matriculation Board (JMB), and the University of London Schools Examination Council (London) all have A-level syllabuses and examinations in engineering science.

The syllabus topics in all three are the same as those found in most A-level physics syllabuses but students are expected to study these topics through their application to engineering; the choice of the applications is left to the individual schools and colleges. Electro-magnetism may well be studied through an examination of the design and operation of loudspeakers and microphones; the properties of materials and structures through consideration of bridge design, and so on.

Practical work is important in all these courses. The AEB syllabus has recently been revised and the JMB syllabus is currently in process of revision, partly to incorporate the National Core Syllabus in A-level physics recently agreed by all the GCE Boards. The title of the JMB examination is Physics (Advanced) Syllabus B.

Syllabuses

The topics may be grouped into the following sub-sections:

- forces and energy
- materials science
- fluid flow, electrical flow and heat flow
- electrical and magnetic fields
- heat, work and engines
- vibrations and waves
- electronics.

In fact, the division into sub-sections and even the names of sub-sections vary from syllabus to syllabus but, apart from the items mentioned below, the topics dealt with are very similar.

Forces and energy deals with ways in which bodies move (straight-line and circular motion) and how they behave in collision processes. It is also concerned with balancing forces and the effects of such balanced forces on ties, struts, beams and columns. AEB asks for a slightly deeper and London a slightly less deep treatment than does JMB.

Materials science is concerned with the mechanical, electrical and thermal properties of materials and, treated very simply, how these relate to the atomic structures of materials.

Fluid flow, electrical flow and heat flow treats the causes of and opposition to each type of flow and stresses the similarity of the laws governing them. All three treat fluid flow over surfaces such as aeroplane wings.

Electrical and magnetic fields is primarily concerned with understanding the principles behind such important devices as the motor, the generator and the transformer. All syllabuses make use of the magnetic/electric circuit analogue and include basic work on gravitational fields.

Heat, work and engines deals with the conversion of heat into work and the properties and behaviour of materials and systems which are of importance in heat engines. The demands of the three syllabuses are very similar.

Vibrations and waves is concerned with the motion of vibrating bodies and the characteristics of waves and the properties of alternating current. AEB is concerned only with the alternating current aspect of this section.

Electronics deals with the use of simple electronic systems, including solid state devices in amplifying, switching and oscillating circuits.

Practical work

Engineering science practical work includes routine measurements, investigation work and project work.

Measurement making is gaining skill in the use of instruments and knowledge of ways of handling the observations. You might well use micrometers, dial gauges, strain gauges, various types of thermometer, timer, ammeter, potentiometer, oscilloscopes etc, and be concerned with zero errors, reading errors and methods of reducing their importance.

Investigation work involves designing and working through an experiment to gain fresh knowledge, eg the effect of annealing on one or more properties of copper. You might be asked to investigate the effect of temperature on the conductivity of glass; at room temperature the conductivity is very low but at red heat the conductivity rises sharply. Very few books give any help and you have to work a method out for yourself, solving a number of problems on the way: size and shape of glass to be used, making connections to the glass, method of heating and method of measuring conductivity. In order to solve these problems you may have to carry out some preliminary measurements and when you have finished you will need to know how reliable your answer is. This, of course, is just one example but the challenges are typical of this kind of work.

Projects

Projects are longer exercises, typically the practical work for two terms, involving a great deal of planning. Projects may be of the design, construct and test type or the extended investigation type. In the latter case it is usually expected that part of the apparatus used will be designed and assembled by the student. A project is a practical problem with a practical solution and the choice of the problem is largely a matter for the student.

Examinations
AEB
There are two papers and coursework assessment.
Paper 1   40% of the total marks. 3 hours.
The paper tests knowledge, understanding, communication, analysis and applications in the topic areas: mechanical properties of metals and polymers, beams and structures, dynamics, thermodynamics and fluid mechanics. Candidates are asked to answer all 12 short-answer questions and four from six longer answer questions.
Paper 2   40% of the total marks. 3 hours.
Similar to Paper 1 in all respects other than the topics tested; these are: d.c. and a.c. electricity, electric and magnetic fields, electromagnetism, electrical machines and electronics and systems.
Coursework   20% of the total marks.
A project assessed by the school and moderated by the Board.

JMB
Paper I Section A   20% of the marks. 1 hour.
Paper I is a multiple-choice examination containing questions ranging over the syllabus. All questions should be attempted.

Paper I Section B   20% of the marks. 1½ hours.
This section consists of approximately 10 short answer questions testing understanding of the syllabus and its application together with aspects of engineering design. All questions have to be attempted.

Paper II Section A   13% of the marks. 1 hour.
This section consists of a comprehension and communication test. Candidates are required to read a short engineering article which may include diagrams, graphs and tables of data and to answer about eight questions on the content and interpretation of the article.

Paper II Section B   9% of the marks. 40 minutes.
This section consists of a single design question which may be related to investigation work, project work or the design of a device or system.

Paper II Section C   18% of the marks. 1 hour 20 minutes.
This section consists of 3 long answer application's questions of which 2 must be answered.

Paper III
This paper tests understanding of the subject matter of the syllabus through the application of physical principles to devices and practical situations.

Section 1   20% of the marks. 1½ hours.
The section contains nine questions, requiring short answers, of which the candidates answer six.

Section 2   20% of the marks. 1½ hours.
The section contains six questions, of which the candidates are expected to answer three. The questions relate to problem-solving and include elements of costing, design and the selection of materials and components.

Coursework   20% of the marks.
Reports on one experimental investigation and a project are assessed by the school and moderated by the Board.

London
Paper 1   25% of the marks. 2 hours.
Paper 1 contains short-answer questions, all of which should be attempted.

Paper 2   37½% of the marks. 3 hours.
Paper 2 contains a number of long-answer questions of which the candidates are asked to answer six.

Paper 3   12½% of the marks. 1½ hours.
This paper is a comprehension test based on a passage of engineering literature.

Coursework   25% of the marks.
Very similar to JMB.

Career prospects
In general terms, engineering science is treated the same as physics as an entry qualification to university departments and the professions. If you wish to study engineering at degree or diploma level you should also study A-level mathematics. Most university and polytechnic engineering departments welcome engineering science as an alternative to physics. The same would be true for applied science courses, metallurgy, and materials science, and for most pure science subjects. On the

other hand, care needs to be exercised when applying for medical faculties as a minority do not yet accept qualifications labelled engineering science for entry purposes. It is always wise to check with the institution in which you are interested.

Engineering science courses give a sound education in the important branches of physics and are particularly appropriate for preparation for careers in the engineering profession. But, as their main emphasis lies in the problem-solving aspects of engineering, they also form a very good basis for careers in management of all types, medicine and applied science. Most people in their work are faced with problems that have to be solved with limited resources and knowledge, and the experience gained by students of engineering science, particularly in their practical work, materially helps them to deal with such problems.

Environmental science and environmental studies
by Keith Barber

Environmental science/studies has been available for about ten years but it is still an unknown quantity in many schools. There is misunderstanding, or a total lack of appreciation, of its sphere of influence and impact upon our way of life. Essentially, the aim at the heart of all current courses is to accept and appreciate the role and effect that the human race has had, is having, and will have upon the physical and finite world we inhabit.

This is a very wide brief and cannot possibly be contained within a course of study lasting two years – but then neither can any of the more accepted, traditional subjects, nor are they expected to. Whether the study of environmental matters be approached from a largely scientific standpoint or, at another extreme, from a humanities angle, it makes little difference to the basic aim and it must all culminate in value judgements, based upon, and interpreted from, a variety of evidence. Thus the links with geography, biology, chemistry, physics, social studies, economics, and history become very apparent. Doubtless the themes of pollution, world population growth, use and conservation of resources, urbanisation, food production, mineral extraction (these are just some examples) will occur in all these 'subject' areas, but it is only by using the environmental approach that the themes become interwoven, and have some real meaning and importance for today's society.

73

Courses and syllabuses

Three Examination Boards offer A-level studies in this field –
London and AEB entitle it 'environmental studies' whilst JMB
prefers 'environmental science'. Numbers attracted to these
courses were around 600 in total for 1983, which was a small
increase on previous years. The broader base of environmental
studies (London and AEB) and the lesser overview of
environmental science (JMB) can perhaps be appreciated by
reference to the main sectional heading in the syllabus.

London

I   The energy flow through the natural environment and the
     limits of the resource base (the physical world).
II   The ecosystem (the living world): field work.
III Man as an organism within the environment (impact and
     change).
IV   Environmental conflicts and planning: field work.

AEB is broadly similar, but with a greater emphasis on
agriculture and food production, and much less field work.

JMB

I   Energy, water, and other resources.
II   Food supply and food production.
III Pollution, waste disposal, and insecticides.
IV   Land use and environmental management.
V   Population.

Practical work

Practical investigation is the keynote of environmental science,
as opposed to the field work of environmental studies. Both
activities have the aims of selection and use of appropriate
techniques for the investigation of problems, and of drawing
conclusions based upon direct evidence (data). The JMB
course is based rather more upon the laboratory, integrating
aspects of the standard sciences of chemistry, physics and
biology into a scientific study of the environment with less
emphasis on social problems. Students themselves devise and
carry out experimental work, seeking to resolve problems such
as sources of pollution, energy balance in a specified activity,
or the effect of man's activities upon the vegetation of a
particular area. No less time is devoted to practical activities
than for the practical work in other A-level science courses.

In London courses, biology is the major standard science

input, especially required for the proper understanding of ecology. Guided field work concerned with habitat studies and the flow of energy is also a prominent feature of this course. Other field work is on an individual basis, related to the student's own choice of investigation. About a quarter of the teaching time is normally allocated to these field activities throughout the course.

Background knowledge and subject combinations

Without any doubt a basic scientific knowledge is desirable, and indeed expected, for the successful study of these courses, and it is of some advantage to have reached O-level standard at least in biology, if not in physics or chemistry. A mathematics O-level or its equivalent will be found helpful, although not essential, as indeed would geography. Experience has shown that an O-level or CSE in environmental studies/science is not necessarily the best preparation for an A-level course and it is certainly not a requirement. Whatever the knowledge and attainment of a student, some parts of the syllabus are certain to be new, and therein lies part of the challenge.

In most situations it will be a case of selecting one or two other A-level subjects for the sixth-form course, and there have been a variety of combinations. The more scientifically orientated will no doubt wish to offer one or two of the standard sciences. Those wishing to study environmental sciences at deeper level would find chemistry useful. Others may wish to select geography and economics, although history, English and art are further subject areas which have in the past also proved satisfactory combinations. The type of study and the demands of the different disciplines must be weighed against the content of the course, especially for the weaker candidates. A real enthusiasm for the subject is perhaps the best criterion to go by – without it it may be difficult to maintain sufficient motivation to see the course through to a successful conclusion.

The examination

Two three-hour papers is the normal practice, with a variety of question style in each, and a varying degree of choice. The JMB's Paper I has a number of compulsory 'short'-answer questions, and a choice of two from four long 'data-response'-type questions, testing an understanding of broad areas of environmental science relating to technology, the natural environment and environmental management. In Paper II there are several compulsory questions of a more detailed nature testing an understanding of the principles of environmental science, together with choice of two from six essay-type questions. Marks for the two papers amount to 80% and the remaining 20% is teacher assessment of the practical skills of the candidate.

In the London Board examination's Paper I there are two compulsory short-answer questions, many of them being of data-response form, which carry a value of 30%. Paper II has a planning question, where candidates are asked to select the site for a major development such as a new town, a country park, the route of a new road, an airport, or an extractive industry, for example, and to justify their decisions in terms of cost, aesthetics, and conservation. Detailed information and maps are, of course, provided. The second half of this paper is a choice of two essays from nine, and the whole paper is valued at 40%. Teacher assessment – with appropriate external moderation – of the field work accounts for the remaining 30%, 10% of which is for the ecology work and 20% for the individual study. These assessments are high for an A-level examination and reflect the value placed upon field work and practical investigations. They are not optional extras, but in both cases are an integral part of the course. The AEB examination has no such compulsory element.

Post-A-level study

Despite its relative newness environmental studies/science is now accepted by nearly all of our universities and polytechnics for entry to appropriate degree or diploma courses. Where a highly scientific qualification is being sought, other science A-levels such as physics or chemistry will be required.

Course titles include – as well as environmental studies and environmental science – ecology, environmental chemistry, environmental health, physics and environmental science, human ecology, environment and resources, computing studies and environmental sciences, applied biology, environmental analysis and monitoring, pollution measurement, urban planning. In a recent (1984) publication by the Education Committee of the Institute of Environmental Sciences, *Environmental Courses in the United Kingdom,* out of 21 courses listed at first-degree level, eight are labelled 'environmental studies' and six 'environmental science'. It will always be wise to make enquiries before embarking upon a set course of action and plenty of information is available in most school career centres.

76

Careers

Without further training it is not likely that an A-level in environmental studies/science will lead at once to a worthwhile job in any environmentally based situation. Broadly speaking, it will be useful in any of the land-linked professions such as agriculture, horticulture, forestry: with bodies such as the Water Authorities or the National Park Boards; with Local Authorities in their planning department; and with conservation organisations such as the Nature Conservancy Council or the Countryside Commission. In many of these concerns competition for jobs is fierce and additional qualifications will be needed, if not at degree or diploma level then at a specific professional grade.

There is a growing need for technicians and officers for the care and maintenance of environmental standards in the sphere of environmental health, consumer protection and health and safety. The provision of recreational activities and facilities for leisure pursuits, particularly in the countryside, is another area that will take an increasing number of recruits. Few graduates with an environmental degree have yet found their way into teaching but numbers are growing slowly, and opportunities will become increasingly available. A very useful booklet on *Careers for Environmentalists* has recently (1983) been revised and updated, and is obtainable from the Council for Environmental Education at the Department of Education, University of Reading, London Road, Reading RG1 5AQ.

Geology
by Tom Shipp

What is geology?

The word geology is taken from two Greek words meaning knowledge of the earth. An understanding of the planet that we live and depend on is also given the title of earth science. In studying geology, students are expected to appreciate the size, shape and principal surface features of the planet, together with its internal structure of crust, mantle and core as deduced from measurements of earthquake waves, gravity and density variations, magnetism and escape of internal heat. The simple chemical nature and properties of two dozen or so minerals will be investigated, some for their importance as raw materials from which are synthesised the metals, building materials, ceramics, plastics, fertilisers and the million and one other manufactured products upon which modern man depends. Other minerals will be studied for their importance as components of the rocks of which the crust of the earth is composed.

The rocks themselves are not as endurable as is commonly supposed. Even the 'rock of ages', granite, crumbles under the onslaught of wind, rain, heat and cold to form clay, sand and water-soluble mineral salts. An important part of the study of geology is to chart the processes of breakdown and reconstitution of rocks in the form of a natural cycle of events. Such processes include the extremes of spectacular volanic eruptions and movement of huge masses of glacier ice, as well as the relatively gentler effects of winds, rivers and tides shifting and sifting rock fragments.

Fossils and time

A link with biology is made in the examination of remains of animals and plants preserved as fossils. For many students, this may prove to be one of the most fascinating aspects of geology. Collecting one's own specimens of fossils as well as rocks and minerals, followed by painstaking checking and identification of them can lead to a profound personal involvement with the subject. Comparison of fossils with living organisms will lead to an appreciation of adaptation and evolution of organisms, as well as speculation on the conditions under which they led their lives.

A feature of any geology course must inevitably be a sense of wonderment at the enormous span of geological time. To say that the earth was formed — nobody knows quite how — 4.6 billion years ago, or that the first shellfish appeared on the scene 570 million years ago, or that dinosaurs were the dominant land animals for some 145 million years puts a new dimension on the study of history — geological history.

One of the most exciting advances made in the science of geology in recent years has been a growing awareness that the crust of the earth is broken up into a series of gigantic slabs which jostle each other, inexorably creating and destroying tracts of territory, giving rise to earthquakes and volcanoes, cracking and bending the rock formations at their margins, and carrying the continental masses slowly across the globe. In the rocks of the British Isles there is ample evidence of ancient tropical forests, deserts, warm shallow seas, volcanoes, glaciers, and the stumps of former mountains of Himalayan proportions.

A mixture of subjects

In reading this outline of the scope of geology, you will have
become aware of the interdisciplinary nature of the subject
which utilises aspects of physics, chemistry, biology, and
technology. Perhaps one of the most important aspects —
man's use of raw materials, minerals, rocks, fuels and water —
should receive special mention. These resources are being
exploited at a rapidly increasing rate and geologists are needed
to locate and evaluate fresh supplies of them. However, the
time is now ripe for geologists, manufacturers and users of
many of the commodities we take for granted, to think and act
to conserve dwindling reserves.

After O-level

The content of many A-level geology courses differs little from
those at O-level; the topics are however studied in much
greater depth and detail. Because of this it is possible to start
geology as a new subject at the A-level stage as many people
do, with great success.

Using the countryside

One aspect of A-level geology which distinguishes it from most
other sciences is that the best geological laboratory is to be
found in the countryside. Geology is, most emphatically, a
practical subject, and the best geologists are invariably those
who have spent a considerable proportion of their working
lives investigating in the field. Several of the A-level syllabuses
specify that a certain number of days shall be spent during the
course on practical work in the field. Students may have heard
on their school grapevine that the highlight of the geology A-
level course is the week spent away in such mysterious regions
as Snowdonia, the Pennines, the Lake District, Arran or Skye.
Field experience of this type is invaluable to the budding
geologist. Nearer home, local quarries, cliffs, road cuttings,
and even kerbstones and shop fronts can provide useful
practical geology. Most geology examinations carry questions
inviting candidates to write about their field observations.

Practical work

Practical work in the laboratory is divided between exercises
involving rock, mineral and fossil specimens; measurement of
the physical characteristics of materials, construction and use
of models, and interpretation of geological features shown on
maps. For reference work, your department and school or

college library is likely to stock geological books to cover all the topics you need. Local museums should not be neglected, and the Geological Museum at South Kensington in London has produced a series of inexpensive booklets of superb quality on a variety of geological themes.

Teaching methods
Your teacher will probably endeavour to divide the syllabus material into reasonably compact topics, introducing new topics at approximately fortnightly intervals and giving you notes and worksheets explaining the theory and practical work to be covered, listing references and suggesting additional information. Students are usually expected to account for the work they have done by periodically submitting completed exercises, essays and practical topic reports. Work in the sixth form is more demanding intellectually and much more time-consuming than it was in the lower school, but much more rewarding.

Having outlined the general scope of a geology course in the introductory paragraphs, the writer would recommend intending A-level students to obtain a copy of the A-level syllabus from their school or college, or from the appropriate Examination Board. The syllabus gives information on the aims of the course, and on the importance and nature of the skills to be developed and on the manner in which they will be assessed.

Examinations
Most Examination Boards rely on end-of-course examinations in theory (at least two examinations totalling five to six hours) and practical (three hours). The practical examination is usually an exercise in observation and deduction involving specimens and photographs, and problem-solving using a geological map. Some Boards arrange for teachers to assess their students regularly throughout the course on specified practical skills and award a separate grade on the basis of this work. The theory examinations usually set out in a variety of ways to probe a student's capacity to recall information, to understand and apply concepts to evaluate data, and to express ideas in an orderly and local manner.

In general, three main types of questions are set. These are, firstly, objective questions where each question has a number of alternative responses from which the appropriate ones have to be selected (ie multiple-choice questions). Secondly, there are structured questions or short-answer questions based on a short reading passage, a diagram or map, or other data, followed by a series of questions, each one requiring a brief answer. Thirdly, there are questions requiring longer, and more thoughtful answers of an essay type. Such questions may be open-ended giving the student free rein to write as much or as little as he can, or they may be directed, hinting to the student what information should be covered in his answer. There is usually a generous choice of essay questions.

The examination is constructed and marked by a panel of examiners employed by the Examination Board. The examiners will have had lengthy discussions about what can and cannot be reasonably expected in A-level candidates' answers, and will mark to a rigorous and uniformly agreed scheme. It is then the duty of the chief examiner to re-mark a large number of the scripts already seen by members of his panel and to report whether individual examiners have been lenient or severe in their marking and whether adjustments need to be made. Reports by schools or colleges of physical difficulties of individual students under examination conditions, for example dyslexia, colour blindness, broken limbs and so on, are then considered sympathetically by examiners. Finally the chief examiner and the secretary or official of the Board decide on the allocation of grades, with a careful check being made on the scripts of borderline candidates leading to upgrading in some instances.

Further courses and later careers

The teaching of geology as an O-level and A-level examination subject increased very markedly in British schools and colleges during the 1970s. Despite this, it is still a minority science subject and is being sorely squeezed by the present financial and other restraints being imposed upon the education service. There are strong arguments for maintaining the teaching of geology at A-level. Geology's value as a cultural science is based partly on its enjoyment as a leisure activity and not necessarily because it leads to a specific career qualification. Career openings in geology for school leavers at 16+ or 18+ are virtually nil. British universities produce between 700 and 800 geology graduates annually, and approximately 30% of these remain at university to study for additional postgraduate qualifications. Sixth formers intent on a career in geology should aim for good A-level grades in science and mathematics. Paradoxically as it may seem, many university departments of geology do not insist on an A-level pass in the subject as a requirement for a degree course, so even if you have no geological facilities at your school you are not automatically debarred from reading the subject at university. Intending geologists should be aware that the supply of trained graduates consistently exceeds the number of posts available. Only those students capable and enthusiastic enough to obtain a good degree, to seek out for themselves the somewhat limited employment opportunities, and to be prepared if necessary to work in remote and inhospitable locations should pursue the subject towards a challenging career.

Despite these facts, geology is a subject well worth considering as part of a sixth-form course. For the very able and single-minded individual, it will provide a challenging pathway to a limited number of career prospects where geology is used in the job. Otherwise, it can be taken as an interesting and relevant addition to physics and mathematics by prospective engineers and technologists. With biology, chemistry, mathematics or geography at A-level it will widen the horizons of those who are thinking of a career in chemical, environmental, biological or marine sciences. Even if taken formally no further than A-level, geology can provide the basis for a fascinating and worthwhile spare-time interest. At the same time it provides an A-level qualification for entry to a wide range of further courses and careers for which most academic A-levels are acceptable.

Mathematics (including pure, applied and further mathematics)
by David Nelson

A very popular choice
There are three standard ways of taking your mathematics up to A-level:

i   As a single subject usually called maths (or pure and applied maths or pure maths with statistics).
ii   As a single subject called pure maths.
iii As a double subject worth two A-levels. Either you take a second subject called further maths as well as maths, or else you take two separate subjects called pure maths and applied maths.

A-levels in maths are very popular. For instance, there were

89,630 entries for maths in the summer of 1983. The particular subject entries were as follows:

Subject	Candidates
Mathematics	60,400
Further maths	6,970
Pure maths	10,260
Applied maths	3,090
Pure maths and statistics	8,910
Total	89,630

What is A-level maths about?

There are two main areas — pure maths and applied maths.

In pure maths you continue the study of algebra, geometry and calculus. If you have not started calculus let me try to give you an idea of it. It is the mathematics of movement and change.

Suppose you sit next to the driver of a car and watch him accelerate from a standing start up to 25 metres per second in 10 seconds. The velocity time graph might look like figure 1. You probably know that the slope of the tangent to the graph gives the acceleration at any time and that the shaded area under the curve gives the distance that you have covered. If you know the equation of the velocity time graph the methods of calculus will easily calculate the acceleration and distance travelled at any time you like.

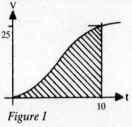

Figure 1

Next, suppose you are designing a cylindrical tin drum to hold say 100 gallons of liquid, and that you want to use as little metal as possible. The calculus proves that the most economical design is the one in which the height of the drum equals the diameter of its circular base. (See figure 2.)

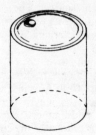

Figure 2

Calculus was invented in the 17th century by the greatest of English mathematicians, Isaac Newton, and is one of the most

83

popular parts of A-level maths.

Applied maths includes mechanics and statistics. If you have taken physics, you will know that mechanics is the study of forces and the way in which forces combine to make things move (dynamics) or stay still (statics). Describing the motion of a shell fired from a gun is a problem of dynamics. Calculating the forces exerted on a front door by its hinges is a problem of statics.

You may have learned a little about probability and frequency distributions (histograms) in your O-level course. The frequency distributions one meets in practice are often one of about six types. The most important one is the normal distribution. It is the sort of distribution you get if you measure such things as the pulse rates of athletes or the heights of 18-year-old boys.

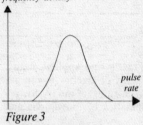

frequency density

pulse rate

Figure 3

A-level statistics goes into the theory of these distributions and, using the laws of probability, helps you to come to sensible conclusions about data. Indeed, learning how to collect, handle and judge a set of figures is one of the most valuable aspects of the statistics part of the course.

What do students find attractive?

Everybody finds maths difficult at times so why do so many people take it up to A-level?

One reason is that maths is a vital subject if your main interest is science, and it is certainly a useful course if you are taking economics or geography.

Many students enjoy the challenge of the subject. They like its strict arguments and the satisfaction of getting problems to come out. They feel that wrestling with arguments and problems is a good training for the mind.

The power of the subject can be very impressive. Over 2,000 years ago the Greek mathematician Eratosthenes performed a remarkable feat. He measured the distance from Alexandria to the Tropic of Cancer, and he measured the length of the shadow of a vertical pole at noon on midsummer's day at Alexandria. Using his knowledge of the geometry of the circle he correctly estimated the circumference of the earth to be 24,000 miles.

Another attraction is that the methods you learn are

effective in so many different ways. The calculus not only finds the acceleration of a racing car, it applies to the flight of a rocket, the growth of populations, the cooling of a cup of coffee and indeed to anything that moves or changes.

Finally, the subject has an orderliness and sometimes an unexpected simplicity which some find beautiful and fascinating. For example, if you add up the first *four* odd numbers 1, 3, 5, 7 the answer is 16 which is the square of *four*. If you add up the first *ten* odd numbers the answer is the square of . . . Well, what do you think?!

What the course involves

The course usually consists of regular classes and homework. The amount of reading is small by comparison with other subjects but to keep up with the classes you will need to solve problems steadily during homework. Most of the classwork is a mixture of discussion, lectures and problems but there is always scope for practical work, especially in statistics. There is scope too for projects. Some of these will arise from discussions in class and you may get ideas from books in the library. Try, for example, *Adventures with your Pocket Calculator* by L Rade and B Kaufman (Penguin).

If you have access to a computer, once you have learned a little programming, there are plenty of ways you can exploit the computer with A-level maths — solving equations, drawing graphs etc.

What O-levels do I need?

Most Boards have two O-levels — mathematics and additional mathematics. To go on to A-level it is essential to have studied the first of these and passed fairly comfortably. Alternatively, a good CSE grade 1 is needed.

Most teachers would agree that it is not essential to have studied additional maths. However, if your school has a pre-sixth-form course in additional maths, try to take it, since it will give you a better idea of what A-level work will be like.

It is easy to start A-level statistics from scratch but it is not easy to settle into mechanics without some knowledge of forces, moments, velocity and acceleration. So it helps to have done an O-level or CSE physics course.

The syllabus for A-level maths

Not long ago somebody counted up and found over 50 variations of maths syllabuses in the UK, so it is only possible to make very general remarks. The six main Boards — JMB, London, AEB, Oxford, Cambridge, Oxford and Cambridge — each provide a range of syllabuses. In addition, the Oxford and Cambridge Board runs the exams for two projects — the School Mathematics Project (SMP) and Mathematics in Education and Industry (MEI). If you have any questions about syllabuses, you ought to obtain a copy of the syllabus for your Examination Board from your school, college or local centre.

Mathematics
Most syllabuses are designed so that everybody does pure maths and is then allowed to do either mechanics, or statistics, or a mixture of mechanics and statistics. An important exception is the SMP syllabus which requires you to do both mechanics and statistics.

If your school offers the choice it is common for students doing science A-levels to study pure maths and mechanics, while those studying arts A-levels go for pure maths and statistics. If you are thinking of architecture as a career, then A-level mechanics could be helpful.

Further mathematics
The syllabuses consist of pure maths, mechanics and statistics taken to a higher level than in maths A-level. As well as extra knowledge, a deeper understanding is expected.

Pure mathematics
Most Boards provide this single subject eg JMB, Cambridge, AEB, London, MEI and Oxford. The syllabus usually consists of the pure maths sections of the maths syllabus and the further maths syllabus.

Applied mathematics
This single subject is available from London, AEB and MEI at the moment. The syllabus usually consists of the mechanics and statistics of the maths syllabus and further maths syllabus.

The choice of syllabus
Each Board bases its A-level syllabus on its O-level syllabus, so it is natural for schools to stay with the same Board throughout the course. But it may be that you are in a school which offers a choice of A-level syllabuses, or you may be moving to a new school, a sixth-form college or a technical college. It is possible

that these centres will offer a choice of say, Cambridge A-level or MEI A-level. What should you do?

It is not possible to give detailed advice in this book: you must go to your teachers for guidance. The right choice will depend on the kind of O-level you did, how adaptable you are, and what you want from the A-level course. But here are some things to bear in mind.

Firstly, the various syllabuses do have a great deal in common. In recent years, steps have been taken by the Boards to agree on and increase the amount of common ground. So the differences between any two syllabuses are usually small.

Secondly, some schools deliberately change to a different Board at A-level. For example, some schools do SMP O-level and then switch to the Oxford and Cambridge Board's A-level, so there are teachers who believe that a change of Board is a good idea.

Finally, a word about SMP and MEI. If you did SMP O-level, and are moving on to a different A-level syllabus, you will need to do some extra algebra and trigonometry. On the other hand, you will be well equipped with matrices, vectors and probability. Similarly, if you start SMP A-level without SMP O-level, extra work will be necessary in some areas. To a lesser extent, the same is true of changes to and from MEI. It is particularly important to go to your teachers for help and advice in these situations.

Assessment
Almost all the Boards assess students on two or three written papers. If a Board sets three papers, then the first is a multiple-choice paper to test the basic parts of the syllabus. (London's new pure maths with statistics syllabus is assessed on three written papers but involves project work).

Courses and careers after A-level maths
Degree courses
Maths A-level is essential if you want to go on to degree courses in maths, engineering or physics. Most university courses in computer science and operational research require maths A-level too.

Two maths A-levels – eg maths and further maths – used to be essential if you wanted to read maths at university. But almost all the universities are accepting suitably gifted students who have studied maths only and have obtained a high grade.

So if at this stage you are not clear whether you want to do maths or science at university, you can safely embark on maths, physics, chemistry and know that you still have the choice before you.

However, if at this stage you are quite sure you are going to do maths at university then you should seriously consider doing two maths A-levels. You go much more deeply into the subject, can spend more time on projects or interesting problems and thus start the university course with more confidence and experience. As a rule, the harder the university is to get into, the more desirable double maths becomes.

Physics, engineering and economics can all involve difficult mathematics at university so if you are strong at maths and firmly intend to specialise in these subjects, double maths and physics or double maths and economics are combinations to consider.

Maths A-level is useful if you are going for geography or social sciences, and some universities require it if you are going for accountancy, business studies or economics. You can check this by consulting your careers teacher or the *Compendium of University Entrance Requirements* which comes out each year (see Appendix E).

Careers
With numbers, statistics and computers so much part of modern life it is not surprising that an A-level in maths is one of the most generally useful qualifications you can get at school. This is particularly true if you go straight into a job at 18.

The main careers where maths plays a significant part are:

Accountancy
Actuarial profession
Air traffic control
Architecture
Armed Forces
Banking
Computing and data processing
Economics
Engineering of all types
Meteorology
Operational research, management, planning
Optics
Sciences of all types
Statistics

Surveying
Teaching and research.

I imagine this list is longer than you expected. It goes to show how much our society uses maths and people who are competent at it.

Your choice
If you decide to take A-level maths, make sure you get off to a sound start. The subject needs good foundations for A-level just as it did for O-level or CSE. So sort out your difficulties with your teacher as soon as they arise. In this way you will be helping yourself to get as much as possible out of this enjoyable and rewarding subject.

If you decide against taking maths, do try to keep up your interest in the subject. Whatever your A-level choice, there are bound to be times when your maths is needed. Your school or college may run simple courses in computing or statistics in the first year of the sixth form. Here are the titles of two books which are enjoyable, straightforward and instructive.

How to Lie with Statistics Darrell Huff (Penguin).
Mathematics David Bergamini (Time-Life).

Physical science
by Mary Munro

Physical science is offered at A-level by three Examination Boards — the AEB, JMB and Cambridge. Most of the entrants for this examination follow the Nuffield syllabus (administered by the Cambridge Board).

Physical science can be defined in various ways but, in general terms, it combines topics usually found in physics and chemistry. The JMB will not allow candidates to take the subject at the same sitting as physics, chemistry or engineering science, and Cambridge operates a similar restriction as regards physics and chemistry, on the grounds that the subjects are too close to each other. The idea behind physical science was to provide a single subject which would be an acceptable background for university courses which require A-level physics or chemistry, or both. As a subject, therefore, it is commonly combined with A-level mathematics and/or biology, or with another subject such as further mathematics, or with an arts or social science subject.

The syllabuses combine theoretical and practical aspects and offer candidates many opportunities to relate their practical work to scientific theory. Students should expect to spend a lot of their time in laboratory work, for experiments and bench-work are an integral part of the course. For the Nuffield syllabus, in particular, there is no practical examination but candidates (who must be at school — at least, on first entry) are required to submit a practical project.

Syllabus

The revised Nuffield syllabus is arranged in ten main sections, including a materials section and a project. The sections are:

- motion and energy
- the periodic table
- electric and magnetic fields
- classification and rates of chemical reactions
- structure
- compounds of carbon
- equilibrium and spontaneity
- waves, photons and electrons
- materials
- project.

The materials section is one of the focal points of the course. It brings together many of the concepts and principles of chemistry and physics that are developed in the course, and gives it an applied-technological flavour. The three groups of materials included as options in this section are: metals; polymers; ceramics and glasses, and you are expected to study one of these.

The project is intended to be either an individual experimental investigation of a problem new to you, or an individual experiment-based study in depth of a topic of your choice outside the syllabus. A future engineer could, for example, choose a project based on electric motors or on some property of concrete. A potential medical student could choose a project in biochemistry, such as the effect of acids on digestive enzymes. The projects are assessed internally by the teacher and moderated externally by the examiners.

The mathematical knowledge required for the course includes algebra, trigonometry, calculus, graphical methods.

Details are given in the Boards' syllabuses. There are sub-divisions of these topics and you should therefore consult the Board's syllabus for further details. Many other topics, which might have found a place in physical science, have been omitted from the syllabuses because the course would have become unwieldy. Even so, the syllabuses tend to be full and demanding. The Nuffield syllabus places emphasis on the handling of facts rather than the accumulation of detail. If you choose to do this subject, you must expect to do a lot of work, both in the classroom and in the laboratories.

In the AEB syllabus, there is a special study and the practical examination is based on it.

The examination
A-level is examined by two or three papers (depending on the Board), typically of two, two and a half or three hours each, plus a practical examination of three hours or, for Nuffield, a project in place of a practical examination. The practical requires observation, accuracy in carrying out quantitative operations (measuring, filtrating etc) and the ability to make estimates and perform arithmetical calculations correctly. The written papers are designed to test knowledge of the syllabus and your understanding of the scientific topics contained in it.

After O-level
It is advantageous for students choosing to take A-level physical science to have done O-level chemistry and/or physics or physical science. It is not absolutely necessary to take A-level mathematics, although this is usual. Students could get by with O-level mathematics or additional mathematics — the syllabuses explain what mathematical knowledge is required to be able to cope with the A-level work in physical science.

After A-level
Physical science is a useful subject to have as a qualification to gain entry to science or technology degree or diploma courses at university, polytechnic or college. Taken with A-level mathematics, it is acceptable for most degree courses in engineering and for degrees in medicine and related subjects. It has the advantage of enabling a student to study topics in physics and chemistry to A-level as well as taking biology and mathematics, without undertaking such a heavy programme as four A-levels.

For more information related to this subject, you should

read the chapters on chemistry and on physics in this book. They give more detailed information about the nature of these subjects, which make up the two parts of physical science. The chapters also tell you in more detail about entry to higher education and later careers.

Physics
by Roger Wakely

What is physics?
Physics is the study of how and why things are, and how they behave. Physicists ask questions like 'Why is the sky blue?' 'Why do some materials conduct electricity better than others?' 'Why does washing-up liquid get the grease off dirty plates?' In finding the answers to such questions, physicists will often go on to ask 'how'. How can the energy of wind, waves and sun be harnessed for man's use? How can new inexpensive memories for use in computers be devised? How can noise from aircraft be reduced? At this point, physicists hand over to engineers who convert an idea which is scientifically possible into something which is practical and usable.

Physics involves designing experiments to make observations and measurements, and it uses mathematics to process the measurements and look for patterns in them. It is important to record accurately what has been measured and observed, and to be able to explain to other people both in speech and in writing what has happened and why. Physics appeals to people who like to know how gadgets work, not only complicated devices like calculators or colour televisions, but also simpler things such as the carburettor of a car or a piezo-electric gas lighter. It also appeals to people concerned about our environment, about the dangers of nuclear energy, the problems of pollution, and the proper use of the earth's energy and mineral resources. Physicists contribute to the understanding of our solar system, of more distant galaxies, and of strange objects such as black holes.

A-level physics
Because physics investigates such a large variety of different things, it is divided into areas for study. Among them are topics such as heat, light and electricity. Alternatively, the subject can be divided up by concepts such as energy, motion, or action at a distance. Many A-level courses take a knowledge of O-level

physics as their starting point, so it would be hard (though not impossible if you are really determined) to begin an A-level course from scratch. A-level courses develop the topics introduced at O-level, going into the theory in more depth and using more advanced mathematics to do so. There is generally much more opportunity for individual practical work than at O-level, partly because the class sizes are smaller, and also because the student is more experienced and can safely use more sophisticated and sometimes delicate equipment. Practical work will probably occupy about one quarter of the teaching time, and will be a mixture of standard measurements and investigations, together with an opportunity to undertake a project to investigate some new problem. In some schools and colleges, technology and other workshop facilities can be used by physics students to make apparatus needed for their projects. Many new and fascinating pieces of equipment are used in A-level physics courses. A student will be using electronic timers, oscilloscopes, apparatus to measure the charge of an electron or the energy of a photon, and perhaps have the opportunity to link this equipment to a computer to monitor continuously the progress of an experiment. The microchip has arrived in the physics laboratory, enabling students to undertake a far wider and more interesting range of experiments.

Laboratory work and theoretical studies
Laboratory work normally runs in parallel with theory in which relevant formulae are worked out and ways of applying them to a variety of situations are studied. These formulae together with examples and problems to illustrate them and the descriptive background are covered in the standard textbooks. However, many of these books do not relate this theoretical work to lab work and to practical applications. It is often left to your teacher to provide this link and to give you the framework and sequence in which to work. Also most A-level syllabuses attempt to give the student some understanding of a broad range of physics topics — mechanics, vibration, waves, heat, electricity, atomic physics and properties of materials.

Nuffield physics
A different approach and a course which links more closely the theory, practical work and applications is known as Nuffield physics. This course selects a smaller number of important ideas (leaving out most of the optics, heat and mechanics in

other courses) and aims to pursue these to a deeper level. The course encourages the students to think for themselves and to use informed guesses if a problem is too complex to analyse fully. It is less formal and uses less mathematics than other physics courses and both the coursework and the examinations try to be more adventurous than the other syllabuses. Nuffield physics provides a structure within which students can follow up their own ideas. For someone keen to do this it can be really exciting, but is a little intimidating for those who like to have what is expected of them clearly cut-and-dried with examples to copy throughout the course. (Around 17% of the entry at A-level is for Nuffield physics.)

How is physics taught?

Whatever syllabus you are following it will often be true that a topic can be approached in a number of different ways. It is therefore a good idea to read other books in addition to your main textbooks. Often the so-called all-embracing textbook leaves out interesting details which shorter topic books explain and illustrate in a much better way. Homework is vital to cover the work with proper thoroughness and this will normally be a mixture of textbook reading, of reading around the topic, of doing problems (both descriptive and mathematical) and writing up accounts of experimental work.

Teaching methods vary widely and to some extent they reflect the syllabus of the A-level examination. Methods vary from the traditional trio of lectures, problem sessions, and lab work, to the almost teach-yourself methods used in some London schools where teacher shortages or very small classes mean that teachers are available only to supervise practical work, to oversee general progress, and to mark assignments. Many schools and colleges adopt a Nuffield approach and encourage open-ended enquiry whether or not they actually use the Nuffield syllabus.

The examination

Most A-level examinations consist of two or three written papers together with a practical examination. The written papers often include one which is 'multiple-choice' ie you are provided with a list of possible answers and have to choose which one is correct. Students who are quick at calculations and who don't like essay-type questions tend to prefer this type of examination, although the questions often involve choosing valid explanations so are verbal rather than numerical. The multiple-choice paper is balanced by a paper in which the emphasis is on explanation and description, and some syllabuses (eg London and Nuffield) have a comprehension paper to test the understanding of passages of scientific writing. The practical examination is a test of skill and practical competence rather than of knowledge. In terms of marks, the multiple-choice paper may carry 30-40% of the total marks and the longer theory questions are awarded between 35% and 50%. The practical and comprehension papers carry most marks (25%) on the London syllabus. As with all A-level examinations, there are five pass grades which in physics range from grade A for a score of about 70% or more, down to grade E for a mark of 40%. Those who just miss grade E are awarded an O-level pass.

Further courses and careers

Physics is often combined at A-level with either mathematics or chemistry or both. Mathematics and physics are essential requirements for degree and diploma courses in all branches of engineering, for courses in physics, applied physics, meteorology, and are extremely useful for mathematics degree courses. Within university courses in physics there are all kinds of options such as astrophysics, geophysics, radiation physics, medical physics, marine physics, solid state physics and many more. If you are aiming at very high-powered mathematics or physics degree courses you would probably combine your A-level physics with double subject mathematics, either pure and applied or mathematics and further mathematics.

Mathematics, physics and chemistry probably opens up the widest range of options of all A-level combinations. They are acceptable for courses mentioned earlier as well as for metallurgy and materials science, geology, chemical engineering, plus all the biological sciences, biochemistry and medicine (with biology at O-level). Physics, chemistry and biology is also a very popular combination and although less relevant for engineering and technological subjects, is useful for agriculture, forestry, biology, pharmacy, optics and dietetics. Other combinations of physics with geography, economics, and other arts subjects are also possible and can be used for surveying, building, architecture, printing technology, photography, textile technology, radiography, orthoptics and many others.

If you are going into a job after A-level, physics is an entry to many careers. Many of the fields of work mentioned above can be entered after A-levels and further qualifications gained by day-release or correspondence courses. Opportunities exist in laboratory work of all kinds including medical laboratory work, the armed services, the merchant navy, environmental health and patent work, to name but a few.

Although there is not a strong tradition of A-level entry into engineering jobs, opportunities are growing for A-level leavers, particularly in electronics. Several large companies now recruit their future senior technicians from those who have studied maths and physics to A-level. Again, further qualifications would be gained by day-release part-time study.

Physics graduates are employed in a very wide range of industries: chemical, oil, construction, aircraft, electrical, gas, food, in all types of job research and development, quality control, production and general management. They also get involved in a variety of research areas from astrophysics to medical physics.

Physics is a subject which is held in very high regard by employers. The scope of jobs and careers is very wide. You should write for two booklets, *Physics Courses in Higher Education* and *Careers with Physics* which are obtainable from the Education Officer at the Institute of Physics, 47 Belgrave Square, London SW1X 8QX. Also read CRAC's *Connections – Physics*.

Last word
Finally, before you embark on your A-level physics course, with all its interest and variety, do find out in detail what the course contains. You should get a copy of the examination syllabus which gives details of the topics covered and the style and marking of examination papers. Your school or college should be able to provide a copy, or tell you where you can obtain one.

Social biology
by Mary Munro

Social biology is a fairly new syllabus offered only by the Cambridge Board, which concentrates on the social and environmental aspect of biology. The emphasis is on man and the biochemical aspects of biology are avoided.

Syllabus
There have been considerable changes in the syllabus for the

1985 exams onwards.

The new syllabus covers the following topics:

● heredity and diversity
● body organisation and function
● human growth and development
● the evolution of man
● the health of mankind
● human ecology
● contemporary issues in social biology.

For the last item, six problems with social and biological aspects are suggested: aggression and altruism; drug use and abuse; mental health; eugenics and euthanasia; race and racial issues; and, finally, the problems of alcohol.

In Paper 1 of the examination there will be a compulsory question on one of these topics and you will be expected to demonstrate in scientific terms an understanding of the social and scientific basis of the topic.

Examinations

Paper 1   2½ hours.
Essay questions which will assess your knowledge and your ability to express yourself in concise scientific terms. This will include the compulsory question mentioned above.
Paper 2   1 hour.
An objective test consisting of 40 multiple-choice questions.
Paper 3   1¾ hours.
Structured questions test your ability to analyse and interpret unfamiliar information, often in the form of data presentations, and apply the knowledge you possess to those unfamiliar situations.

There is no final practical examination but examiners are looking for evidence of practical experience and understanding of scientific method.

There is an optional scheme of individual studies for which candidates are required to submit a written report on a project. A good project can enable the student to improve the final grade in the examination. Projects can involve such things as study of indications of pollution in a local river, or a study of air pollution by looking at lichens, or projects with a more sociological bias such as a study of local facilities for caring for old people.

Classwork
There is as yet no single textbook which covers the course and
you must be prepared to follow references from a range of
texts. Teaching will be mainly in the classroom, although you
will do some laboratory work and some field trips to collect
material and data for study. Visits could be to museums,
sewage works, old peoples' homes and hospitals in order to
give students some first-hand experience relating to the topics
in the syllabus.

Subject combinations
With such a wide-ranging syllabus covering topics in zoology,
biology, sociology and geography, the question obviously
arises about which other subjects you should take with social
biology. At present neither biology nor zoology will be counted
as separate subjects, although geography and sociology are.
The overlap with sociology is greater than the overlap with
geography, although this depends on the options taken in the
social biology syllabus. Social biology could be taken with a
wide range of subjects including other sciences, maths,
geography, history, economics and modern languages. It would
help to have studied O-level biology or human biology but it is
not essential and most sixth-form centres will consider the
ability of each individual applicant to cope with the course.

Careers and further courses
Social biology is obviously very suitable if you are considering a
career in a paramedical field (physiotherapy, nursing, occupational therapy, speech therapy etc) and if you have not had
the chance to study much science at O-level or CSE. It is also
suitable for a career in primary teaching and for environmental
studies or ecology courses at university, polytechnic or college
of higher education. However, it is unlikely that a university
department will prefer social biology to a pure science A-level
for these or other science courses and it is doubtful if it would
be acceptable for any course where general biology was a
requirement unless it was well supported by physics and
chemistry at O-level. There are one or two degree courses in
social biology at colleges of higher education.

Finally
Social biology is not a wise alternative to biology if you can
cope with the chemistry content of this and if you need an A-
level biology for entry to a science-based course in higher

education. It is, on the other hand, a very attractive alternative if you are interested in man and the environment and it is very suitable for many paramedical and educational careers. It would also have a role in widening an otherwise arts biased A-level course for some students. It is a wide-ranging and interesting course of a topical and important nature, but should not be undertaken with the illusion that it will lead automatically to jobs in organisations concerned with conservation and the environment.

Statistics
by Peter Holmes

Which of these two drugs is better?
What is the best concentration of this fertiliser?
How many teachers will we need in five years' time? Where? In what subjects?
Is this machine set correctly? At what level should I set it to maximise profits?
How has the cost of living risen over the past two years?
What is a fair insurance premium for my car?

The answers to all these questions require the use of statistics. Statistics is concerned with measuring and with data. It is the subject which helps you to make decisions in the face of uncertainty. One of its great attractions is that its applications can come from almost any field of human endeavour. It is essentially a practical subject. It considers general questions. What are the appropriate data? How can I obtain them? How can I use them most efficiently? What do they tell me about the inferences I can draw?

The nature of statistics
Statistics is an interesting subject in its own right, especially for people with enquiring minds, because it can involve familiarity with many different backgrounds in which the data arise. Quite often, the context in which the data are collected will affect the inferences that are drawn. For example, data that 40 out of 100 people say they will vote Conservative from an opinion poll is inherently less accurate than data that 40 out of 100 ball bearings are below a certain weight, and should be treated accordingly. A good statistics course can make a student a jack of all trades and a master of one (statistics). It is the inherent

usefulness of statistics that makes the subject an excellent A-level choice for students whose primary interest is in one of the fields of study which are increasingly using quantitative methods. These subjects include geography, economics, biology and the life sciences, psychology, medicine and allied subjects, social science and commerce.

Mathematics

To study statistics at A-level, it is not necessary to have studied it first at O-level. However, those students who have taken an O-level statistics course will come to the A-level with a greater appreciation of the nature of data and of underlying statistical concepts and techniques. They will not suffer as much as others from the problems of being exposed to a large number of new ideas in a short space of time. Nevertheless, most students of statistics start the subject at A-level. A-level statistics, however, does require a background provided by O-level maths, since it is a subject which requires a lot of mathematics.

At A-level, the subject takes a fairly mathematical character. There are many courses in mathematics and statistics which clearly contain a substantial amount of mathematics. There are also, however, A-levels specifically in statistics and it is these that this chapter is about. References to the other type of syllabus will be found under the chapter on mathematics.

A-level syllabuses

The syllabuses of the three Examination Boards which offer statistics vary in the emphasis placed on theory and techniques. The Cambridge Board is almost entirely theoretical, whereas the AEB approach expects the students to carry out more calculations. From the student's point of view, the amount of practical work completed in class will depend on the approach used by the teacher. Calculators will be required and students who have access to a computer may have a chance to use it for statistical problems, or to try some of the many statistical packages being developed for use on microcomputers. As yet, no syllabus requires the use of a computer. The main aim of the syllabus is to give students a theoretical background to what is involved in the various processes statisticians apply to data of all sorts. The JMB has a compulsory project which the student has to carry out and write up as a report. This is seen as part of the teaching process where guided help from the teacher is given. The choice of subject for the project is left to the student.

All these courses contain simple measures of sample distributions (such as the mean, median and variance) and elementary probability theory which extends to some simple probability models such as the binomial, Poisson and normal distributions. The theoretical distributions are then used in simple cases of hypothesis testing to help draw inferences about the actual values obtained in a sample. There is also some work on regression and, in some cases, correlation, which are concepts used to examine the association between variables, for example the yield of a plant and the amount of fertiliser applied.

For full details, students should obtain a copy of the syllabus for the A-level examination from the Board, school, college or local centre.

Classwork
Students can expect to be involved in some practical work. This can vary from simple experiments, tossing coins or throwing dice, to more substantial fieldwork, such as conducting a traffic survey. Most of the course time is spent on establishing the theoretical basis behind simple statistical methods. This is usually reinforced by time spent working out simple exercises based on the theory just learned.

Some examples of this kind of work are evaluating a set of quality control measurements of the diameters of newly minted coins, calculating the error involved and assessing its acceptability in terms of material costs, labour costs etc. Discussion of the most suitable methods for particular problems and the pitfalls of the methods of taking samples such as those mentioned above will also be an important part of the classwork. Homework could consist of collecting data for analysis, practising similar examples to the type tried in class, or writing conclusions in a comprehensible form after annotating your calculations.

Examinations
Formal examination papers form part of the assessment procedure for statistics. Each Board expects students to take two three-hour papers and gives a choice of questions on each paper. The Joint Matriculation Board also requires all its candidates to carry out a project and submit a report on their work. This report is first assessed at the school or college and then moderated by the Board.

Subject combinations and further courses

Statistics may be combined with A-level maths and computer science or computer studies. However, it is more often taken with arts or social science subjects. Other subjects that are beginning to use statistical methods at A-level are geography, economics and psychology. A-level statistics is therefore an excellent support subject for these and for entry to courses in higher education which use quantitative methods, such as sociology, social administration, business studies, accountancy, agriculture, environmental sciences and computer studies. The choice of other subjects to be taken at A-level would also depend on the requirements for the main subject of interest. Statistics itself is not likely to be an entry requirement for any degree or diploma course, even for a degree in statistics, but it is an exceedingly useful A-level, none the less.

Further courses

Statistics can be studied at universities and polytechnics as a degree subject. At this level it is usually highly mathematical and is often studied in conjunction with mathematics. In order to study statistics at degree level, it is therefore essential that the student has an A-level in a mathematical subject. In this respect, A-level pure mathematics with statistics is considered as a mathematical qualification but the A-level statistics course described above is not, although it is a useful background. Anyone wishing to study statistics in its own right as a degree subject and who wishes to study A-level statistics should also study an A-level in mathematics.

Statistics can also be studied further on higher diploma courses in mathematics, statistics and computing in many polytechnics. Again, A-level mathematics is a useful background.

Careers

If you are starting your career after A-level, statistics is particularly useful for statistical posts, laboratory work, accountancy, market research, as well as for many Civil Service and local government jobs. It is possible to qualify further in statistics by taking day-release or evening classes and studying for the examinations of the Institute of Statisticians. On completion of the stage III (three-year post-A-level) examination, you would become a fully qualified statistician.

As a statistician, you could be employed in industry in the field of quality control, in market research (finding out and analysing people's opinions), in government service (collecting and analysing data to make planning decisions), in insurance (deciding on appropriate premiums and forecasting), in medical research (in designing and assessing experiments to develop and test new or better treatments), and in many other ways. For further information, a free booklet *Careers in Statistics* is available from the Institute of Statisticians, 36 Churchgate Street, Bury St Edmunds, Suffolk IP33 1RD.

Surveying
by John B Garner

The Associated Examining Board is the only Board to offer an A-level in surveying. The syllabus is designed to promote an understanding of linear, angular and height measurements and their combination in the production of maps and plans. Literacy, numeracy and practical skills all play an important part in the assessment of candidates taking the examination. The subject is offered by several Boards at O-level, and some candidates for the A-level course will have studied the subject to this level. However, O-level is not a necessary prerequisite for the A-level course: it is useful but not essential.

The syllabus
The syllabus is divided into three sections:

Section A covers the historical development of the subject and the physical bases on which observations are made. Linear, angular and height measurements are covered and their applications in surveying practice. In addition, the computation, adjustment and plotting of surveys are included.

Section B deals with photogrammetry, or the use of aerial photographs for producing maps and plans. It also covers the use of aerial photographs as a source of information for various purposes.

Section C covers engineering surveys and setting out on site.

The syllabus and examinations are structured such that Sections B and C may be considered as alternatives and it is not necessary that both are studied.

The examination

There are two three-hour written examination papers and a prescribed programme of practical work. The distribution of the marks between the various components is as follows:

Paper I   35%
Paper II   35%
Practical Work   30%.

Paper I is based entirely on Section A of the syllabus with most of the questions requiring analytical solutions. Paper II contains three essay-type questions based on Section A of the syllabus, together with optional questions from Sections B and C.

Practical work

The practical work is carried out during the course and is supervised and assessed by the centres but subject to moderation by the AEB. The work involves a series of prescribed projects dealing with the basic elements of map and plan production, together with one piece of work selected from either engineering surveying or photogrammetry. The three compulsory projects involve theodolite traverse levelling; braced quadrilateral observation and adjustment (using methods of equal shift); and either a horizontal highway curve (design and set out), or an air-photo interpretation project.

Equipment

In addition to the basic equipment such as chains, tapes and ranging poles, the only other equipment you would use would be a level and staff, and a theodolite.

Further courses

It is unlikely that this subject would be required by selectors for courses in higher education. It seems to be perfectly acceptable, however, as a third or possibly fourth subject, and since it involves elements of mathematics, physics and geography, it would be an excellent subject to complement any combination from these subjects. In addition, there are a number of students who are already studying surveying as part of a certificate or diploma course who are able to take the subject further in order to take the A-level examination.

Careers

In addition to those who take further courses in land surveying, and make it a career, there are many more who go on to take courses in other areas leading to careers in a wide variety of professions where surveying constitutes an important part. Such disciplines include geology and the earth sciences, geography, building and building surveying, civil engineering, mining and applied mineral sciences. The A-level course in surveying would, therefore, serve as an extremely useful introduction to those students aiming for careers in any of these areas, although for the more technical ones it should be combined with mathematics, physics, or other science subject. Further information about careers in surveying can be obtained from the Careers Department, Royal Institution of Chartered Surveyors, 12 Great George Street, Parliament Square, London SW1P 3AD.

Chapter 7

Modern and classical languages

Greek (with classical studies)
by Elisabeth Henry

The special qualities of Greek

To describe one language as more subtle, rich, or expressive
than another might seem too subjective to mean very much;
but some qualities of language are measurable. Greek has a
much larger vocabulary than most languages; it has an unusual
number of inflexional forms, and an extremely wide range of
grammatical alternatives for expressing identical or similar
structures of thought. Above all, it has a unique wealth of
idiom to convey written equivalents to a tone of voice, such as
the two-letter particle suggesting 'yes, but at least one has to
admit . . .', or a three-word phrase that says 'of course that is
so, and how could it possibly be otherwise?' This makes Greek
prose vivacious and poised; there is also immense scope in the
language for poetic imagery of every kind during the thousand
years or more which are embraced in the term 'ancient Greek
literature'.

Start with O-level

These qualities of Greek make it very hard to reach the stage of
reading without a dictionary, but not at all hard to learn to
respond to a Greek author's mood or intention or level of
seriousness. (A good translator can clarify for us the response
that the author demands, but anyone who is interested in words
will find intense pleasure and satisfaction in a direct encounter
with the original writer.) The early stages of Greek, taking you
to O-level, may not make these characteristics of the language
entirely clear to you, because the vocabulary required for O-
level is deliberately limited. The one or two authors chosen for
study will use only a small range of the more straightforward
literary styles. A-level Greek will require not merely more
words but different kinds of words and will enable you to meet
more complex and sophisticated literature.

The difficulty of the A-level course, then, will not be the
amount that has to be covered, but the nature of the language
and the extent of its difference from English. For this reason it
is not really practicable to take A-level from scratch without
doing O-level first. An O-level course provides tools which are
indispensable.

Those tools, some of which can be acquired through the
study of Latin, can be used for linguistic analysis in other

languages as well. The habit of scrutinising words, exploring the scope of their meanings and their history, often leads to illumination of hidden senses and references in English words or phrases such as: 'climax', 'anode' and 'cathode', 'ostracism', 'thou art Peter, and upon this rock . . .' The Greek element in English does not go back to the earliest roots of our language, but it provides the words needed in a later age when English speakers wanted to describe what they were doing in the arts, religion, politics, medicine and science.

The A-level course

Reading Greek forms a large part of all A-level courses, whether in the form of practice for traditional unseen translation tests or as study of prescribed authors. Nowadays, these are usually examined by comprehension-type exercises and by essay-type questions as well as, or instead of, the translation of passages from the work studied. The third element which used to be equally important with unseens and books was translation into Greek. However, this is no longer compulsory, and with most Boards it has become an alternative to an additional paper on literature, requiring wider reading in Greek from a prescribed author or a particular period or group of works. Translation into Greek really means learning to handle one or two distinct styles such as historical narrative (you must write like Xenophon, more or less!) or dialogue on social or political themes (like Plato, again more or less!) or, in rare cases, verse in tragic or lyric metres, which is a very esoteric and delightful skill. Anyone who successfully practises translation into Greek has gained a real grasp of grammatical structure (English as well as Greek) and is likely to read more perceptively as a result. However this demands much time, like all arts; many students and teachers think it more valuable to read two more plays in Greek perhaps, or another book of Thucydides.

Some will take this train of thought even further: why not read six plays, and three books of Thucydides, by using English versions all the time? There are many very good translations in print, and often several available for a single work, so that one could read the *Odyssey*, for example, in many English styles from Tudor to present-day American. To read in English extends the quantity and range of the reading enormously, and enables the reader to avoid being enmeshed in language and to attend to what the author has to say. Euripides in *Medea* expresses the heart of conflict in women's liberation; Plato's

Apology presents Socrates as a timeless prisoner of conscience; Homer makes us know war, both heroic and degrading.

Classical studies

The importance of this literature in content and also in its historical context may be good reason for many to choose a syllabus in classical studies (or some such title) in preference to Greek at A-level. Whatever it is called, this subject will include many topics of wider scope than A-level Greek can allow time for. These may start from prescribed authors, read in English, but they will go on to themes like the Greek theatre, ancient democracy, or the visual arts such as sculpture or architecture. Study of this kind needs a historical framework, and part of the course will use historical methods; the A-level papers usually require most answers in essay form, though passages for comment from source-authors are often included. The syllabus is usually equally divided between Greek and Roman topics.

Combining Greek with other subjects

Because of the creative diversity of Greek culture, there are many different A-level subjects which can relate equally well with Greek or classical studies. English, history, and Latin are the most usual companions, but there are many other rewarding combinations, either at A-level or in a degree course. A modern language course gains from Greek in the same way as English does, through comparison of grammatical usage and the growth of awareness of idiom and vocabulary. There are also immense literary debts to Greece, especially in the study of German. The more modern fields of study which relate to history (archaeology, sociology, politics) are greatly strengthened if the student has the ability to read even a small part of the source material which exists for them in ancient Greek.

University courses

Greek at A-level is required for most degree courses in classics (if not at A-, then necessary at O-level).

Subjects which may be started at university, and which benefit exceptionally from an A-level groundwork in Greek, include linguistics, philosophy, and theology. A-level classical studies is a strong and a natural base for degree work in any of a dozen subjects in a faculty of arts in universities, polytechnics and colleges. It is a valuable support for a professional course in art or education, and is acceptable in any combination of subjects as a qualification for university entrance, even for such apparently remote subjects as law or mathematics. (As a supporting subject on an application form it must be recognised also that Greek has for some admissions tutors a kind of charisma or special quality which commands notice.)

Do you have the choice?

All this has been written as if the choice of A-level Greek were readily available in any school or sixth-form college. This of course is very far from the truth; it may be very difficult to find the opportunity for A-level teaching or even O-level in the language. Classical studies can be made available much more easily if students ask for it with persistence. It is worth remembering that many universities now offer beginners' courses in Greek, and there are several well established summer schools for Greek beginners or near-beginners, mainly attended by students of sixth-form age. These can lead to a more advanced course later for those who missed the chance of A-level when they were at school.

Careers

For entry to jobs requiring A-levels, Greek is most unlikely to be asked for specifically. However, it is undoubtedly accepted as an A-level pass for careers which require this and, furthermore, it is likely to impress employers. Some apparently believe if you can do Greek, you can do anything. People with an A-level in Greek can be found in such diverse jobs as computer programming, marketing and social work.

People who have taken degrees in classics, or general degrees with a classical component, are not always recognisable at first sight in later life. They won't all be teaching or working in museums. They may be journalists or politicians, bankers or public relations officers in the Civil Service or in industry. They may never have to open a classical book or read a word of Greek in the course of their working lives. However, a good many of them will read new books on ancient history, go to Crete or Etruria for their holidays, join a local archaeology group, see classical exhibitions and perhaps remember Plato's writings at election time. Many will say that they think they do their non-classical jobs better because they once studied classics, and many will say it has made their lives more interesting. An A-level choice which can lead in that sort of direction is worth a good deal.

110

Latin
by Denis Henry

O-level and A-level compared

Latin up to O-level is mainly an investigation of the Latin language. If you have studied what has come to be called traditional O-level Latin, you will have analysed passages either through comprehension — thus gradually elucidating the detail and more general meaning of a passage which is at first obscure to you — or by translation, thus making your understanding more continuous and complete. The authors you will have read are likely to have been Livy, Ovid, and perhaps Virgil. If you have used the Cambridge Latin course, you are likely to have rehearsed Latin in a more dramatic way as a series of fables. This method seeks to reproduce at first the tone of the spoken, and later the written language, with fable put aside and authors like Pliny, Virgil, Tacitus and Catullus to study. You will have been encouraged, no doubt, to link what you read of these authors to relevant and familiar domestic, social and historical situations. In responding to those situations you will have enlarged your interest in the life they describe and contrasted it with the life you see around you now.

Language skills and imagination

Doing A-level Latin will combine features from both methods, and demand both sorts of response from you at the same time. Latin at A-level is demanding; it requires a clear, precise and extensive knowledge of the language. This is why it cannot be done without having previously studied O-level. It also encourages and fosters a further and more special kind of understanding through the imagination. To illustrate. There is in one of the books you are likely to read as part of the A-level course (Virgil *Aeneid* Book VI line 743) a phrase which has become famous: *quisque suos patimur manes*. Anchises, Aeneas' father, is explaining to his son what the large gathering of ghosts on the bank of the river of Hell, Lethe, means. They are, he says, waiting to be reborn into life. At the time, Aeneas is visiting his father from the world of living men and is alive. Anchises is dead and is looking sadly at the dead who will return to life. Anchises speaks in the light of the experience of his own lifetime now ended. It is simple to translate the words I have just quoted as 'We all endure our own ghosts'. To say what they mean, however, is a task of some difficulty and involves an understanding of this great epic poet, as well as of Roman religion and its concepts of sin, the nature of death, human relationships and human experience. It requires an imaginative act of understanding and one which will be individual to you.

Grammar, words and meanings

Latin is an inflected language in which a change of termination of nouns indicates a change of case. At first sight it uses this characteristic to pay little attention to word order as a vehicle for establishing sense. Objects in the accusative case may precede subjects, verbs may linger so far behind that you despair sometimes of ever reaching them. Almost every Latin sentence, however simple, demands of the reader that he finishes the whole before he can understand any part. In this way the unit of sense is lengthened in comparison with an uninflected language. Undoubtedly this makes the process of translating Latin slower than, say, French or Spanish. In compensation, however, it contributes to an unusual range of feeling and expression.

Just before the passage I have quoted from the *Aeneid*, in line 318, Aeneas asks his guide to the Underworld about another crowd who are waiting to cross the stream that lies between a Limbo and a Hell. 'What is the meaning of the crowd by the river?' His words in Latin do not match the English order. The (to us) bleak disorder of the words may themselves suggest the bleakness of this borderland between nothingness and death. One could perhaps also say that the words in Latin only form themselves into intelligible shapes of sense in the mind after they have been thought, spoken or read. Rapid reading is not a device that lends itself to the Latin language.

Learning from literature

So far, we have spoken of the Latin language studied in the A-level course as a means of exciting the imagination. But in a different way it encourages what is today known as a structuralist approach. It is the literature of a people living amid unusual violence and having the likely prospect of dying before the age of 30. It presents material and evidence (added to constantly by archaeology) to those who have other interests as well. To the economist absorbed in the problem of inflation, the galloping inflation of the Roman Empire reflected in the satirist Juvenal is another, and distant, view. There are interesting parallels for the social analyst alert to the difficulties of a mixed society and immigration.

A psychologist will be concerned to explain the mental aberrations of a Nero or a Domitian in terms of the excessive concentration of power in one man's hands. A student of political administration may want to explain how a unit of government of the immense size of the Roman Empire could be controlled from a small administrative centre, but a centre with a memory bank so that the regulations for the Bithynian fire brigade were not too conspicuously different from those in force elsewhere. For others, the most challenging problem that the study of Latin A-level will provide, will be to show how an uninspired and rapidly decaying religion of Jupiter and the Olympian gods could with such extraordinary speed give rise to Christianity and help (even through its words) to form its structure. Students of A-level could well find themselves exploring from Rome to Christianity the development of the word 'genius'. No one should do A-level Latin without being prepared to use original thought and go beyond the range of what is set as the formal, agreed and recognised syllabus.

The syllabus

Much of the A-level syllabus of the various Examination Boards is concerned to assess a candidate's ability in language by presenting him with passages for translation (as at O-level) which he has not seen before. Unseen translations offer passages in prose and verse from central writers in the Roman literary tradition. It is not only language ability that is being assessed. Skill in the analysis of meaning, in deducing from evidence available in the unseen itself the tone, range, quality and appropriateness of the words are all looked for. The exercises make demands on a candidate's ability to discover an English meaning which matches the Latin in idiom and succinctness. Succinctness is one quality of Latin literature. Read the brief sentence in the *Annals* of Tacitus describing the Roman nobility in the age of Nero: *quasi per virtutem clari honoratique agere.* 'They lived famous and honoured as though for virtue.' Were they virtuous or not?

If you find yourself skilful in this process of transference of Latin into English, you may avail yourself of the option offered by most of the Examination Boards, that is the opportunity to reverse the process and translate from English into Latin, translation being in this case transmutation. 'Life dawns anew'

113

becomes in Cicero's words: *Alterius vitae quoddam initium ordimur*. But that isn't the way the words go.

The study of set books

Any literary subject must encourage, as part of a course which may lead on to a university course, the continuous and concentrated reading of what are unromantically known as prescribed books. The University of London examination syllabus, for instance, refers to this as a study of authors 'in some depth'. All of the Examination Boards differ in the way they attempt to direct this reading. Some link the detailed study of particular books with topics: for example one links the reading of Propertius Book I with the topic of love poetry and advises additional reading, not necessarily in Latin, from Ovid and Catullus. The aim clearly is to offer the opportunity for wider reference and the understanding of what a tradition is. Other Boards favour the reading of a single author such as Virgil *Aeneid* I-VI for comment and appreciation; a third group emphasise the topic and associate with it the works to be studied. All Boards offer an S paper which includes more difficult unseens, and a few Boards have a project-essay on a subject to be studied during the course and written about without notes during the examination. Subjects recently set have been transport in the Mediterranean world and town planning of Pompeii. The marks awarded to the prescribed texts are generally slightly more than those allocated for the language papers.

On to the university

Latin at A-level can be taken with a wide variety of other subjects and leads to a greater variety of university courses. The UCCA handbook is rather misleading as it indexes only Latin and you have to look under the separate universities for the many combined courses. Latin may lead to university courses in classics, law, theology, religious studies, archaeology with or without anthropology, ancient history with or without medieval history, Mediterranean studies, classics and drama. Combined with mathematics and further mathematics it could lead to courses in economics and computer studies (where Latin is a very useful introduction to computer languages). With French, German, Spanish, Italian or other languages, it could lead you into single subjects — or language combined courses. Taken at A-level with history or English, your study of Latin would give you entry to a great variety of combined or integrated arts courses. To take just one example, the recently introduced combined English and Latin degree course at Warwick University leads on directly from the study of these subjects at A-level. Other suitable courses are in law, archaeology, classical studies and civilisation, and philosophy.

Careers and jobs
What careers can you have in mind if you start on the study of Latin at A-level? Well, that will depend on circumstances at the time and the direction you follow. Careers in which the study of Latin and Greek have a direct bearing are archaeologist and museum curator, but of course you would need to go on first to a university course in history, archaeology or classics. Other careers in which classical scholars have made their mark are journalism, Civil Service, law, librarianship and teaching in university departments and in schools.

However, A-level Latin or a degree in classics is usually taken to indicate a person's considerable academic ability. This in itself could take you into banking and insurance, broadcasting, business, law, accountancy and a wide range of other non-technical careers.

Modern languages
by Robin Derbyshire

To start you thinking about studying languages at A-level here are answers to six major questions which are often asked by prospective students.

Grammar and vocabulary
Firstly: 'Will the course be any more than the acquisition of more and more grammar and vocabulary, and is such a course likely to sustain my interest?' It's important not to enter the course thinking that you will only have to study grammar and learn vocabulary. The range of study for the keen linguist is very wide and demanding. You will be for ever on the look-out for more sophisticated ways of expressing ideas, and satisfying your personal curiosity about their interrelationship. You must be enterprising in your researches, and acquire knowledge not just by chance encounter with words, but by asking yourself 'What is the French for . . .?' and seeking out the answers. You must also be industrious in learning by heart words, phrases, sentences and even passages, since a great deal of success

comes from accurate imitation. From close attention to what a Frenchman says and writes, there comes an ability to express yourself in French which is every student's aim.

It's also important to realise that the study of languages is based only partly in the world of abstract linguistic forms. You will also be dealing with real-life situations through your reading and also through face-to-face encounters with people. The modern language courses no more consist of pure abstractions than does the study of history or geography, and you should not choose languages as a means of escape from problems of the real world. Indeed, it is most desirable for you to be interested in current affairs and social and moral questions.

Linguistic skills

Secondly: 'Is the course going to make me into an efficient practical linguist? Will I be able to translate and interpret and negotiate on a professional level? Will I acquire useful knowledge of the countries as they are today?' Most courses do aim to give you an understanding of the country, but they do this partly through the study of literature. This in itself reflects the thinking of writers' wider problems. In addition, some courses try to relate texts to historical and contemporary events and conditions. You might, for instance, be asked to read George Orwell's *Homage to Catalonia* about the Spanish Civil War, books on the modern history of Germany and Italy, or on the Russian revolution.

Knowledge of the language

As far as a working knowledge of the language is concerned, A-level courses don't deal specifically with oral skills. You won't become an interpreter by the end of the course although you will acquire a reasonable grasp of modern colloquial phrases and the language of everyday speech. Interpreting is a highly skilled job requiring specialist postgraduate training. Professional translators are people with not only a very sound grasp of English and another language, but often with a technical or professional knowledge of a specialist field such as law or chemical engineering as well. However, translation into English and from English into the language will be part of the course and you should certainly be well able to negotiate at the level required by ordinary people visiting the country, even if not at the level required for the subtleties of international diplomacy.

Fluency

Thirdly: 'Is a good oral standard important, and is there any guarantee that I shall ever become orally fluent?' Some students enjoy speaking, and quickly become fluent (if not always accurate!). But others are shy about their accents and fumble for words. 'I enjoy reading and writing, but I don't expect ever to be taken for a Frenchman (or woman).' This need not inhibit you: for being taken for a native is extremely flattering for a linguist, but it is not the only sign of success. However, when you have studied a certain topic, you will find that you have become fluent in that area. It's a sign that you have learned the work thoroughly. Gradually, with an effort, your range will extend to more advanced and specialised topics. Your teacher will aim to create an atmosphere where the foreign language is a natural medium of expression, and you will no longer feel any embarrassment.

Literature

Fourthly: 'Do I have to read literature, including texts over 300 years old, and if so, will they be relevant to me?' The role of literary studies has undergone something of a change from the days when all students studied the classics, with, at most, one modern text, and used these as the model for all the language which they learned. Nowadays, the texts are mainly modern, and students find, sometimes unexpectedly, that they are one of the most enjoyable parts of the course. This is because they depict life so vividly and make interesting comparisons with Britain. An older text, if chosen, may also turn out to be favourite: for example a Molière comedy can be enjoyed and acted as well as any modern work, and you will be getting to know the literature familiar to any educated French person.

Contemporary topics

Fifthly: 'You don't just read old books do you?' No, you'll also study texts about family life, town and country problems, international affairs, the changing roles of the sexes, crime, unemployment and food and drink. In other words you'll read and talk about important issues which are discussed in Britain and which are experienced in similar, or in different, ways abroad. There are many ways in which your course will link up with the present day. Your school may provide, or your teacher may help you to subscribe to, a foreign magazine such as *Paris Match* or *Stern*. You will have the satisfaction of knowing that the language in magazines such as these, while sometimes difficult, is authentic and up-to-the-minute (your teacher may also be learning from it, since languages are still developing whilst you are studying them). There may also be a foreign language assistant on the staff of your school who can help you with your oral skills and background knowledge of the country.

Studying abroad

Sixthly: 'Will I be expected to visit the foreign country as part of my course?' Examination Boards do not require you to show direct or indirect evidence of a stay abroad. You should therefore not give up the idea of doing languages because you are prevented by financial or personal reasons from making a foreign visit. At the same time, a visit will make your studies come to life more than anything else. You may already have been abroad at the pre-O-level stage and will have observed differences in the way of life. To take only one example, there's the different rhythm of young people's daily life caused by the morning-only schools in Germany. If you go again, or if you go for the first time, your observations can be at a more adult level. You will be able to discuss quite sophisticated issues with native speakers, read newspapers and watch television critically. If you stay with a family, you can discover how your outlook would be different if you had been born into this family. Your fluency will improve, especially if you make a conscious effort to learn. (You should not assume though that the visit will automatically improve your grammar, which still needs to come under the discipline of your school studies). If your school does not arrange its own visits, there are many sources of information on alternatives, and you may even find some organisation such as your local education authority, which offers scholarships.

To sum up this section, it's clear that if you study modern languages, you are acquiring a key to the minds of people brought up in another tradition. There are many personal interests which you can follow up: the links and comparisons with both history and English literature will be obvious, but all kinds of contemporary studies such as geography, politics, economics and sociology take on another dimension through your access to original sources and your ability to ask your own questions. In this way, you are very much more than just an interpreter and translator for others. You will be far better equipped to form your own judgements and standards of comparison.

Do I need O-level?

To succeed at A-level in a language, it is generally necessary to have studied it to O-level and got a grade A, B or C pass. In some languages, such as Spanish and Italian, fast 'starter' courses are sometimes offered to linguists of proven ability, leading straight to A-level in the two years available. If you take one A-level language only, you'll find it will become a subordinate skill in your later career. Two A-level languages are desirable for the more academic university courses, and future teachers of modern languages will find their prospects greatly helped if they can offer two languages.

Although it's possible, you would be advised to think very carefully before embarking on a three-language A-level course, since this tends to turn you into an extremely narrow specialist at a comparatively early stage.

The A-level course

You will ask, 'What does the A-level course consist of? What will be the form of the examination?' It's impossible to give a single answer because there are variations depending partly on the different syllabuses of of the Boards and partly on the fact that teachers have different methods of reaching the same objectives. But a typical course would include the following:

1 *Texts* Intensive study of texts, to bring out new grammar points and new areas of vocabulary. These will lead to analysis, oral discussion and essays. You will be aiming all the time to develop your skill in expressing things with greater complexity and exactitude. This means in turn that you have to inform yourself on many different issues, and think deeply about them. Of course, your written or oral work will not be as long and complex as it would be if you were writing or talking in your mother tongue, but within the scope of about 300 words you must aim for careful, orderly argument and opinion.

2 *Translation into the language ('prose translation')* The majority of students do not practise this skill for O-level. But, provided that basic grammar rules have been learned and such things as genders and parts of verbs are known, this side of the work should hold few terrors. It's the aspect which most develops the ability to analyse complex grammar. At a later stage it also gives an opportunity for comparing the idioms of the two languages, so avoiding the clumsy and inauthentic word-for-word translations.

3 *Translation into English, and comprehension* Teachers and examiners argue about whether translation is just as much a test of English as of the foreign language, but it is still on most syllabuses. Other forms of comprehension exercise and tests have recently been introduced, including the summary, which means that you have to make a precis in English of a long passage and answer questions on it. There may, too, be multiple-choice questions on heard or read passages. The important principle to bear in mind is that as in English, your reading and oral comprehension in the language will be greater than your own powers of expression. In making an assessment of your standard, teachers and Examination Boards always give credit for showing that you have understood the meaning. Thanks to the tape-recorder, you can now practise listening to a passage over and over again, until you can follow it at a natural pace, a skill which formerly could only be developed face-to-face. It should be emphasised that the good student will always read outside what is the basic minimum, adding to his or her vocabulary book.

4 *Literary studies* Most courses prescribe four literary texts, although there are often alternative texts on history, politics, geography or other aspects of life and civilisation. The effort required to understand these texts linguistically helps other aspects of the course. All written examination questions are in English, but your teacher may conduct some of the oral discussions in the language.

5 *Oral work* Increasingly, teachers use every type of lesson to develop oral fluency. In particular, you are likely to be asked to give short prepared talks on specific topics. At A-level, about 10-15% of the marks are allocated to oral work. Boards are currently experimenting with new methods of improving oral standards, and you should find out, by asking the teacher, what your Board is doing.

6 *Background studies* Some Boards have introduced, or are thinking of introducing, syllabuses which reduce the element of literary studies and give more opportunity to explore non-literary backgrounds. The Southern Board French syllabus B leaves a wide choice of reading to candidates and expects them to discuss topics orally. They also award 20% of marks for a project written in French or English. The Joint Matriculation Board French syllabus permits a written dissertation in English on a non-literary subject in place of one of the set books. Other Boards are reviewing their requirements and trying out new ideas.

French

From a career point of view, French has a great usefulness, especially in commerce, diplomacy and technology. It is very widely used not only in Europe but throughout the world and it is, and will remain, in very strong demand. When you progress from O-level to A-level, you are unlikely to find that vocabulary or sentence-structure become suddenly much more difficult to grasp, and you will increasingly enjoy the elegance and wit of many of the French idioms. French literary culture has a long pedigree, and makes a very interesting contrast with our own. It has traditionally been characterised by logic and discipline, whereas the English genius has been less subject to rules and precepts. The way in which the French seem to proceed by clear-cut reform and revolution, followed by a period of reaction, throws an interesting light on our own more gradual development. It has been said that the French, though nearest to us geographically, are a people who by temperament and tradition are one of the furthest removed from us. This may give a reason why our points of view and interests, in Europe for example, seem so often opposed. It's essential that there should be educated people in the professions, business and politics who understand the French way of thinking and pride in their tradition.

Of course, French is also the key to an enormous richness of culture: 'cuisine' and 'couture' are not by accident French words. Painting and music also feature prominently, and for the linguist and devotee of 20th century creativity, the French cinema is full of interest, achievement and pleasure — a fact which the Associated Examining Board recognises in setting an optional topic on the French cinema in its syllabus.

The syllabus and examination in French

To give you an idea of an A-level French syllabus, a typical Board sets three papers and a separate oral examination. There is, firstly, a literature paper, lasting three hours, with one question on each of four prescribed books, taken from a list of about twelve from the 17th century to the present day. Authors commonly prescribed in the syllabuses of all Boards include Molière, Voltaire, Balzac and Maupassant, and from the 20th century, Camus, Anouilh, Ionesco, Colette and Beckett (amongst a very wide selection). Some Boards, though not all, include a study topic, counting as one of the books, such as post-war politics in France, a French province, the French Impressionists of the Cinema in France since 1945, and these require study of relevant books or other documents, written in English or French. The wide choice of subject matter allows flexibility in catering for different tastes and interests. All your answers on this paper are to be written in English. A second paper of three hours sets translation into French and a free composition of about 300 words in French, on a general topic. A third paper, of two hours, sets translation from French and comprehension tests of written and also sometimes of heard French; the latter may be of a tape recording spoken by a native speaker. The oral examination covers reading aloud and conversation on general topics, which may include your set book reading.

German

German has for a long time lagged behind French in the importance attached to it in British schools, and yet surveys in the field of business and commerce show that the demand for the two languages runs neck and neck. The reasons are obvious. Today, German is the most widely spoken language in Western Europe. It includes the energetic and inventive West Germans, Austrians, and a large slice of Switzerland. It is also the only language to sit astride the Iron Curtain (in East Germany). In business, science and technology it is a tremendous asset.

For some students, German at A-level might seem to be difficult. This is partly because of short two-year O-level courses, compared with French. It is partly because the vocabulary, as it becomes more abstract, builds up words from elements which are often not recognisable from the English. These words do, however, have their own logical pattern which the student will soon understand. Again, a thorough grasp of case and endings becomes essential, as they are used in more and more subtle ways. Having mastered these points, the student comes to appreciate the succinctness of the language (often contrary to its reputation!).

Many German writers deal with moral and social issues and students appreciate this, feeling they can recognise and understand the writers' views. The rise of Nazism, the recovery of Germany after 1945 and German literature and culture are very important topics. In the wider cultural field, German literature, especially poetry, has strong connections with the immensely important field of German music.

The syllabus and examination in German

As with French, the A-level German examination usually consists of three papers, plus an oral examination. Again, the same range of skills are tested:

- oral language
- written communication
- comprehension of spoken and written language
- knowledge and understanding of literature and background (history, music, life of the people and so on).

The German A-level examination takes similar form to the French, as outlined above. Authors commonly chosen include Goethe, Schiller, Kleist, Mann, Kafka, Brecht, Böll, Frisch and Dürrenmatt (two German-speaking Swiss dramatists), and there are study topics such as the Weimar Republic, 1918-33, the mass media in the Federal Republic, and West German government and democracy since 1945.

Russian

Russian became popular in British schools in the 1950s and 1960s, but entries are now on the decrease. If you are lucky enough to be doing Russian successfully as an O-level subject, the scarcity value of an A-level makes it well worth considering. It is undeniable that Russian demands a good linguistic mind and perseverance because the grammar is detailed and there is a large vocabulary. University departments are anxious to promote Russian studies, and you may find the local university particularly helpful in providing additional lectures or other enrichment to your course. In the same way, they are keen to obtain good students, and point out that the political, scientific and commercial importance of Russia offers good career prospects. There's every encouragement that you could make professional use of your Russian, if it is of a good enough standard.

It's very unlikely that, in the course of your A-level studies, you will have opportunities for informal contacts with ordinary Russian people, although package visits or tours are available. You will, however, be able to read Russian newspapers and magazines in the original. Although these present the official view, they do give shrewd insights into the Russian mind and Russian condition. The literature prescribed will be from the pre-revolutionary classics and more modern writers.

The syllabus and examination in Russian

The objectives of the examination are the same as for French and German: oral and written communication skills; comprehension of the written and spoken language; knowledge and understanding of the culture, literature and background of Russia. Again, too, there are usually two papers of about three hours, and one paper of one and three quarter hours. These cover the prescribed books which are studied for themselves in relation to literary history. There are usually questions about the Soviet Union as part of the background, for students are expected to know something of recent Russian history. Within the same examination framework as for other languages, the student reads texts by authors such as Pushkin, Gogol, Turgenev, Chekov, Pasternak, Solzhenitsyn and Yevtushenko. Boards which set background study include topics such as 20th century history (Tsarism, the 1917 Revolution), Lenin, Stalin and the condition of USSR after Stalin's death: also the Soviet cinema and Soviet Socialist Realism in the arts.

Spanish

Spanish is a language with a strong literary tradition based on a long and important history. It is, however, not uniformly easy to find schools offering O-level courses, and serious academic students may have to study it from scratch to A-level in two years. This is usually regarded as a quite acceptable university entrance qualification, although in terms of breadth of background study it leaves something to be desired.

The early stages of the language are usually found quite easy, especially to someone with a good standard of French, although there will be more problems later both with syntax and with the wide vocabulary. Spanish is of course the key not only to Spain, but also to much of South and Central America. In addition to classical and modern Spanish authors, the Examination Boards increasingly set modern Latin-American texts and topics, thus affording the chance to study developments in non-European countries. However, it must be added that keeping abreast of the situation in up to 30 Latin-American countries, some of them very volatile and with little mutually common ground, is a highly complex undertaking, only possible to some extent given the time and resources available later in a university.

Spanish has considerable commercial importance reflecting its Latin-American associations, and you may find an opportunity to use it in business, but as with other languages, this is likely to be as a sideline to other activities. Intending teachers should not expect to be in demand in the profession without another language, probably French, to a good standard.

Pupil and student relationships with Spain are not well developed, so this is not a likely channel of contact. (You will not of course expect to further your serious knowledge of Spanish and Spain on a typical package holiday!) There is speculation that political liberalisation and entry into the Common Market may improve the position, but as yet it is difficult to point to any positive signs of change, and you may have to rely on your own resources as an informed visitor and seeker of the cultural treasures of the country.

The objectives for the A-level examination are the same as for other languages — oral and written skills, comprehension of spoken and written language, and knowledge and understanding of Spanish literature and life. The type of examination papers is similar to that for French. Texts are chosen from authors such as Lope de Vega, Blasco Ibáñez, Espronceda, Machado, Lorca, Cervantes, Laforet and Vallejo. Topics which may be set for background study include the Spanish Civil War, Modern Spanish painting, recent Mexican history and Castro's Cuba.

Italian

Although there are about 40 departments of Italian in British universities, it is only a minority of schools that offer an opportunity to study this language. A few schools, especially in areas where there is a significant immigrant presence, offer courses to O-level, but otherwise the maximum provision is likely to be a two-year course from scratch to A-level, often with O-level taken at the end of the first year. Inevitably, this means a strong concentration on essentials, and it will be worth asking the teacher of such a proposed course about the amount of Italian background and culture which will be included in such circumstances. Most university departments will accept an A-level gained under such conditions as a qualification for their course, although they may occasionally query its breadth. Alternatively, most universities offer Italian courses from scratch (so called *ab initio* courses). Students with an O-level in Italian are quite likely to find themselves allocated to these courses.

It must be regarded as something of a risk to embark on a single subject language course such as honours Italian at university. Your chance of language teaching with this narrow qualification (ie one subject) will be very low. You will also find that very few employing organisations will expect you to have only one language, which is a highly specialised but narrow expertise.

You will find a knowledge of French and/or Latin very helpful in your Italian studies because of the language similarities. But you will discover there are very large regional differences, so that your academic standard Italian may only be a starting point to an understanding of the language as it is actually spoken.

As your studies progress, you will discover that Italy is a country of great cultural riches and traditions, especially in the world of art, and with a strong literary tradition. As a nation, however, it is young and struggling with problems of economic inequality and backwardness, and with political instability. These factors are reflected in the contemporary literature which is likely to be prescribed for A-level. The student who visits Italy (and the opportunities for school exchanges are unfortunately not very great, though the Italian government is making some effort to promote youth links), will find that young people are very interested in politics and public affairs, and may shake the comparative complacency of some young British people.

In the examination, there are normally three papers, plus an oral. The objectives of the examination are to test oral and written skills, and understanding of the spoken and written language, literature and background.

Boards set a similar scheme of papers as for French. Among the authors whose books are set for study, you would be likely to find Dante, Machiavelli, Petrarch, Leopardi, Moravia, Pirandello, Verga, Vittorini and Lampedusa, that is, authors from mediaeval times to the 20th century. Study topics which appear on the syllabuses of the various Boards include Mussolini and the rise of Fascism, the Second World War and the Resistance, the problem of the Mezzogiorno, Church and State since 1918, and politics and society since the Second World War. The papers test translation into and from Italian, and free composition in Italian. In the oral examination (Cambridge Board) candidates read aloud a passage and converse on everyday topics such as sport, fashion, popular music, films, Italian cities, country life and politics.

Going on into higher education

For single honours degree courses in French, German, or

Spanish, it is usually essential that you have studied these subjects to A-level. Russian and Italian can be a little more flexible. For joint honours (ie studying more than one subject) it is often possible to take a second language on from O-level, or sometimes start from scratch. For very unusual languages such as Japanese or Norwegian, the university will probably want evidence of an ability to learn languages, rather than any background in the particular language. This usually means success at A-level in one or more of the 'commoner' languages.

At university or polytechnic you can study a single language or a combination of languages. You can also link up a language with another subject such as linguistics, drama, history, geography, economics, business studies, science and so on. Your A-level course in one or more languages will be an admirable preparation for all of these courses.

There are also a variety of higher diploma courses such as business studies, or tourism with options in languages, and linguist-secretarial courses for which an A-level language pass is required. A foreign language is also useful, but not essential, for degree courses in history, history of art, librarianship, anthropology, marketing and business studies. Students with strong science interests who are also good at languages will find a small but increasing number of science and engineering degree courses which offer the chance to develop language skills, often from O-level, and include a year's study or working experience in a laboratory in the particular country as part of the course. As it is not always necessary to study the language to A-level, students can concentrate on science at A-level and return to language study at university.

Careers

There are very few jobs for which a knowledge of a foreign language is the main skill required, but there are many for which it is required in addition to other kinds of experience and training. Translating, interpreting and teaching languages are the main careers where language skills are the major requirement. However even within these careers there are other qualities and training required. Britain is less in need of interpreters or translators than other countries because so much of the world speaks English (or American). Competition for posts in international organisations, (the EEC — Common Market, United Nations etc) and as linguists in Civil Service departments is very fierce.

People who enjoy learning languages are also often naturally sociable and communicate well with others. They are therefore attracted to careers which make use of these skills. Many of these careers may require specialist training and work experience. This does not mean to say that A-levels or degrees in languages are not useful, but in order to use your languages in a job you may have to train for another career first.

If you look at the 'appointments' or 'situations vacant' columns of a newspaper such as *The Daily Telegraph* or *The Times,* you will see jobs where special mention is made of people who can speak and write in a modern language. These are secretarial services, sales and marketing staff (especially in export services), accountancy, engineering, banking, insurance and many more. To make special use of languages, you could also consider airline service, travel agencies, tourism and courier services, hotel reception, broadcasting, journalism or library work.

Chapter 8

Art, crafts and music

Art

by Norman Laing

Syllabus aims

The different Examination Boards adopt somewhat different methods of examining in A-level art. However, the similarities in what they are looking for are more important and more frequent than any differences in examining techniques or systems. All syllabuses are designed in the hope that they will stimulate, in both teachers and students, the desire to develop an ability to create lively, imaginative and above all, personal visual images. These can be paintings, sculptures, graphic designs or carefully observed analytical studies.

In addition, it is hoped that at A-level this development will take place in the context of a knowledge of the long history of man's attempts to create visual images which clarify or comment upon his reactions to the human condition, his reactions to his environment (both physical and spiritual), and above all demonstrate the limitless variation and capacity of the human imagination. This is an important aspect whether the syllabus has a formal 'history of art' component or not, for the visual images we create and the visual language we use are products of the past as well as the present.

All this sounds demanding and even somewhat unexciting but what, in fact, does it really boil down to? It means that A-level art, perhaps more than any other subject, is concerned with truly individual and personal ideas, reactions and concepts. True, some degree of technical ability is necessary but it must be borne in mind that quite often the power and conviction of a personal and imaginative idea can be expressed in relatively simple technical terms. Equally, the strong desire to communicate the idea will enable the individual to acquire the necessary technical skills.

Similarly, what may seem a purely academic pursuit, namely the 'history of art', can take on a new, lively and personal meaning when we realise that what we are looking at are attempts made in the past to express those very ideas and concerns that we ourselves are seeking to comment on by creating our visual images.

The attraction of studying art

Who then will find benefit and above all, excitement, in studying art at A-level? The answer is anyone who is capable of reacting personally and imaginatively to the environment and times in which he or she lives, and finds these reactions can be best expressed in a visual language. Similarly, art should attract anyone who is fascinated by the forms and structures of the natural and/or man-made objects which surround us, and finds satisfaction in making visual and analytical representations of these objects. There is also, of course, the sheer personal pleasure that can come from developing the skills of image-making with the wide variety of materials and equipment available to the A-level student.

Naturally, within a formal examination format, the syllabus and the examination itself have to separate out the various areas of self-expression so that they can be fairly assessed one against the other. This enables a clear course of study to be followed. However, a glance at the syllabus of a few of the Examination Boards will show that the scope, variety and combinations offered are very comprehensive indeed and offer opportunities for nearly all forms of individual visual self-expression. Naturally, again, in the majority of cases some selection has to be made before a course of study and practice is embarked upon but this rarely proves to be seriously restrictive.

Having decided a course of action, the emphasis is on studio work and above all, on personal private practice, where you will seek to develop your technical skills and the ordering of your individual thoughts, ideas and concepts. There is no way of avoiding the truth of the statement that 'the way to do it is to do it'. Though formal homework may or may not be set, the potentially successful A-level student is one who is constantly seeking to feed his or her visual memory and improve his or her technical skills by concentrated observation, sketch-book work, reading art books and magazines, visiting exhibitions and so on. There is no substitute for experience and time cannot be reclaimed. In practical work you cannot swot up shortly before a forthcoming examination.

If the course of study is directed towards an examination which has a specific history of art section, then, of course, a substantial amount of time has to be spent on this aspect of the work. Even if the examination is in the form of a traditional timed written answer this does not mean that formal classwork and practice in writing essays are all that is necessary. What is looked for at A-level is not the regurgitation of remembered facts, but an expression of personal opinion or a view-point, based upon knowledge and experience. Much of this experience is gained outside the classroom by being aware of what is going on in the art world. This means reading newspapers, books, magazines and visiting galleries, museums and exhibitions.

The personal study and fieldwork

With some Boards, the history of art component can be undertaken as a personal study on a selected topic, so the need for personal investigation and fieldwork is essential. Here is a real chance for personal enthusiasm, interest and expertise. Here also the skills of other disciplines such as English, geography and history can be harnessed to produce a successful study. Remember, however, that what is looked for is a personal study presenting your own personal opinions arrived at over a considerable period of time and from your own investigations. A last-minute collation of bits from a range of standard textbooks will not satisfy the requirements of the examination.

Coursework and examinations

In most cases it is expected that the student entering an A-level course of study will have successfully completed an O-level course in art. This is probably essential if the course involves a history of art requirement. Where the syllabus is concerned with solely practical components, it is possible that someone who has seriously practised some form of art as a hobby or recreation may be considered as a potential A-level candidate. If you need guidance, ask to see a member of the art staff of the school or college. They will want to see visual evidence of your ability and skill to assess your standard. Some of the Examination Boards make the history of art a compulsory part of the course. If so, it is examined by means of a written examination or a personal study. Other Boards offer history of art as an alternative to part of the practical work submission. On the other hand, some Boards require practical work only.

Within the history of art option or compulsory section, you may find your Board will require the study of a specified period or periods in the history of art. Others offer alternatives such as the history of painting, the history of architecture or the arts of daily life. (These examples are from the syllabus set by the Joint Matriculation Board).

Practical work

The Examination Boards also vary in the range of practical

work expected and tested. Some restrict it to drawing and painting, usually object drawing, plant drawing and imaginative pictorial or still life painting. Other Boards offer a whole range of options under the general heading of 'art', such as pottery, sculpture, embroidery etc. It is essential to obtain a copy of the syllabus for the A-level art examination for the appropriate Board from your school, college or local centre.

The other essential piece of information which can be discovered from the printed syllabus is what exactly has to be submitted in terms of pieces of work. Some Boards accept only work done under examination conditions within the time limits specified, which can be up to 15 hours. Others may require preliminary sketches or studies on various items of work to be submitted along with the examination pieces. Some Boards require a specified number of sheets of course work, that is work done in the normal course of study. This course work contributes to the total marks awarded to a particular examination component. In addition, there are special syllabus examinations which may well be a combination of the methods outlined above together with some internal assessment. This means that some work is marked by the staff involved in the teaching. These marks are moderated against the work of other schools submitted to the Board. The variations of syllabus and submission requirements are too many to detail them all here but it is essential that you know which particular examination requirements have to be met, at the outset of the course of study.

Once the work of a candidate has been submitted to a board for assessment, the detail of the marking procedures varies from Board to Board. There are built-in safeguards to ensure that the marks awarded for each piece of work from each candidate are fair and consistent. As with all external examinations there are systems to ensure that each examiner marks to the same standard and to an agreed marking scheme. Checks are made on every script to ensure that there are no clerical errors. In addition, sampling and comparative statistical techniques are employed to maintain fair and consistent standards throughout.

Classwork
Much of the work done for A-level art is completed in the artroom or studio. However, it is also expected that students will work outdoors, completing assignments in painting and drawing in the natural environment, if they are candidates for

plant drawing, imaginative pictorial or still life painting. In the examination, as in course work, students are expected to show skill in figurative, non-figurative or abstract terms. Some Boards specify that for one paper, students' work should reveal direct and analytical observation of one of these: objects arranged in a composition by the student; drawings or paintings of living models in everyday costume; natural forms, and manufactured articles. During their course, students will practise this kind of work in various settings.

Further courses and careers
Art can be combined with almost any other subject or subjects. Students aiming for a career in art or design probably intend to go on to art school for more advanced training. For most degree and diploma courses in the various different specialisms of art such as graphics, sculpture, textiles, fashion, silversmithing etc, it is necessary to have completed a foundation course. These are either one- or two-year courses available in colleges of further education or in art schools and can be done either after A-levels or after O-levels. Some colleges offer two-year courses which include A-levels, usually art and history of art. Foundation courses vary from one part of the country to another but entry is usually competitive requiring minimum GCE qualifications as well as the presentation of a folio of work. Because of the grant system most people have to undertake this stage of their art training locally. So it is best to find out what the system is in your area, before planning your art training.

But not all A-level art students are budding designers. An A-level pass in art is accepted by most higher education institutions as a full A-level although some universities insist that the syllabus must have a written component. Occasionally faculties list it as an additional or technical subject. Art can be taken as a second or third subject in almost any combination of subjects either for career reasons or for personal satisfaction.

It could be amongst the A-levels of those going on to degree courses in architecture or landscape architecture (probably taken with maths or science), history of art, fine art, or many other fields where the other academic subjects are of primary importance.

Careers which may interest the student of A-level art could be teaching, occupational therapy, beauty therapy, art restoration, cartography, photography, home economics, window display, fashion buying, retail management, printing, publishing, advertising or public relations. Many of these will require other specific subjects at A-level. Employers who want a person with some creative and critical ability are often willing to take A-level art as an indicator of an applicant's potential. For many of the competitive careers mentioned above other qualities of personality will also be necessary for success.

Craft, design and technology (with woodwork, metalwork, technical drawing, engineering drawing and graphical communication)
by Keith Dixon

Different courses — different titles
There are several courses at A-level with overlapping areas of study, but with different titles. Two of the Examination Boards (the JMB and Oxford Board) have named the course design; the London Board's title is design and technology; the Welsh JEC's is design, craft and technology, and the AEB call it design — communication and implementation. All of these syllabuses have developed from the traditional subjects of woodwork and metalwork; however, variations between them are now considerable.

In addition, all of these Examination Boards (with the exception of London), plus the Cambridge Local Examinations Syndicate also offer A-level courses in woodwork and metalwork. It may seem a confusing picture, but you can pick your way through it, once you know which Board's syllabus is used in your school or exam centre. The wide variation in titles reflects the differing stages of development of these subjects.

No matter which of these craft, technical, technological or design subjects you do at A-level, you will be required to complete the design and the construction of at least one major project. The assessment of the project in the form of a mark or a grade counts towards your final A-level award. This practical coursework within all the craft and design courses marks the difference between them and the academic subjects taught at A-level.

The new syllabuses
The syllabuses for some of these courses have been undergoing revision. The newer syllabuses have added more intellectual rigour to these practical subjects. This has been attempted by

placing greater emphasis on design which demands the fullest use of a student's creative and analytical abilities. These are measured by careful assessment of the planning stages of coursework projects. The Boards vary in their allocation of marks for these sections, but at least two thirds of the total marks are given to coursework and the design papers. In this way, the new syllabuses and the exams based on them are looking to students' ability to think and create, rather than testing knowledge of materials and processes.

Design

Since design is such an important part of the syllabuses, it is necessary to consider it in some depth in order to appreciate the special demands it imposes on students. In fact, design means many things to many people. There are the technological advances in microelectronics at one extreme and the aesthetic puzzle of an abstract sculpture at the other. Between these are transport systems, communications, urban planning, civil engineering, architecture and interior design. Nor is design the exclusive preserve of the man-made world because nature provides an unending source of inspiration for designers of fabrics, wallpapers and jewellery.

The scope of the design syllabuses

Teachers involved with design education are firm believers in the value of the design experience. Therefore, syllabuses have been planned to allow students to pursue their own interests throughout a wide range of options. This brings together young people with very different experiences and interests who can contribute different points to discussions, either formally in organised lesson time, or informally over a cup of coffee. These discussions play an important part in the growth of understanding of what design is all about, and how designers work.

You will study lines, shape, form, space, colour and texture, and learn to apply these to the creation of fabrics, furniture, jewellery and a variety of domestic goods. At the same time you will develop critical faculties so that you can apply aesthetic criteria to new projects. There will always be differences of opinion about a shape being attractive or ugly and you must be able to argue with reason and knowledge.

Most objects in our lives have a function. A designer analyses the nature of the function and thinks about the problems which are revealed. Then he or she goes on to design an object to fit the needs. This process requires creative talent and a wide knowledge of materials, processes and constructions. There is no right answer to a design problem, only a number of solutions which may vary in simplicity, size, cost, effectiveness and so on. Possible solutions should be invented, carefully considered and rejected until the best one is left. Many students will have enjoyed this kind of experience from their early years in secondary school and will find the opportunities and problems of A-level design challenging and rewarding. Others may struggle in the early stages until familiar with a problem-solving approach.

As products are designed for use by people, a knowledge of ergonomics (the scientific study of man-machine relationships) is necessary. This means knowing how to work out the height for a chair, a table or a work surface, and how to make a handle comfortable according to the way it is held. Another feature of the course is learning about the capacity of the human body, its size, and shapes, its need for fresh air, food, light, rest and the effect of fatigue. Industrial designers must consider all these points thoroughly because it takes more than functionalism to make a successful product.

Drawing and presentation techniques

An essential part of the course is the ability to communicate ideas and discuss solutions to problems. This means developing ability in freehand sketching; learning to draw in perspective and isometric projection, and using colour effectively. Annotated sketches are the quickest way of communicating solutions to problems. A sound knowledge of BS (British Standard) 308 is essential to make a working drawing and a knowledge of presentation techniques is very useful. Students with a knowledge of technical graphics will have a sound basis for this part of the course.

A-level technology

A new kind of syllabus is now available from the Cambridge Board. Called technology, it is a demanding and interesting syllabus, and there is evidence to show that some university and polytechnic engineering departments are prepared to accept this subject as equivalent to an 'academic' A-level. However, to gain entry to a degree course in engineering, students should always take A-level maths in addition to technology.

The syllabus offers a choice of modules. Two are to be chosen from four:

- structures
- automation
- electronics (instrumentation)
- materials processing.

The syllabus has a design core, but in the sense that design means technological design with decision-making aspects closely tied into the coursework. A case-study is included, and this requires the student to present a technological project.

The work involved in doing this course can be very exciting for students with engineering interests. Certainly, this syllabus should not be confused with others in metalwork or engineering workshop theory and practice. In some ways, technology is similar to applied science or engineering science, with a larger weighting on project work, and with a section on automation which is very up-to-date.

The examination and the project
The first paper of the London A-level is a six-hour design paper which requires solutions to a chosen problem. This paper is preceded by a Design Research Paper distributed about three months earlier. It provides problems for investigation. Candidates choose at least one topic and carry out as much research as possible, so that they do not enter the examination room with no knowledge and facts to draw on. The Design Paper sets a specific problem and candidates have to make a thorough analysis; determine a specification noting key priorities; and provide various solutions and evaluations of them. The chosen design has to be developed and a production drawing is made with notes on suitable materials, constructions and types of finish.
Two examples of recent problems set to students:

Design a hand-operated hydraulic lever kit to free trapped passengers involved in a major accident.
Design for a nursery school a stacking chair, and also a table which could be used singly or in a group.

The same methodical approach to problem-solving is employed with the coursework projects, but because more time is available, greater research is expected. Information can be gathered from a variety of sources and used as starting points. Students are encouraged to try different kinds of projects and use different materials.

Students without an O-level need to put in extra time to

acquire craft skills. Reading a chapter on cutting a set of dovetails or silver soldering a joint will give the relevant information so that a student knows what to do, but doing it successfully takes a good deal of practice — just like playing a musical instrument. The mark for this section varies between 33.3% and 60% of the total marks and reflects the importance attached to research perseverance, intellectual ability and original thinking which are not easily judged in the time-limited examination.

The final part of a project is the evaluation. Does it fulfil the original terms of the brief? How successful is it? What unexpected problems were encountered and so on?

The Examination Boards set a written paper to test candidates' knowledge of materials, tools and construction processes. A detailed knowledge of at least two materials (wood, metal or plastics) is required. This covers the structure, properties and testing of materials. Students are required to know about the methods of shaping by rolling, drawing, extrusion, forging, forming, casting, moulding, laminating and cutting by hand and machine. In addition, they are asked about joining materials by jointing, welding, soldering, riveting, screw threads, knock down fittings and adhesives. Other aspects of knowledge expected of candidates are measurement, mass production techniques, quality control and inspection. The marks awarded for the section vary from 20% to 33.3%.

Design and technology: the revised syllabus
The London Board has now introduced a much revised syllabus which will provide a choice of two modules from materials; general design; electricity and electronics; mechanisms and energy. The two chosen options build on a common core to provide a grounding in design and in technology. As with the earlier syllabus, an important element is a major design project, with a practical part to it. There has been a distinct movement away from the artistic side of craftwork towards technology. Students who are good at art but poor at science will find this new syllabus difficult.

It is too early to provide evidence of how universities and polytechnics will rate this new syllabus. However, the early reactions are that higher education authorities are impressed with the new course and you would be safe in taking it. But students are again advised to make specific inquiries at their target university or polytechnic departments to find out the present position.

140

Classwork and homework

Craft, design and technology is not an easy option at A-level. The technology syllabuses are very wide and usually absorb at least half the teaching periods allocated each week, with reading and note-making to be done as homework. Another couple of periods are usually given to design methods and drawing, leaving perhaps only two periods for practical work. Students therefore need to spend a lot of their free time in the workshops or drawing office in order to complete the projects on time.

Subject combinations and higher education

Craft, design and technology can be combined with a variety of other A-level subjects. Those interested in engineering careers would need to take physics and mathematics as well. For architecture or industrial design there would be more flexibility but maths or physics would be useful.

The Joint Standing Committee on University Entrance Requirements accepted the London University syllabus several years ago for general entrance purposes. However, all university faculties are free to make their own decisions so that the picture is confused and some will not accept design and technology as a suitable entry qualification for some courses. If you intend to take a degree, you must therefore check with a university on the acceptability, or not, of this subject as an entry qualification. Many polytechnics have a more enlightened attitude and accept the London and Oxford syllabuses, in particular, for a wide variety of courses including various kinds of engineering, art and teacher training. There is no doubt that because of this lack of complete acceptability many able students play safe, particularly for engineering, and the growth of the subject has been severely stunted. However, progress has been made over the last ten years and a number of official bodies are now trying very hard to persuade able students to go into technology rather than the pure sciences or arts. If you are in doubt do check in plenty of time with the appropriate university or polytechnic department.

Besides engineering, students of architecture, social sciences and applied art have found that this A-level gives them valuable background information. Students at A-level also gain valuable experience in design and during the course many see career opportunities which they pursue later in furniture design, jewellery and industrial design. It could also be an excellent subject for general education because so much is relevant to the way of life in a modern industrial society.

Woodwork and metalwork

Methods of examination
The AEB, Cambridge, JMB, Oxford and Welsh JEC Boards offer syllabuses in these subjects and the methods of examining are similar. All the Boards set a theory paper, a design and drawing paper, a practical test, and all except Oxford award a coursework mark. The syllabuses outlined below are considerably shortened and the actual syllabuses and past papers should be examined for further details.

If you are thinking of proceeding to university or polytechnic, you must check up on entry requirements of particular institutions. Woodwork and metalwork are not normally acceptable as full A-level subjects for entry to universities.

Woodwork
Materials — common timbers, structure and properties, conversion, seasoning and manufactured boards, screws, nails, adhesives, etc.

Tools — evolution, construction and maintenance of common hand and power tools.

Constructions and processes — frame and carcase construction of all kinds, together with turning, inlaying, veneering and polishing.

History — a knowledge of the development of the common articles of furniture or of particular items such as the chair.

Drawing, design and practical work — students are expected to be able to make formal working drawings according to BS308 and to be able to draw in isometric and oblique projection. They must be able to produce freehand sketches and design components as well as complete pieces of work. The mark for the drawing paper varies from 20% to 33.3%. Some Boards do not expect the same amount or standard of design work as required for design and technology courses. However, all design analysis, preliminary drawings and working drawings for coursework projects must be available. The mark for this section varies between 20% and 40%.

The AEB set a specific design problem to be solved and constructed while other Boards supply the drawing of the test piece to be made. This section of the examination calls for considerable skill and expertise because the student must work to high standards at speed and in the correct sequence.

This subject is particularly suitable for students who wish to pursue a career in furniture design and construction or teaching after an appropriate higher education course.

Metalwork

Some Boards set a general section to be studied by all candidates and a specialist section in either engineering or silversmithing, and forgework. This allows for the different facilities found in schools and makes it possible to study in greater depth.

Syllabus

Metals — common metals and alloys, properties and uses, the heat treatment of steel.

Tools – use, care and maintenance of common hand tools, measuring tools, lathes and drilling machines.

Constructions and processes — all the common methods of joining metal, shaping by cutting, casting, hot and cold forming.

History — this usually involves the study of famous engineers or the development of crafts such as silversmithing and blacksmithing.

Then follows deeper study of the chosen specialist area.

Drawing, design and practical work — see the appropriate section under woodwork.

This subject is particularly suitable for students who wish to pursue a career in teaching metalwork or some areas of art and design such as jewellery and silversmithing, three-dimensional design, industrial design and furniture design. All of these fields would require further training at a college of higher education or at art school.

Career progress

Where entry to degree courses for teaching is intended, students should check on the acceptability of these A-levels in advance. Ask the opinion of the university, polytechnic and college departments which you have in mind.

At this time, there is a shortage of teachers of craft, design and technology subjects. Opportunities to train in order to teach these subjects in schools should therefore not be overlooked.

To assist you further with this confusing group of subjects

within craft, design, technology and engineering drawing, overleaf is a chart which shows the skills, activities, work, examination courses and career prospects.

Technical drawing, engineering drawing and graphical commmunication

Technical drawing
Several Boards (including Cambridge, AEB, JMB and the Welsh Board) have syllabuses at A-level which cover much the same ground although the titles are different. In some cases the syllabus is called technical drawing; in other cases it is engineering drawing, and a further title (Cambridge) is geometrical and engineering drawing. There are courses, too, in engineering science (see separate chapter). In addition, there is a syllabus in elements in engineering design (Cambridge). You should find out which Board's exams are taken at your school/college, and try to get a copy of the syllabus.

Graphical communication
At the present time, this area of the curriculum is in a state of change. In the future, some of the Examination Boards (such as the London Board) are likely to introduce a new kind of A-level with the title of graphical communication. The syllabuses will be broader than engineering drawing or technical drawing. They will include references to work in town planning, electronic symbols, flow charts associated with computer work, logos (that is, the characteristic symbols which carry a company or organisation's activity, such as the well-known British Rail logo), and other modern elements.

Where do these subjects lead?
All these courses have been designed for students interested in design, draughtsmanship and engineering. The courses are very useful for entry to careers in a wide range of jobs within mechanical engineering. Among other jobs, careers and professions for which this is a valuable qualification are the aerospace and vehicle-manufacturing industries, electrical and electronic engineering, computers, shipbuilding, architecture, surveying and draughtsmanship.

However, university and polytechnic departments vary in their willingness to accept these subjects as A-levels for entry

CURRICULUM STATEMENT ON CRAFT, DESIGN AND TECHNOLOGY	GENERAL RESOURCE SKILLS	AREAS OF EXPERIENCE (SPECTRUM)	SCHOOL ACTIVITIES	EXAMPLES OF PUPILS' WORK	EXAMINATION COURSES	CAREER PROSPECTS
CRAFT	Manipulative skills	Engineering workshop practice	Tool making Machining	Engineers tools Model engineering	O-level and CSE Engineering workshop practice	Fitter Toolmaker Draughtsman
	Material processing skills Hand and machine tool technique Constructional	Motor vehicle education Metalwork Woodwork Building studies	Motor mechanics Machine work fitting Constructional Woodwork Building projects	Stripping down and building up car engines Tool making Furniture making Carpentry Joinery Brickwork	CSE Motor vehicle courses O-level and CSE Woodwork Metalwork AEB Building studies	*Operator* Machine operator Production worker *Craftsman* Mechanic Welder Electrician Toolmaker
DESIGN	Creative	Building drawing Technical drawing	Plans and elevations Building details Plane and solid Geometry Mechanical drawing	Building project drawings Engineer component drawings	O-level and CSE Technical drawing Engineering/building	Building draughtsman Surveying Engineering Draughtsman Teacher of design and technology Technical illustrator
	Aesthetic Creative Analytical	Graphic communication	Design and graphics techniques	Design drawings	AEB Graphic communication	Designer
	Communicative Discriminatory Constructional Manipulative	Aesthetic design Product design	Design drawing Pictorial Perspective Development Colour washing	Carving Sculpture Enamelling Jewellery design Furniture design	London O- and A-level Design and technology Oxford A-level Design	Design draughtsman Furniture designer
TECHNOLOGY	Technological Scientific Mathematical Creative Inventive Analytical Investigational Communicative Discriminatory Constructional	Industrial design Systems design	Ergonomics Production techniques Flow diagrams Critical path analysis	Chair design Machine tool design Traffic flows Container systems	London Design and technology Electronics	Industrial designer Production planning Systems engineer
		Structured technology Technology and society Industrial engineering	Control technology Modular technology Technology and man Industry studies Manufacturing technology	Electrical switching gears Structures Electronics Mechanisms Pneumatics Technology and society Industry jigs – presses, punches	AEB O-level Control technology Cambridge O-level Technology East Anglian CSE Technology Cambridge Elements of engineering design	*Technician and technician engineer* Draughtsman Teacher of design and technology Estimator Inspector Test technician Electrical/electronic
		Applied science Engineering science	Materials science Energy Mechanics Electricity Metrology	Metallurgy Timber technology Polymer science Measuring and engineering experiments	Oxford O-level (282) Applied science Oxford, London NJMB, AEB Engineering science	*Technologist or professional engineer* Mechanical Production Electrical Electronic

Reproduced with the permission of Jim Flood, senior advisory teacher, Cambridgeshire County Council, and the Association of Advisers in Design and Technical Studies.

to degree courses. Students would be well advised to check with universities and polytechnics where they intend to study later, to find out if these places accept A-levels in the subjects. On the other hand, many students who have completed degree work in engineering have said that the experience of taking engineering drawing at A-level was a very valuable preparation for their degree work.

Syllabuses

The *geometrical* aspect of the syllabus deals with topics such as:

1   Geometrical drawing, where students are expected to draw projections involving geometrical solids in specified positions, and deal with problems associated with planes and solids and the curve of their intersection. This work will include prisms, pyramids, cylinders and cones.
2   Harmonic motion.
3   Cam synthesis and motion.
4   Straight spur gears.
5   Kinematics of simple plane mechanisms, and velocity diagrams.
6   Statics — force diagrams for simple framed structures.

In the *engineering* drawing syllabus are topics such as:

1   Projections — students practise different projection methods in machine drawing and sketching used in the design, manufacture, assembly and maintenance of engineering items.
2   Knowledge of conventional representation of machine parts and their various features.
3   The interpretation of drawings, both of components and the whole assembly.
4   Composition — the selection of views and sections; the use of dimensions on drawings; lettering and layout. The preparation of detailed drawings to scale.
5   Machines — the accurate representation of bearings, belts, gears, keys and splines.

After A-level

For A-level work, candidates should have passed O-level in mathematics, and it is almost essential to have studied the same (or a related) subject to O-level. Technical drawing is often taken by students who find three academic A-levels a heavy burden.

University and polytechnic departments usually accept engineering science as a full A-level equivalent to, say, physics, for a science or engineering course. However, the same cannot always be said of technical drawing. It is more often acceptable as a third A-level for entry to courses where two other A-levels are required. Check carefully with an institution (university, polytechnic or college) which you may be thinking of for later entry to find out their opinion of technical drawing at A-level as an entry qualification.

Home economics
by Judith Christian-Carter

Names and titles
Home economics is to be found in a number of different guises under a whole host of names. Basically, there are two aspects to home economics at A-level: (i) home economics or domestic science (or as one Examination Board defines it, the home, the family and society) and (ii) dress and textiles which is variously named as fashion and textiles, domestic science (fashion and fabrics), or just dress. However, a most important point is that both types of A-level course are now designed with male students in mind, and should no longer be regarded as exclusive female-only subjects.

If you are interested in studying a subject at A-level which not only has growing vocational worth but is also preparation for life, then this chapter will be of assistance in helping you to make your decision. Although both aspects can be dealt with under the one heading of home economics, it is simpler if they are treated separately. Therefore, the first part of this chapter will look at home economics and the second part at dress and textiles.

Home economics

A-level courses
All A-level courses in home economics are designed to allow students to develop the abilities which are required to manage a home and to feed a family efficiently at a time when the society in which we live is daily becoming increasingly complex. In addition, considerable emphasis is placed upon increasing students' appreciation of the aesthetic aspects of making a home within a particular environment, the importance of

personal relationships within the family, and the place of the family in today's society. You will soon discover that you are required to develop logical and independent powers of thought along with knowledge of the principles of modern home management. Most definitely, this is not just a theoretical study: it will demand your active and complete participation. You will need to apply accurate observation, scientific investigation and undertake experimental work as well as food preparation during the whole of the course. It is no push-over. You will be expected to do hard but extremely rewarding work. Home economics covers so many aspects of living in modern society that all students with enquiring and lively minds will find it to be a real challenge.

Study topics

One major section of study is food and nutrition. In this part of the course, the scientific and social aspects of nutrition are studied in depth. To achieve success in the practical part of the course, the composition and use of animal and vegetable food commodities are also covered, along with the preservation, storage and supply of various foods. Knowledge is needed, too, of how to plan meals in relation to nutritional requirements of various groups of people. An increasing number of syllabuses are putting a greater emphasis on the practice of current nutritional thinking and advice, which means that practical work is a lot more than just 'cookery'! Part of the practical work in the course is concerned with, and based on, kitchen planning and design.

Some knowledge of chemistry is needed before starting the course. In addition, knowledge of physics and biology is required in order to understand the scientific basis of the subject. Other useful subjects to have studied up to O-level are history, art and mathematics, because these are all applied to the study of home economics.

Another area of study looks in detail at the family: its role, structure and functions in a changing society. Other topics for study are child development, leisure, finance, employment, budgeting, consumer protection, housing, buying a house, renting, homeless families, health and welfare services, poverty and social security. Additional topics often included are design in the home, materials and finishes used in equipment and surfaces, cleaning materials, domestic heating, lighting and fuels, water and detergents.

Syllabuses do vary, however, so it would be wise to obtain a copy of the syllabus for the A-level examination studied at your school, college, or local centre from the Board.

Coursework and teaching methods
With such a range of topics to be covered, reading a variety of books is a feature of the course. You will be asked to do your own research in local libraries by reading journals, surveys, reports, etc. Practical work will take up anything from one quarter to one third of class time, and it will also require time spent at home in planning and preparation. Teaching methods vary according to the preferences of particular teachers, but include some, or all, of the following: class lectures, group work, individual research and assignment work; visits to exhibitions and research establishments; study weekends; viewing and listening to television, films and radio; the use of computer programmes on diets, and experimental work in food science.

O-level
It is not absolutely necessary to have previously studied O-level food and nutrition or home economics although, obviously, this is a help. Provided you have the interest and are prepared to put a lot of effort into the A-level course, coupled with a general educational background with a few qualifications of O-level standard, then you should find access to A-level open to you.

Examinations
Assessment usually takes the form of a written and practical examination, although some syllabuses do give marks for practical work completed during the course and which is assessed by your teacher. The practical examination can account for between 25% and 40% of the total marks, depending upon the syllabus being studied. The usual pattern is that a planning session of two and a half to three and a half hours is arranged a few days before the actual practical examination. The exam itself usually lasts for between two and a half and two and three quarter hours. During the exam a meal or various dishes are made and/or experimental work is undertaken.

The rest of the course is assessed by two written papers which deal with, either separately or together, food/nutrition and family/social aspects of home economics. These written papers are usually three hours each and require both short answers and essays. In some cases all questions have to be answered, while in others three or four questions have to be selected from the six or eight questions.

Subject combinations
Home economics combines well with many arts and science subjects. Those interested in the family and society part of the syllabus may like to combine home economics with a social science subject such as sociology, economics or social history. Chemistry is obviously a useful combination for those who wish to go on for further training in home economics, dietetics, food science and nutrition, or environmental health. If you wish to take home economics beyond A-level, mathematics and chemistry to at least O-level are an advantage.

Further courses and careers
An A-level in home economics is accepted by most universities as an entry qualification. However, some faculties of some universities are a little hesitant to accept the subject. If therefore, you have a particular subject in mind which you wish to study at degree level, it is best to check first with the particular university. For a degree in home economics, which can be studied at various colleges of higher education and polytechnics, an A-level pass is useful but not absolutely essential. A number of colleges and polytechnics offer courses leading to the National Certificate in Home Economics Education (NCHEE) and higher national diploma courses awarded by the City and Guilds and the Business and Technician Education Council. For entry, previous study to A-level is preferred but, again, is not essential.

With a qualification at A-level or a degree, there are opportunities to work in education, teaching at higher/further or secondary level, industries such as food, textile, fuel, and equipment manufacturers, retail trade, food, clothing and furnishing stores and departments of large chain stores, community welfare services, journalism, television, public relations, advertising, hotel management and catering. There are various kinds of research and testing work in large manufacturing and retail companies such as United Biscuits, Rank Hovis Macdougall, Sainsbury and many more. Indeed, home economics is an A-level which offers a qualification as well as a preparation for life, so do not pass it over until you have given it serious thought.

Dress and textiles

A-level courses

Titles for this course may vary but the syllabuses currently available are fairly similar and are also now designed with both sexes in mind. They aim to give a comprehensive grounding in the field of textiles, textile science, costume, dressmaking and aspects of soft furnishing. The A-level course helps you to develop a taste and appreciation of clothes and fabrics, and the ability to choose and create garments and furnishings suited to modern life and individual needs and tastes. It will also help you to appreciate design through a historical study of social conditions, industrial development, technical and scientific progress. As with home economics, emphasis is placed not only on theoretical knowledge but also on experimental and scientific investigation coupled with practical application.

Syllabuses

The topics covered in the majority of syllabuses are: the study of fibres (natural, man-made, synthetic), yarns, fabric structure, selection and use of fabrics, current fashion trends, the use of decoration, the use of commercial patterns, equipment, making clothes and household items, handling of different fabrics, linings, care of clothes and fabrics, finishing processes, colour in textiles, the textile industry and the development of the clothing industry, fashions and dressing habits in relation to social and economic change, fashion design and fabrics in relation to art and literature, the means of communicating new styles of dress, the work of various designers, constructional features in men's and women's dress, and design discrimination.

O-levels

Some knowledge of chemistry up to O-level standard is of value before this course, as well as the study of art and history. Some Examination Boards recommend that study up to O-level in dress, needlework/craft, fashion and fabrics is necessary, because of the practical element of the course. If in doubt, consult the syllabus and ask your teacher/lecturer for advice.

Classwork

Because of the emphasis on assessment of coursework,

practical work will constitute anything from one third to one half of the class time. In addition to reading relevant books, especially in the field of costume, visits to museums and art galleries will also form a part of the course. One syllabus requires an illustrated essay of about 2,000 words on some aspect of historical costume from 1600 to the present day. Other syllabuses require a two- or three-piece outfit (which you wear at the end of the practical examination), an item of clothing either for yourself or for a child (which shows a particular form of decoration), or an item of soft furnishing, household linen or embroidery. If you like working on your own, and have plenty of initiative to complete both practical and written work out of the classroom, then you will find this course much to your liking. Some of the work on fibres will take place in the science laboratory. Films, television and radio programmes are used to supplement the teaching of these topics. A close liaison with the art or design workshop will probably be maintained as most syllabuses encourage you to exercise and develop your own skills in design and pattern construction.

Examinations

The practical examination and/or course work can account for anything between 25% and 60% of the final marks, so you can probably appreciate that this is very much a 'doing' course. If a practical examination is conducted it is preceded in most cases by a three to three and a quarter hours' planning and preparation session. The practical examination lasts from three to four hours. The rest of the examination consists of two written papers of either two and a half or three hours each on fashion and fabrics/garment construction and science and textiles and/or English costume since 1800, depending upon the particular syllabus being studied.

Subject combinations

Dress and textiles would combine well with art or history of art, for those interested in design, or with economics or science subjects for those more interested in the business or technical side of textile manufacturing or retailing. If you are also studying other purely academic A-levels it offers an interesting extra subject with a useful practical aspect.

Further courses

Acceptance of A-level dress and textiles by universities for entry purposes is not widespread, although more and more universities are coming to recognise the value of this A-level, particularly for degrees in art or design and as a part of an all-round education. It is best to check first with the particular universities if you wish to study A-level dress and textiles with a view to studying for a degree at university at a later date. For courses at many colleges and polytechnics, this A-level is a most valuable one, especially if you wish to embark on an art, or design, or textile-based course.

Careers

An A-level pass in textiles will help you to gain entry to several careers, and if you have a higher qualification obtained at a college or university, your chances will obviously be much better. You can pursue a career in the textile or clothing industry, fashion design, or in teaching at secondary or higher/further level. There are openings too in journalism, public relations and advertising.

Apart from giving you a life long interest and hobby for your leisure moments in the future, this A-level can also open many doors in the job market for both males and females alike. The days of just sewing are well and truly times of the past.

Music
by John Turner

Areas of study

The study of music at A-level offers an appreciation of the subject in various ways, and the options built into most syllabuses create opportunities for students to select a course which will best suit personal interests and requirements.

Broadly speaking, there are four main areas of study:

● musical performance
● the history of music
● written skills
● aural.

Performance

The performance requirement is normally a pass at Grade VI standard (Associated Board of the Royal Schools of Music or Trinity College etc) or in the case of the London 509 syllabus, a Grade V and Grade VIII pass on two instruments. These practical options are an interesting and rewarding way of following the course.

The history of music

The study of the history of music is followed in both a general and relatively detailed manner. A panoramic view is taken from about 1500 to 1980. In addition, a period such as Baroque — classical — romantic or modern music is studied in greater depth. A set work such as Beethoven's third symphony is studied alongside the chosen period and in this way a more informed appreciation is realised. The study of the set work develops students' powers of analysis and this is a most important part of a musician's training.

The bird's eye view of the growth of music from 1550 to 1980 is essential in order to establish a perspective. The recent introduction by the London University Examination Board of 30 selected extracts as the basis to the study and examination of the broad span is an interesting approach. It is essential that the student is aware of changes in musical styles and the extracts test students' knowledge. It is very important to study developments in the history of music through the score, the recording and the performance. An accurate and developed historical awareness of the subject is an important factor in any later course of study or career to be taken up.

Written skills

Written skills form an important aspect of the course and are essential in the development of aural accuracy. It is important that harmony and counterpoint should have been studied at O-level before embarking on the A-level written skills course. The approach to this part of the syllabus is by:

i   The ability to re-create a style of composition such as: an Elizabethan madrigal, a Bach chorale, a trio sonata, a string quartet, an accompaniment to a Schubert song and so on.
ii Original composition.

No matter which Examination Board syllabus is being followed, the common aim is the development of contrapuntal and harmonic skills. For the student who intends to read music at degree level, close attention to this part of the syllabus is essential.

Aural accuracy

The development of aural accuracy is an essential part of a musician's training. For this reason considerable emphasis is placed on this part of the syllabus, and some form of dictated test is a feature of the final examination. A regular, systematic approach to aural training must be a feature of any A-level course and will enable the student to improve on this essential aspect.

The syllabus

Students should closely examine the syllabus of their particular Examination Board. The London A-level syllabus, for example, includes the points which have been made. London offers five alternative syllabuses. Four of them offer variations on the themes which I have outlined and options vary according to the syllabus. In this way a tailor-made course can be selected. An attractive feature of London's package is that two of the syllabuses (508 and 509) may be taken together and count as two separate A-levels. This two A-level feature obviously applies to students entering upon graduate courses at London University, and recent enquiries have confirmed that the London Music Colleges (RAM; RCM, Guildhall School of Music and Drama, Trinity, and the London College of Music) also accept this qualification. However, it must be pointed out that many universities have not adopted the London 508 and 509 formula as a two-subject qualification, so the student is strongly recommended to seek written confirmation of entry requirements before embarking upon any particular syllabus.

The distinctive feature of syllabus 509 (which, like the others, may be taken separately) is its practical bias. Students must obtain a Grade V and VIII pass on two instruments to qualify.

The course goes on to deal with the historical development of instruments, styles and performance, and the aural tests relate to the performing situation. Recognition of musical styles and ensembles is also tested by means of recordings. This is a useful syllabus to follow for students who intend to make their careers as performing musicians and also for students interested in offering a performance as an option in a BMus degree course.

The London A-level syllabus has been used as a model. Students should examine the courses offered by other examining bodies, and observe the ways in which the variations operate.

Classwork

The teaching methods adopted obviously depend on the style of the individual teacher, but in broad terms these are the most common kinds of approaches:

1 *Aural work* This part of the syllabus will be taught by using the keyboard and recordings. It is essential that regular training is given in order to increase accuracy and sensitivity.

2 *Musicianship (written skills)* The approach to this will be in two ways:

  i   Harmony and counterpoint will be introduced in a formal, structured manner to build up the necessary vocabulary.

  ii Students will be introduced to the compositional styles (techniques) of various periods, and will be expected to imitate them. Considerable use will be made of scores and recordings to help develop this facility and skill.

3 *The history of music* Awareness of historical detail will be expected. Teachers make use of scores and recordings to demonstrate and illustrate different periods and styles. Students are expected to build up their informal background knowledge by attending concerts, listening to radio broadcasts, listening to records and by classroom work. Studies will be undertaken into the work of some of the composers whose work has led to significant changes in the evolution of musical styles or periods. Students are expected to take notes as the course proceeds, and these notes add up to a considerable body of work on the history of music. Class discussion and interpretation of composers' work will also be part of the course.

4 *Set works* Set works are studied in some depth. A detailed knowledge of the work under discussion will be expected from students. Everything is centred on the score and recordings, and the teacher will introduce each work with a description of the background and the main structures on which the music is built. Wherever possible, students are encouraged to perform the piece of music set for study. This is possible when the scoring is for a solo instrument or a small ensemble.

Homework

It is impossible to be specific about a time pattern or scale for homework. This is because teachers have different expectations, and students vary so much in ability, motivation and attitude. Generally speaking, however, you should realise that with such diverse and different spread of musical skills required

156

by the syllabus, everyone's commitment over the full time of the A-level course is absolutely essential.

1 *Musicianship and written skills* Students are expected to produce written exercises on average about one a week. They are of rather a formal kind but occasionally you may be asked to write an original short composition. This work will take from two to three hours a week.

2 *History of music* Students are expected to add to their classroom work by a programme of regular reading. Essays to be done at home will be set on a regular basis, and on average this work will take you two or more hours a week.

3 *Practical work* For pupils/students who are following a syllabus which involves some practical or instrumental element, the standard or grade of the work determines the amount of time spent in preparation. Generally speaking, one would expect any instrumentalist at this age and level to devote from one to two hours a day to concentrated practice.

Time and commitment

It will have become obvious to you that an A-level music course will take up a lot of your time. The extent of the course demands a serious commitment on the part of the student. The interlocking and supportive nature of each part of the syllabus is encouraging, because students soon appreciate that they are learning about music in many different ways. The amount of specialisation built into any part of the syllabus makes the study of music a very rewarding experience. The broad-based nature of the A-level provides an excellent 'spring-board' to further study at depth later on at college or university.

After A-level

The courses of study which lie beyond A-level are centred basically upon:

- university
- music academy or college
- polytechnic or college of education
- a Kneller Hall kind of establishment for people interested in a career as a military bandsman etc.

Universities offer courses leading to a music degree, BMus, BA etc: most courses offer options as at A-level, so that you can follow a particular interest or specialisation.

The music academy or college course is obviously geared to

those with high technical skills and it is from their ranks that orchestral players are usually recruited. You can also read for a degree at these institutions, and this should be borne in mind by students who are both highly proficient as performers and are also good at academic work.

Polytechnics and colleges of education offer various kinds of courses. For example the BEd degree is an alternative course of study for prospective teachers and the study of music occupies about half of the curriculum time.

The Armed Forces provide fine opportunities for musicians interested in a service career and establishments such as Kneller Hall offer scope and facilities to develop musical skills to a high standard.

Careers

As you can see, the careers in which music has a direct link are mostly in teaching (in a school, college, university, music school or as a private teacher), and in performance in orchestras, quartets, operas, or as soloists or conductors. Competition in all these areas is severe, particularly for those with skills on the more common instruments. The world of popular music is even more uncertain.

There are some opportunities for trained musicians to use other skills in the BBC (radio and television), independent broadcasting, the recording industry, music publishing, music libraries, the retail trade, concert management, musical instrument technology and music therapy. The services look for performers, and there are attractive careers in the Royal Navy, Royal Marines, Army and Royal Air Force for bandsmen and women.

For entry to other jobs and careers, music is a fully recognised A-level qualification. It is accepted for entry to courses in further and higher education along with other arts subjects such as history or English or occasionally with maths and physics. It is particularly useful for primary and nursery teaching. Music graduates who do not want to make music their working life can be found in a wide variety of graduate jobs typical of those taken up by arts graduates generally.

A useful overview of careers using music is *Careers with Music* published by the Incorporated Society of Musicians, 11 Stratford Place, London W1N 9AE.

Final words

It should be said that music provides great pleasure to people in every walk of life. Tastes vary. Some people love orchestral music, others enjoy choral music — either listening or performing — and millions of people like to listen to or play jazz, folk, pop and many other kinds of music. To have studied music to A-level deepens your knowledge and appreciation of music, and for most people their enthusiasm lasts a lifetime.

Theatre studies
by Nova Beer

The A-level course in theatre studies (offered by AEB) builds upon the work done in drama throughout the secondary school. Although it is not essential to have studied drama to CSE or O-level, those students who have had some basic training in drama skills and practical experience of improvisation techniques will obviously find themselves at an advantage initially.

The essential qualities a student must possess in order to study drama at this level are a lively interest in all aspects of theatre, both technical and practical, a sensitive appreciation of dramatic literature on the page as well as on the stage, as well as an interest in the historical development of theatre in relation to society.

It is important that intending theatre studies students understand that this is not a 'soft option' as an A-level and, that although there is a large practical component to the course, there is also a demanding academic content. It is also a very time-consuming subject – students must be prepared to give up quite a lot of time outside formal lesson hours on such activities as theatre visits, rehearsals for course productions and research for their individual studies or extended essays.

The course
The theoretical study includes: the interpretation for the stage of set dramatic works; the examination of the work and theories of major theatrical practitioners including the most influential contemporary ones; and a study of the development of theatre socially and historically in a choice of periods. The course also involves a detailed individual study of an aspect of contemporary theatre in the form of an assignment.

Practical work, which accounts for 35% of the final examination, aims to give experience of all sides of theatrical practice and to stimulate the student's growth in both group and individual work. Technical aspects, such as design, lighting, sound, costume work, make-up, stage management, etc, are incorporated according to the particular interests and needs of the individuals on each course.

The overall aim will be to extend and deepen students' knowledge, imagination, sensitivity and insight into the complexity of drama and theatre by exploring the nature of dramatic experience both through study and discussion and practical participation in a variety of workshops and presentations.

The syllabus and examination

The examination consists of four main components: a practical examination, two written papers and a written assignment.

The first of these (known as Paper I Theatre Presentation) counts for 35% of the total marks and has two parts to it, which are equally important. One part is known as the Group Project and for this students work together in groups of between five and nine to present the examiner with a short original drama programme (lasting between 15 and 30 minutes) which they devise entirely by themselves. This tests not only their theatre ability but, just as importantly, their ability to work together in cooperation with other people. Most students find this the most dynamic and challenging part of the whole course and the end-product brings a feeling of achievement! The second strand of the practical exam is where each student demonstrates to the examiner an individual theatrical skill, which may be acting, directing, lighting, costume, set-design, mask-making, etc, according to their own particular interest and ability. The examiner will visit the school or college to see the demonstration of the group and individual skills and to talk to students about what they have shown him, look at designs, models, working notebooks, etc. This is usually a very pleasant informal day, taking place in the period March – May of the year in which the student is sitting the examination.

The two written papers count for 50% of the total marks and between them will be testing the student's ability to appreciate a play from a director's or actor's viewpoint through analysis of prepared and unseen texts; their knowledge of theatrical influences, conventions and styles related to specific periods in the development of the theatre; their appreciation of the changing role of director and the theatre in the 20th century.

Finally, the fourth component of the examination is what is

known as the 'individual study' (worth 15% of the total). This is basically an extended essay of between 3,000 and 5,000 words on any subject of the student's own choice related to post-1945 theatre and drama, which can be chosen from topics as varied as the study of the work of a living actor, an evaluation of an extant theatre company, an appreciation of a specific production seen, or a comparison between different styles of presentation adopted by different set designers or directors. The emphasis in this part of the examination is very much on personal research and evaluation of course material, and most students find this an enjoyable task and a way of following a particular interest in depth.

Subject combinations and careers

Theatre studies combines well with most other arts subjects, particularly English, languages, history and art, and, although a relatively new subject (at present offered by only one Board, the AEB), is accepted for matriculation purposes by most universities and polytechnics. It also provides a good grounding for those students wishing to go on to drama schools or colleges of higher education. In more general terms, students should find it an asset in careers where public relations matter, since the practical element of the course will undoubtedly increase their self-confidence and ability to present themselves in public and to relate sensitively to other people.

Chapter 9

Arts and humanities

Archaeology and ancient history
by Alan Jamieson

'I have always wanted to be an archaeologist. How do I start?'
Hundreds of letters like this are received by the organisers of
the Young Archaeologists Club[1]. The answer they give is to
join the club, and to take part in meetings or excavations run
by local archaeological societies. Some schools, too, have
history or archaeological societies or clubs which arrange visits
and fieldwork. If you are still interested, you should plan to
study archaeology at college or university and so prepare
yourself for a job in a museum, university or a research trust.

All about archaeology
Archaeology is the scientific study of the past based on
evidence, (objects such as pottery, weapons, ornaments,
utensils, brooches, tools) and the physical remains (buildings,
fortifications, roads, tracks, earthworks, barrows and so on).
The study of these objects and remains is part of prehistory
(before the coming of written evidence) and can be seen in
bones, stone, bronze and iron, and history which covers the
time of written records. You should realise that the work of
archaeologists at this level is very scientific. They date
materials by using radio-carbon and thermo-luminescence
methods, analyse soils and rocks, identify bones, and use
microscopes to investigate the remains of plant, animal and
human life.

Most people think of archaeologists as unusual people,
rather eccentric and scholarly, digging holes all over the place.
This is very far from the truth. Being an archaeologist certainly
means you need to know a lot, so scholarship is very important.
But it is also very hard work. It means being prepared to spend
hours, days, months, studying in museums and libraries, and it
means working in cold, wet weather on 'digs' or excavations.
And the reward for living rough in tents or huts usually ends up
in a low salary. Many keen amateurs do it all for nothing! And
yet the evidence of the great interest of many people in
archaeology can be seen in the large number of local societies
which flourish in all parts of Britain. These meet regularly to
hear lectures, to go on visits to sites, and occasionally to take
part in 'digs'. The student who is sufficiently interested and

[1] *Write to Dr Kate Pretty, New Hall, Cambridge.*

keen to read archaeology at A-level (very few) or AO level (rather more) may well eventually join a local society because it is likely that his or her interest will be aroused and strengthened by studying this subject for a public examination.

A-level archaeology

The A-level course is available at present in very few schools and colleges, and is offered by only two Boards, Cambridge and JMB. Other Boards offer the subject at AO (Alternative O-level) or include archaeology as part of a general studies course. If you are very keen to take archaeology and there is no A-level course locally, you could keep it as a leisure interest by joining a local club or society, or by listening to a course of lectures at the local university, if there is one. Some organisations (such as the Workers' Educational Association) arrange lectures or courses. Try, too, the extra-mural or adult education department of the local university or college. If you want to study archaeology at university, you will not be expected to have done the subject at A-level, but you will be expected to show evidence of having taken a keen interest in it in your spare time. Many archaeologists do not read this subject at university; they come through from taking degrees in history or classics (or other subjects), so you could think at A-level of preparing yourself by opting for these subjects: history, ancient history, Greek, Latin etc.

Course content

What do you study? Here are some typical questions from the Cambridge Board's papers. 'What are the main results which can be achieved by excavation or by field surveys, with reference to a region known to you?' Another question asks: 'Discuss the uses made of bronze or iron in prehistoric Britain'. Another will ask about aerial photography, or Roman coins, or the scientific methods used to date hill forts, pottery and barrows. You could be questioned on famous sites such as Stonehenge, Sutton Hoo, or Roman forts, walls, palaces, temples and villas. You would be expected to know something about archaeological sites in Africa, Western Asia, and Europe, and the evidence found in them. In classwork, you would be given air-photographs and be asked to identify special features — lines, shading etc. In this way, you are trained as a detective, able to show your knowledge and skill, and learn how to make judgements about the evidence you see and read about.

The syllabus and examination

The A-level syllabus of the Cambridge Board has been designed to test students' knowledge and understanding of the nature of archaeological evidence. It expects students to know about the skills and techniques used in archaeology, and of ways of interpreting the evidence. Candidates for the examination are expected and encouraged to take part in professionally organised excavations which are advertised in a leaflet.[2] In addition, students are expected to visit local museums, excavations and sites, and, if possible, to take part in an excavation and handle the material found there.

The Cambridge Board A-level exam has three papers. Paper 1 is on the principles, methods and chief discoveries of archaeology. You will be shown how archaeologists reconstruct the past from remains; the meaning of terms such as artefact, culture, industry; how to date materials, and so on. You will be asked about fieldwork techniques, including how an excavation is set up, and how and why particular methods such as air photography are used. For this paper, too, you would study various methods of work used by archaeologists, such as stratigraphy, the technology of flint, stone, clay and metals, Carbon 14, pollen analysis and other methods of dating. Furthermore, you would study the Old and Middle Stone Ages, the domestication of animals, and the growing of plants in the neolithic period. You have to know about the rise of civilisations in Western Asia down to the end of the fourth century BC and their cultures as seen in metallurgy, pottery, writing and urban society.

Paper 2 is on the archaeology of the British Isles. This means studying the sites, tools and other remains of the earliest peoples in Britain, the hunters and farmers, their settlements and religious places. On the syllabus are the Bronze Age and the Iron Age — hoards and round barrows, farms, cemeteries and hill forts. You will need to know about the tribes which lived in Britain before the coming of the Romans, and also the way of life of the Romans and the archaeological evidence from the excavations of towns, villas, forts, roads and other remains.

Paper 3 is a fieldwork project. Each candidate has to submit an individual piece of work or a completed project involving some fieldwork. This should be connected with some aspect of

[2]The Council for British Archaeology, 112 Kensington Road, London SE11 6RE provides details of all kinds of fieldwork and other activities.

local archaeology or at least be on a subject where the student has some access to actual material. The project could be an account of a surface exploration of a local monument or site, or the study of material in a local museum and the publications of an archaeological society. In their project book, students are expected to keep a record of visits to sites, and all references to published work and to museum materials have to be recorded.

Further study
Archaeology can be studied at about 20 universities or colleges of higher education in Britain, where it is a three- or four-year course. To gain entry to a few of these courses, an A-level pass in Latin is required. Other universities demand O-level Latin. Some look for a pass in maths or a science subject at O-level, particularly for the newer archaeological science courses. Almost all universities want an O-level pass in a modern foreign language. For more information, read the *Guide to University Courses in Archaeology*, published and available from the Council for British Archaeology.

Archaeology is a very interesting subject at A-level for students going on to read history, classics, ancient history or other arts courses at universities, polytechnics and colleges. It is fully recognised as an A-level subject for entry to all kinds of courses in further and higher education, equivalent in this way to A-level history.

There are few opportunities in archaeology as a career, and most of these are for people who have university degrees. These jobs are described in a CBA booklet.[3] For people going into jobs immediately after A-level, archaeology rates as a perfectly acceptable qualification alongside other arts A-levels.

[3] *A job in Archaeology*, published by the CBA.

Ancient History

Ancient history with other subjects
Ancient history is offered at A-level by six of the Examination Boards: London, Oxford, Oxford and Cambridge, Cambridge, JMB and the Welsh Board. In addition, JMB has a separate A-level in ancient history and literature. The total number of candidates for these examinations in 1983 was over 1,800 people. Some of these students were also studying classical languages, taking Latin and Greek at A-level alongside ancient

history. However, a substantial group of students are known to take ancient history with other arts subjects, such as English, modern languages and others. Another combination is with economics or government for students interested in public and political affairs. It is certainly not necessary to have passed Latin or Greek at O-level to get on to the A-level course, nor is it expected that these subjects will necessarily be combined with ancient history at A-level. As you can see, therefore, this is a very open subject, and teachers of it will welcome all-comers.

Six Boards also offer classical civilisation, which is very similar in content and had an entry in 1983 of another 1,600 candidates.

The course of study
The syllabuses of the different Boards cover very similar ground. Greek and Roman history are at the core of the course. Alongside the close study of selected periods of ancient history, students are also expected to acquire some under-standing of the nature of historical evidence — archaeological and written — and be able to show some skill in interpreting and commenting on the events and people they read about.

Within Greek history, some of the topics and subjects which you would be expected to know about are Sparta; the long history of the city of Athens; the way of life of the Greeks who lived in the islands, or in Ionia, Crete etc; the wars against Persia; the Peloponnesian War, and the life and campaigns of Philip of Macedon and Alexander the Great. Other topics for study are religion, literature, domestic life, trade, and the lives of some famous men — Solon, Pericles, Themistocles and others. The syllabus of each Board covers a slightly different span of years; the JMB, for example is 600 to 323 BC. To find out exactly the period to be studied, you should look at the syllabus of the Board whose exams you will be taking.

In Roman history, most courses cover the major events in the history of Rome, again within start and end dates. The JMB syllabus is 264 BC to AD 68, and the London Board's paper 2 is Roman history outlines from 146 BC to AD 96. Among the topics for study you might find Marius and the army, the Gracchi, politics and society in the republic, Caesar, the rule of emperors such as Nero and Tiberius, religion, the economy of Italy, and overseas contacts and conquests.

The London Board's course is on Greek and Roman history outlines, and also includes special subjects. These are topics

167

such as the culture of Athens over a period of about 50 years, or the reigns of Philip and Alexander (in Greek history), and Roman Britain, or the rule of Augustus (Roman history).

One of the big attractions of ancient history is its remoteness from modern times and its completeness. This means that you study a civilisation where you can see its start, history and end. This makes possible the kind of discussion which cannot take place for topics in modern history. Similarly, classical civilisation contains topics on Roman and Greek history, but in addition candidates study the literature, philosophy, architecture and way of life in the ancient world.

Examinations

In ancient history examinations, candidates take either two or three three-hour papers, and in each paper have to answer four or more questions. Typical questions might be, 'How far can you justify the murder of Julius Caesar?', and 'What were the major problems facing Rome on the Rhine and Danube frontiers, and how were they met?', and 'What efforts were made by Alexander the Great to spread Greek culture in the lands he conquered?'.

In the special subject papers (London), extracts (in English) are set on documents such as Caesar's account of the conquest of Gaul and Britain, or the writings of Plutarch, Thucydides, Aristotle and other Greeks. Interpretative questions, with short answers required, are set on these extracts, and candidates are expected to show knowledge and understanding of the context of the writings: this comes after close study with the teacher of documents (again, in English!) of the period.

Classwork

Methods of teaching are similar for ancient history and classical civilisation. You will be expected to read widely: textbooks, biographies, specialised books, pamphlets and books of translated documents. Most of your work will be in preparing essays or exam answers. In class, too, there will be discussions, and students will be expected to prepare papers in order to lead a discussion on a topic.

Higher education and careers

Ancient history and classical civilisation are accepted like any other arts subjects for entry purposes to further and higher education. They rank alongside history, English, modern languages etc. They are obviously useful subjects to have if you intend to continue with the study of history, ancient history, classical studies or classical languages at university or college. But they are not required for entry to these courses. There are degree courses in ancient history at several universities (see the *Compendium* mentioned in the book-list at the end of this book), and in some universities there is a joint course in ancient and medieval history.

For other courses they are acceptable subjects, and for jobs immediately after A-level, or indeed after taking a degree, A-level ancient history or classical civilisation rank alongside the other arts subjects already mentioned. Clearly, as a subject they do not lead into a vocational kind of job or career, but a pass in these subjects shows that you have the ability to handle facts and ideas and present them in a coherent and intelligent way.

Economic and social history
by Rex Pope

Economic and social history bridges the gap between history on the one hand, and social science disciplines on the other. Like other types of history, it is concerned with the examination of change over a period of time (eg in attitudes towards education) and with the study of particular situations (eg the reasons for and the content of the 1944 Education Act). Unlike some branches of historical study, economic and social history does not have much to do with kings and queens, politicians and statesmen, political parties, or foreign policy. The economic and social historian does, however, study society and its organisation. In this he or she shares a common interest with students of such social science disciplines as economics, sociology, human geography or public and social administration.

Economic history
The economic history part of any course involves an examination of changes in the organisation of industry — in technological organisation, in scale, and financing. This is generally approached through the study of particular industries such as agriculture, coal-mining, textiles, iron and steel, electrical and electronic engineering or motor car manufacture. Linked to this is a study of changes in the home and overseas markets for goods. Then there are developments in transport (roads,

canals, railways, shipping, motor vehicles) which affect the location of industry and markets for products. The economic historian also looks at changes in economic theory and government policy over questions such as intervention to protect an economy against overseas competition. Other examples are the regulation of industrial practices or financing, or more recently, a government's ability to regulate the economy as a whole.

Social history
Social history is really a study of the ways in which economic change affects individuals and groups within the community. Social historians look at the way economic change can lead to unemployment or the growth of towns, and the resulting social problems. They look at the interaction of industrial organisation and developments in industrial relations, including the growth of trade unions. They study the changing position of women and children in society. Social history is also concerned with the causes and effects of changes in everyday life in town or country; with attitudes towards religion; with leisure activities including holiday-making; and with the causes and influence of developments in mass media communication.

In addition, social historians study demographic changes, the reasons for and consequences of changes in the size of the population or its distribution by age, sex, occupation or geographical location. Finally, they study changes in social attitudes and in the role of the state. They examine the evolution of attitudes towards the treatment of poverty from dependence on charity or the Poor Law to 20th-century developments in pensions, social insurance or other forms of assistance or benefit. They look at changes in government policy relating to housing, public and personal health, social work and, last but by no means least in importance, the growth of the education system.

Although economic and social developments are inter-related, it is possible to concentrate on either the economic or social aspects of the subject. This can be done through a choice of syllabus or through selection of topics within a syllabus.

Syllabuses
Most Examination Boards offer a syllabus for economic and social history which deals with Britain during the past two or three hundred years. Students examine the industrial revolution and its consequences together with the more recent period

when British economic performance has been less impressive than that of some other countries. They examine reasons why there has been increasing attention given by governments to the social consequences of economic change. The exact coverage does vary. In 1984, for example, the Southern Universities Joint Board syllabus covers the period 1650 to 1950, the JMB 1700 to 1951, and that of the AEB from about 1750 to 1970. London requires candidates to answer questions from a much broader time span (including the medieval or early modern period) in its examination paper 1 but allows quite a choice of specialisation in paper 2 including options in medieval and early modern economic and social history as well as in the more recent periods such as economic history since 1914 and social history in the 20th century. The Oxford Board, in what is at present probably the most flexible of the schemes, offers a fairly conventional route to A-level (1700 to the present day) but also gives the opportunity for medieval or early modern study (from 1300) and/or a special study option, 'social movements and economic change in Britain during the revolutionary period, 1776 to 1848'.

For two reasons, the variations in the period covered by syllabuses and the revisions presently being made by some Boards, you should obtain a copy of the syllabus used at your school, college or local centre. Some Boards (eg Oxford and Cambridge, JMB) have introduced documentary and/or statistical elements while others (eg AEB, Cambridge) are planning to do so. This, of course, affects the nature of the examination.

Debate and discussion
History students (whether political or economic and social) are not concerned with certainties. Therefore, much of an economic and social history course will be taken up with areas of debate, particularly on issues where historians disagree. Much of the debate stems from the incompleteness of the evidence which is at our disposal. Students are expected to understand the arguments put forward in these disputes, and their strengths and weaknesses. Issues examined in this way can include the effect of industrialisation on the standard of living, the characteristics of 19th-century trade unions, the efficiency and far-sightedness of British businessmen in the late 19th century, economic performance between the wars, the effect of the war on the position of women, and developments in educational or social provision.

Coursework

At A-level, students depend quite a lot on teachers and textbooks in following the course or investigating historical debates. Economic and social history does, however, offer scope for practical projects either on a local or a broader basis. These can involve the use of industrial archaeology, oral history (talking to people about their experiences of the war, unemployment or past leisure activities) and old newsreel or feature films. All these techniques enliven the study of the subject and enrich understanding. Students reading and talking about economic and social developments will, like all history students, benefit from close analysis of sources and materials (mainly written) which date from the period being studied. There are many readily-available collections of this type, not only in libraries or local record offices, but also in edited and printed form in paperback editions.

An economic and social historian, like any student of the social sciences, should be numerate. Arguments sometimes depend on the interpretation of figures. Some work, therefore, is likely to be based on statistical information and some GCE Boards (eg Oxford and Cambridge, AEB, London, Oxford) include questions which invite students to demonstrate skills of this type.

Examinations

The examination will generally be in the form of two three-hour unseen papers. For most Boards (but not London or Oxford), paper 1 at present deals with the early industrialisation period up to about 1850. Paper 2 covers developments after the mid-19th century. Questions are normally of the essay type although one or two structured questions on statistics or short passages do occur. Candidates are usually given a free choice of four questions out of approximately 15 on each paper. All questions are worth equal marks unless the examination paper specifically states otherwise. The JMB scheme allows for an approved personal study to be substituted for one examination question.

In marking papers, examiners look for evidence of knowledge, understanding, relevance and coherent argument. The last two qualities are vital for candidates hoping to acquire higher marks. Good use of examples will always strengthen an answer and appropriate local knowledge (eg drawn from a project undertaken during the course) will be welcomed. So, too, will evidence of a wide study of either books or documentary sources.

A-level combinations

You will find that economic and social history can be very helpful as part of an A-level package of subjects. If you are taking subjects such as sociology, economics, government and politics, geography, public and social administration or English (where you might be studying 19th- and 20th-century literature), then economic and social history interacts with other studies. It will reinforce your understanding and enjoyment of them, and improve your academic technique. This assumption is supported by the practice of some Boards which do not offer economic and social history as a separate A-level syllabus, but instead offer it as an option paper within other subjects, as in economic and political studies (Oxford and Cambridge Board) or in economic and public affairs (Cambridge Board). Don't worry, incidentally, if you have not taken economic and social history at O-level. This will create no problems; indeed, coming to the subject fresh can actually be an advantage.

Higher education

The content and methods of A-level economic and social history can be useful in preparation for a number of subsequent courses and careers. It is an expanding part of the history programme in all branches of higher education. This subject or part of it (either by name or under an alias) appears in many courses in the social sciences. Among them are vocational and semi-vocational areas of study such as social work, public and social administration and environmental or urban studies. It appears, too, in some art and design courses and, in the form of history of education, it constitutes part of the curriculum of teacher training institutions.

Apart from degree courses in history, it obviously provides a preparation for economics, business studies, law, politics and sociology courses. It is also appropriate to courses in higher education in a wide range of business studies, public administration and management and similar subjects.

Careers

For careers starting after A-level, economic and social history doesn't provide a ready-made entry qualification. However, it is fully accepted like any other arts A-level such as history or geography for entry to careers where one or more A-levels may be required — banking, insurance, the Civil Service, accountancy, building societies, local government and commercial companies. It would also be a useful background for careers in journalism, libraries and social work.

English
by Mike Torbe

Until now your English courses have involved you in several
different kinds of work. You will have written stories, poems
and essays; read various books, some of them immediately
interesting, some of them — especially for O-level literature —
difficult and demanding; you may have had drama lessons; you
may have enjoyed talking about all kinds of topics; you may
have done various kinds of language work.

The A-level English course, however, is generally not an
extension of all of these. With very few exceptions, it is a
course in English literature only. The exceptions are some very
new A-levels in English language, which are not yet widely
available. Most of this article, therefore, refers to the more
common A-level English literature. In this course you will
spend your time reading, discussing and writing about great
literature of the past and present.

The syllabus
The organisation of the course varies slightly from one
Examination Board to another. To be quite clear about the
details, you'll need to get a copy of the syllabus used by your
school or college, or from the Board itself. In general there are
three parts to the final examination, and that affects the way
the course is taught.

Paper 1 is usually compulsory. You will be expected to
answer questions on all of the books you have studied in this
paper. Normally, you will find that you will be studying two of
Shakespeare's plays, and the work of one other writer, perhaps
Chaucer, Milton, Gray or another. A typical group you might
find would be *Hamlet* and *The Winter's Tale* by Shakespeare; if
the examination syllabus includes Milton, you might find you
will be reading some of *Paradise Lost* (a long poem about
Adam and Eve) or *Samson Agonistes,* a poem about the blind
Samson and the Philistines. If you are to study Chaucer, you
will read one of his *Canterbury Tales,* written in what will look
to you like a different language, which is, in fact, an older form
of English. Or, you may study a poem such as Gray's *Elegy in a
Country Churchyard,* or T S Eliot's *The Waste Land.*

The paper 2 syllabus contains a lot more books, but you will
not be expected to answer questions on all of them. Instead,
you will only have to write essays in the final examination

174

about four or five of them. You can choose from a long list of books of all kinds — novels, poetry, and plays — written at any time over the last 500 years. Some of the writers' names you may already have heard of, but some will be new to you. You will find poets like John Donne, John Dryden, William Wordsworth, T S Eliot and Seamus Heaney. There will be novelists from the past like Jane Austen, Henry Fielding, Charles Dickens, and from this century like D H Lawrence, Joseph Conrad, Virginia Woolf, George Orwell, E M Forster etc.

Finally, you may find there is a paper on practical criticism. For this, you will be expected to read and respond to passages of prose or poetry which are quite new to you, to show how closely and critically you can read, and how clearly you can express your understanding. Some Boards recognise that a sixth-form course can help to develop your ability to write in an original way, and sometimes an optional paper in creative writing is set.

The work of the course

The most obvious thing about the course is that you will have a good deal of reading to do. There will be at least seven different books to read, and maybe more, depending on how your teachers choose to approach the course. In addition to this essential work, there will probably be times when you will be discussing the books you have read, either with each other or with the teacher. There will be other occasions when the teacher might want to talk to you about all or part of the text. You will certainly be writing essays in which you will be exploring various aspects of the book and its meaning. Your teacher might want to lead a discussion about one of the texts, or to do some extended work on one or all of them in a project. You might have the chance to go to the theatre or the cinema, to see a performance of one of the plays you are studying or a version of a novel. Finally, you may be asked to read other books in addition to the basic texts. This could be other literature by the same author or by other authors of the same period. You will be asked to read what critics have written about a text, to help you to assess and extend your own response and understanding. In this way, you build up an extensive — and deep — knowledge of literature.

What happens in class?

Different teachers will deal with the course in different ways:

you will need to find out, for example, if the teachers will expect you to read all of the books on paper 2, and then choose in the examination which to write about, or whether they will themselves choose just four books and study them in great depth, so that you will be expected to answer questions on those books only. Equally, some teachers may start straight away studying the set books, whereas others may spend the first term or half-term introducing you to a more general approach to reaching complex literature.

In the same way, the style of the teacher will make a difference to the way he or she conducts the lessons. Here are some of the things you might find yourself doing in lesson-time, not in your own study time:

- taking notes while your teacher talks about a text
- discussing as a whole group the meaning of parts of the text
- working in small groups, preparing your version of your understanding of a poem, or a part of a play or a novel
- writing about texts in special ways; for example, writing about an incident from different people's points of view
- participating in a seminar; that is, a specific kind of discussion in which all the participants have previously studied one thing, so that there is some understanding in common
- preparing for, or making a presentation: that is, you alone, or you and one or more of your friends will be expected to *lead* a discussion
- having tutorial sessions with your teacher in which you and the teacher together discuss your work, either as a general discussion, or perhaps talking about an essay you have written.

What happens in private study?
In your own time, out of class, you will be expected to do things like this:

- prepare and write essays
- involve yourself in longer and more sustained pieces of writing, if your teacher suggests it; a project on an author, or a text, or a period
- write up and expand notes
- read around the texts, perhaps looking at what critics have written, or at other works by the same author. You won't be expected to do too much of this, because your teacher

will be aware of how much time this takes but you might find, if you get very interested, that it will help you to read other books.

What else do I want to know?
In this next section, you will find some questions that people like you have asked in the past, and some of the answers that can be given.

Exactly how different is A-level from the English course I've done so far?
The main difference is that it will be almost exclusively about *literature,* unless you are doing one of the alternative-level courses. Another difference is that you are unlikely to write creatively, unless your teacher is particularly interested in creative writing or the syllabus includes a creative writing option. You will spend most of your time in analysing and exploring the texts.

If I've enjoyed creative writing, and want to make my career by writing, will A-level English be a suitable course?
This depends; some people will tell you to do other courses and carry on writing in your own time. But most degrees which might be suitable, and professional courses like journalism for example, will welcome you if you have done an A-level English course.

Does it make a difference if the books are several hundred years old?
It's bound to; literature from the past took different things for granted, in what the writers expected their readers to know and to understand. But that doesn't make them either impossible to read or irrelevant to you today. It just means that you'll find it harder at first to see what the writers are getting at. Console yourself with the thought that if the books have survived, and are still being read after hundreds of years, it must be because they've got some permanent value, and you are likely to find that as you study them, you'll begin to understand and enjoy them.

How much work will be involved?
You know now about the amount of reading — at least seven quite hard books; in addition, there will be varying amounts of writing. It varies because of the approach of your teacher.

Some teachers expect an essay every two or three weeks; others will expect about three a term. Any course that involves reading and writing essays will probably take up rather more time than a course that involves practical work.

Can I do it if I don't enjoy reading?
Yes, but you'll have to find a way to compensate for the difficulties you have with reading. The important thing is to recognise that reading is the way you become familiar with the text, and that what determines success and failure in the examination is the understanding you have of the text, and the way you can express that understanding.

What kinds of essay will I have to write?
Some teachers will ask you to work through questions from past papers, so that you become familiar very quickly with the sort of thing the examination will ask of you. Others will start you slowly and work up to the difficult ones. At first it will seem impossible to you. You may feel that you'll never be able to write at the length and the complexity that the examination will demand of you; but in two years you will change a lot, and it will be within your reach.

What will the proportions of drama, novel and poem be?
The syllabus will offer you a wide range of each; some Boards might split them up so that you meet an equal number of each in your studies. Your teachers may decide for you, or they may leave quite a lot of the choices with you. If you feel at the moment that you are anxious about (say) poetry, don't let that affect your decision too much. You may not have read very much poetry at the moment, but after the course you will feel much more comfortable with it.

What's the examination like?
Difficult, mainly because you have to conccentrate two years' work into just eight or nine essays, each one written in about one hour or less. It can be particularly hard for slow writers, or those who like a long time to plan an essay before they start. At the moment, that is the way examinations are conducted, and after all, it's the same for all subjects, and all students. However, some Examination Boards provide coursework assessment in A-level, so that writing done during the course can be considered too.

What do you have to do to be good at it and get a good grade?
You have to be very familiar with the books; that is, to know very thoroughly what happens and who the people are in novels and the drama. You have to understand the basic ideas that the author is expressing. You have to be able to have a point of view of your own, but also to know what points of view other people have had about the book. You need to be able to balance your views with others, and judge which offers the more satisfactory interpretation. And you have to be able to build, sustain, and justify your own point of view by careful reference to what is there on the page, quoting the text so that it supports what you are saying. Finally, you will have to learn during the course how to construct an essay which states clearly your view and persuades your reader that what you think is worth considering.

Alternative A-levels in English
AEB provide an A-level in English language and literature, which involves the candidates in wide reading of newspapers and periodicals, and essay writing on topics of general contemporary interest. The syllabus is much closer to the sort of work you have been used to at O-level, combining language work like essay-writing and summary, with a study of literature.

London will soon offer an A-level English Language studies examination, which will involve 'preparation for courses with linguistic elements, and for careers in which knowledge of and sensitivity to language will be required'. This is quite different from anything else currently available, and you will need to be very clear about what is involved if you are interested in taking this examination.

Other A-levels
English literature is the second most popular A-level subject and it combines well with most other arts or language subjects. It is commonly taken with history, French or other languages, geography, classics or economics. It can be combined with science subjects, although as in all cases of mixed A-levels, the career and further education course implications have to be carefully considered. For some careers, such as primary school teaching and/or speech therapy, English and a science subject is an ideal combination.

If you wish to go on to study English literature at degree

level at university or polytechnic, it is usual to have studied it at A-level. Most university departments also ask for a foreign language, at least to O-level. There are all kinds of other courses for which English is an excellent subject for entry. Some of them are closely related, for example: linguistics, drama, philosophy; others less obviously so — history, politics, languages (classical and modern), law, American studies, theology, social sciences, and business studies. In short, English is a very well-known and respectable A-level, welcomed by most university departments and employers.

Jobs and careers

If you leave school at 18, there are many jobs where the study of English to A-level will be an advantage: banking, secretarial work, personnel, commercial jobs in building societies, insurance companies, advertising, marketing and sales. In other careers such as the Civil Service, the Health Service, local government, journalism, library work, legal work and so on, you would find your knowledge and qualification useful. Personnel officers who recruit school leavers into industry and other careers often say that students who have taken English show a willingness and ability to discuss ideas openly with people both older and younger than themselves.

General studies
by Frank Vigon

The special quality of general studies

As an A-level subject, general studies is very different from other A-level courses. It offers the greatest variety of topic areas of study, educational experience and teaching methods. It also offers students the opportunity to study several subjects for their own intrinsic value, at the same time as acquiring an examination certificate.

Until the sixth form most students do not have time to consider how the various subjects complement each other. General studies aims to compensate for over-specialisation and give students a broader educational perspective. It is not intended to be 'science for artists' or 'arts for scientists', but rather aims to examine a wide range of issues spanning the whole spectrum of the curriculum. The context of the major part of general studies courses is chosen to be immediately relevant to contemporary issues and problems which affect young people and the rest of society today. It follows that general studies can be a very stimulating part of the A-level course, and at the same time form a useful cohesion between other subjects being studied.

Do you need O-levels?
General studies can be of value to students of all specialist backgrounds since it covers some aspects of every part of the curriculum. Depending upon what is offered in your own particular school, general studies could be taken as an additional A-level to provide wider educational enrichment rather than as part of entry qualifications to higher education. In this respect although AO (Alternative Ordinary) levels do exist there is no necessity for students to have taken AO level. Some schools operate a system whereby you take AO level in the first year of the sixth form and having taken and passed the examination you convert it to A-level in the second year of the sixth form. Then you would take the A-level examination along with your other A-levels at the end of the sixth year. Apart from this two-part system, students can take A-level general studies without having any previous experience of general studies. There are no indications that not having taken general studies before as an AO level would limit your success at A-level.

Syllabus
Unlike the other subjects on the timetable, there is no one common agreed syllabus for A-level general studies. The content of the A-level general studies course will be deter-mined by the expertise and interests of the teachers, the character and interests of the students and in some instances by the Examination Board which the school chooses to adopt. The variations in subject matter are infinite. Obviously, teachers will aim to give a balanced course but subjects could include: astronomy, political affairs, pollution, scientific responsibility, culture, ethics, philosophy, literary appreciation, linguistics, a foreign language, mathematical reasoning, spatial relation-ships, aspects of scientific research, history, genetic engineer-ing, sociology, psychology, general knowledge, the theatre, the cinema, the media, religion — the list is endless. Students who are interested in taking general studies should talk to their teachers to find out what is offered and this will help to determine whether or not the course will be suitable.

The course of study and teaching methods
The nature of the work involved will vary from institution to institution and much will depend upon the preferences of the teaching staff and their particular specialisms and interests. Textbooks will vary according to subjects studied. In most cases the schools will provide these resources. In many courses teachers prefer to use either their own materials in the form of booklets, handouts etc, or they will use kits produced by commercial publishers. Since much of the subject matter is contemporary, materials will change frequently. Lessons will vary considerably, and although the class lecture can form an important part of the general studies course, most general studies courses will offer a wide variety of approach such as talks by outside speakers; visits to places of interest and relevance to the course being studied; films, visits to the theatre; sound and film strips; experimental work (physical and human experiments); 'happenings'; drama work; group work; discussion groups; debates; lectures from guest teachers; visits to universities; research work in libraries and museums; visits to courts, councils, parliament; preparation of surveys, interviews; self-produced films and video programmes; viewing of television programmes and many other possibilities.

The work load will vary from school to school. Some schools will require a collection of essays over the two- or one-year course. Some schools will organise their courses in terms of options so that the student can choose as he or she wishes, with a requirement of so many essays per option. Other schools may require projects; some a combination of projects and essays; others may include group work in their marking. Homework will be a matter of negotiation in individual schools and can take the form of research work, watching a television programme, talking to friends and relatives, writing pieces of prose or completing work as an extension of the work taking place in the lessons. Again the methods of work are infinite and the list given here is only a small sample of what might be on offer.

Examinations
As far as examinations are concerned there are wide variations between the different examinations offered. Five of the Boards offer A-level general studies. These are: AEB, JMB, Oxford Local Examinations Board, University of Cambridge and University of London. The format of the papers varies considerably. Some examinations test knowledge in areas of

arts, sciences and social sciences, other ask questions along more general lines. At least two of the Boards have a special syllabus that will form part of the examination. The special syllabuses will be taught by all schools taking those two Boards' examinations. Some examinations involve only essay type questions, some have language translations, mathematical questions, science questions of a specialist scientific nature, and science questions of a very broad general nature. Some of the examinations include objective questions where candidates are given several possible answers and are asked to underline or indicate the correct answer. Projects can form part of an examination. All in all, in order to discover what examination is being offered, students should approach their general studies teachers who will be only too pleased to show them copies of past examinations and explain the requirements of future examinations.

The marking of the examination will vary from Board to Board, but students should be aware that the standards expected in other examinations will apply in general studies. Marks are awarded for accuracy, use of evidence, the ability to construct a coherent answer, standard of language, spelling, neatness, and handwriting is taken into account by some Boards.

Further courses and careers

It is difficult to be precise about the particular use of general studies either as a background for a future career or for an entrance qualification to higher education. Much will depend upon the employer, or the university or institution of higher education. If you are in any doubt about the relative advantage or merit of taking A-level general studies you should consult your general studies teacher, your head of sixth form or your careers officer. Give them specific details about what you intend to do when you leave school and they will be able to make the necessary enquiries to help you with your decision.

University entrance

Students who are aiming at university entrance would be wise to consider general studies as a third or even fourth A-level subject. The original JMB examination (JMB is the Board whose examination is now taken by nearly four fifths of the 46,000 students entering for general studies) was designed as an alternative to the O-level requirement to provide evidence to the universities of width of study undertaken by the applicant.

It was offered in addition to at least two other A-level subjects, and is still acceptable. Nowadays, however, most applicants also offer a range of O-levels as well and regard general studies as a widening of their A-level course.

This width of content can also be helpful to students faced with a bewildering choice of subjects which can be started at university level. Social sciences, business studies, politics, law, engineering, are just a few examples of subjects which may not be available in your school or college. A general studies A-level course could well give you some insight into the sorts of ideas some of these disciplines are concerned with, and help you to choose an interesting degree course.

If you are taking general studies as one of two A-levels, you should check very carefully about its acceptability for further courses or careers. For polytechnics and colleges this will vary from one institution to another. General studies is acceptable as an A-level to the CNAA, but it may not be favoured by admissions staff for particular courses. It is unlikely to be accepted as the only A-level pass required for entry to a higher diploma course in, for example, catering or business studies.

If you are going into a job after A-level and wish to qualify through the relevant professional examination, it is very important to check its acceptability, particularly if it is to be offered as one of only two A-levels. At present it is not accepted in this instance by several of the accountancy bodies, the Civil Aviation Authority, or the Royal Navy. It is, however, acceptable to the other Armed Services, the Chartered Insurance Institute, the Institute of Bankers and the Civil Service. This is far from a complete list and acceptability does change from time to time. The other A-level subjects and supporting O-levels will also be important, so do check each case carefully with the help of your careers teacher or careers officer.

This note of caution should not put you off choosing general studies at A-level as long as the aim of its purpose as a widening of an A-level course is fully understood. Many employers would welcome it as just this. For others who are not familiar with the course, it may be necessary to be ready to explain it in some detail. This may offer you the opportunity to sell both general studies and yourself to a likely employer!

Geography
by Peter Bryan

Most people study geography for some part of their school career, and large numbers go on to take it at O-level or CSE. Despite its popularity, most students and teachers find it difficult to give a precise definition of the subject, not least because in the past 20 years it has been one of the most rapidly changing and developing subjects in the curriculum. It is perhaps easier to say what you will study in A-level, although changes in the subject have introduced considerable variety into the syllabuses, which now differ quite a lot in their content and approach.

Different kinds of geography
It is true of all syllabuses that they involve the study of man and his activities, together with the physical environment within which they exist. The study of the physical environment — land, sea and atmosphere — is called physical geography. This can be taken as a separate discipline or can be integrated with the human aspects of the subject. Regional geography studies man and his activities in particular areas, such as continents, and seeks to identify how and why areas differ. Human or systematic geography studies man and his activities in a different way, looking at such topics as urban or agricultural geography. It seeks to recognise distributions and patterns across the world, in order to explain their origins, processes of development and relationships with other phenomena. All these branches of geography can involve description, measurement and explanation; generally they involve all three.

You should appreciate that geography tends to be a concrete factual subject. Despite this, there are not many people who find it lacking in interest because the world itself is a fascinating place. It is certainly a wide ranging subject, lying on the frontier between the observational sciences and the critical humanities. Because of this breadth of subject matter, there are few students who cannot find substantial areas of interest in it, so long as you remember few A-level students are likely to enjoy every single part of their course, whatever the subject! Human geography overlaps on to such fields as history, economics, politics, sociology, agriculture, architecture and planning to name but a few. The study of the physical environment combines well with scientific interests, especially in the biological and environmental fields, to which geographers often contribute.

Making geography your A-level choice

Although it is helpful to have studied the subject at O-level, it is certainly not essential. The A-level course does not demand previous knowledge, and although for a short while you may experience some unfamiliarity with basic ideas and terms, this should disappear in a few weeks, especially if you admit your lack of background and ask for help. It can even be an advantage to take geography from scratch, for you can approach it with an open mind, free from prejudices about previous courses and teachers. Many students with little or no previous experience have been very successful at A-level and have also found it a fresh and challenging experience. In choosing geography as an A-level, you should also look beyond at the effect it could have on your career, particularly if you are thinking about higher education and degree courses.

The A-level course

All syllabuses include physical geography, which comprises the development of landforms (geomorphology), climate and meteorology, vegetation and soils (biogeography). On the human aspects more choice is given. Some syllabuses offer the study of major areas of the world in detail (regional geography); a common alternative to this is the study of major aspects of man's activities, such as population, settlement, industry, agriculture, and transport, illustrated from appropriate areas of the world (human/systematic geography). Practical studies are common, and some syllabuses offer the chance of submitting original practical studies in place of a written paper. It is important to realise that because of the syllabus options offered by some Boards, it is possible for two centres in the same town entering students for the same Board, to run courses with very different content and approaches.

Teaching methods

Most of your work will be in the classroom, although fieldwork is popular with many schools. This offers students opportunities for visits of varying lengths up to a week to see at first hand areas which are relevant to their coursework. Many field excursions are also based on practical exercises of an investigative nature, singly or in groups, and students often look back on field trips as the most enjoyable parts of the course. Geography is usually taught in a specially equipped classroom, for a wide range of techniques are used in its teaching. Audio-visual methods are widely used, together with the study of maps and photos. Project work, group study, simulation and gaming exercises are common, all of which place emphasis on self-learning.

Contrary to rumour, most syllabuses do not place any emphasis on mathematics, although some schools are placing more weight on this aspect because they wish to do so. Students with an O-level or CSE grade 1 pass in maths will find no problems with the course. Equally, the idea that geographers have to be good at drawing maps is just as untrue, since nowadays most maps are duplicated for us. The subject makes great use of books and other written sources, so you will be required to read widely and deeply, and a willingness to read is therefore important. Both in the classroom and at home you must be prepared to spend a lot of time reading, writing notes and essays.

Examinations

In many ways, the final examination will not be very different in style whatever syllabus you take. All have two or three written papers, and considerable emphasis is placed on essay-type questions. Marks are given for the content, but also for the ability to select relevant knowledge and to organise it into coherent logical essays which blend facts and assessment. If you are hopeless at writing essays, geography may not be a good subject for you! There is some variation of the essay format: some syllabuses include short structured questions which stress ability to think rather than write; many offer material in the form of maps, diagrams and photos as a stimulus to thought or to set problems. But in most cases you cannot escape the essay-type question entirely, so be warned! Because it is a factual subject at this level, knowledge is essential for a good result, and this involves a good deal of learning. But learning will not produce much of a result on its own, because examiners look for evidence that you can use your knowledge — that you can select, organise, analyse and argue. From this they learn whether you can think.

A-level combinations

Geography combines well with many A-level subjects. On the arts side it is commonly taken with English, history, or a foreign language. It also goes well with social sciences such as economics or with pure sciences, mathematics or statistics. It is important before deciding on taking geography with a combination of sciences to make sure that you are not narrowing your choices of further scientific courses or careers. It is also important to ensure that you have the right O-level subjects for any intended careers. Many semi-technical areas which attract geographers need maths and science passes at O-level or CSE grade 1, even if not at A-level.

Further courses and careers

A-level geography is usually needed for a degree in geography, and it is considered an excellent preparation for degrees in subjects such as economics, history, politics, town planning and surveying. But difficulties can arise for those likely to go on to science degrees, including subjects like geology, and earth or environmental science. The more specifically scientific the degree, eg medicine or engineering, the less likely geography is to be regarded as a useful or even acceptable qualification. Even in related sciences, such as geology, environmental sciences, or meteorology, where geography is accepted as a useful subject, lack of scientific knowledge of the right kind can cause a student some uncomfortable problems with parts of the degree course. There is virtually no degree course for which the subject is an essential entry requirement, although there are many for which it is highly valued. Some students may therefore have to accept that it is not a wise A-level choice for them, however great their interest in it. This still leaves a vast number of students for whom it is a stimulating and wide-ranging subject which will enhance their career prospects — the fact that geography is among the top ten subjects in A-level popularity is proof of this. For those starting their careers after A-level, there are very few jobs for which geography is a required A-level subject, although there are many for which it is a sound preparation. Commercial careers such as banking, insurance, shipping, freight forwarding and travel agency work welcome the subject. It is particularly useful for air traffic control (with maths), cartography, land surveying, general practice surveying and many careers in local and national government.

Career progression in many of these will require further qualifications often taken part-time or by correspondence course. Some of the examinations for the commercial qualifications include examinations in branches of the geographical subjects, especially economic geography.

In conclusion

How can we sum up all this? Geography is not a difficult subject at A-level, but don't confuse difficulty with worth! You don't need any special talents to tackle it. Although it helps to have a reasonable mathematical and scientific background, it is not absolutely essential. Full and wide-ranging syllabuses mean that there is a lot to learn, so it is not a subject for the work-shy. You should enjoy reading, because you will do a lot of it, and you need to be fairly good at writing notes and essays. You should have an interest in the world around you and the desire to find out more about what happens and why. If you are not scientifically minded, there are parts of the course where you can develop these interests; if you are more interested in man and his activities, the human aspects of geography touch on almost every aspect of life. It is a lively inquiring subject for lively inquiring minds, so if this chapter has not answered all your questions — start inquiring.

History
by Alan Jamieson

'There is a history in all men's lives' wrote Shakespeare in *Henry IV*. Some famous men — and women — have made a distinctive mark on history and their names feature in thousands of books. Millions of other people — peasants, soldiers, workers and builders — in their own way contributed to making history, but their achievements are unsung. Many students are attracted by the fascination of studying what happened in the past, of finding out about people's lives, and of reading and thinking about great ideas and achievements. In the summer of 1983 for example, over 43,000 students sat the examination for history or economic history at A-level. Among the syllabuses they followed were British, Scottish, Welsh, Irish and English history; ancient, European, Commonwealth, American and world history. In addition, millions of other people find history an absorbing subject, reading for pleasure and interest the works of famous historians, historical biographies and historical novels.

Why history?

Why is history taught in schools? Plutarch, an ancient writer who described the Romans, had one answer. He said that Cator wrote a *History of Rome* 'with his own hand and in large

189

characters, that his son might have in his own home an aid to acquaintance with his country's ancient traditions'.

History is still seen as a means of finding out about one's own country — its greatness on land and sea, its empire, its kings and soldiers. 'Traditions' means more than this, too. It means learning about the system of government, about farming and industry, about the way of life of people over many centuries, and also about literature and art.

All these subjects come into history at A-level. But you will find your study will go much wider than British history. Some historians think history should be worldwide, that it is important to know about the civilisations of ancient Egypt, Greece and Rome, about India, China, Russia, Africa and America. Other people think we should concentrate on 20th-century history because momentous changes took place in the political, religious, scientific and artistic life of the world in the last 80 years, and these have important consequences for today. The entries for the different syllabuses at A-level compared over the last few years show that there has been a swing towards the study of 20th-century history.

The examination syllabus

Your A-level work will be dominated by the external examination set by one of the eight Boards. Each Board offers a group of different syllabuses, and the teacher can, in theory, choose freely. But of course he or she will be influenced by several factors: personal interests is one; class and library books available will be another; a third is the traditions already established in school or college.

You may find that a teacher prefers medieval or ancient history because they are worlds so different from our own. The Tudors and Stuarts are popular because of the dramatic events, the religious and political changes, and the personalities — Elizabeth, Shakespeare, Drake, Cromwell, Marlborough — that one meets. Many teachers prefer to study the 19th and 20th centuries because of the insight this gives into the modern world.

Some — a few — schools cover the same ground as the O-level course. This could be deadening but it is likely that the A-level syllabus will cover a wider period, and certainly in much greater depth. There's so much to choose from in history that it seems unimaginative not to change. However, where a sixth-form college or FE college takes students from several 'feeder' schools, it may well be possible that some of the A-level course will cover the O-level period. But you should expect much more scholarly teaching at A-level and your own work will be in greater depth. It is not essential to have passed O-level history before starting an A-level course. You can start A-level from scratch.

You will probably find that the course has two parts: a study of a long period, say Europe from 1789 to 1945 for one paper, and a special study or topic, such as the Renaissance, the American War of Independence or the British trade union movement, for a second paper. A shorter period is sometimes referred to as a special subject. This gives time for detailed work, whereas a long period allows you to take a broad view of events across a hundred years or more. A special study usually requires the study of documents — in printed form — of what people saw, said or wrote at the time. In this way you get at the roots of history. Some Boards also accept evidence of a project. This usually takes the form of a loose-leaf file or folder or work completed on a special topic.

Papers

To give you an idea of the range of history which a Board offers, here is the list of the main papers from one Board. Candidates can be entered for two or three papers, with one paper chosen from each group. In the examination three hours are allowed to answer a paper.

Group 1
1 English history to about 1500
2 English history 1500-1714
3 English history 1660-1832
4 English history 1783-1964
5 English history 1450-1964
6 History of the USA 1783-1945
8 Ancient history

Group 2
9 European history 337-1500
10 European history 1450-1715
11 European history 1648-1815
12 European history 1789-1964
13 European history 1450-1964
14 World affairs since 1945

Group 3
15 The Normans in England 1051-1100
16 Mid-Tudor crises 1536-1569
17 British society 1815-1850

Group 4
18 France in the age of Louis XIV
19 Bismarck and German unification
20 The origins of the Second World War

Teaching methods
History teaching has always suffered from the need to 'cover the syllabus'. This can sometimes lead to a situation where fact is piled on fact, and notebooks are filled with information on the politics of an age, on peace treaties, people famous and infamous, economic changes, the cultural life of the people and so on, until history seems to be measured in notebooks.

But history doesn't have to be like this. You certainly need to get to grips with the facts — they are the raw material of history. But most of what you need is contained within the pages of the textbooks you will be given. You can add to them by keeping a notebook to jot down extra information taken from additional books, but don't think that history at A-level is just note-taking and note-making.

Reading
To study history, you must like reading. First of all, there's the textbooks. You may be set assignments: 'read chapter 4 for a discussion tomorrow' will be a regular instruction. If the course is, say, world history from 1870 to 1970, the teacher will recommend two or three textbooks, and you will return to these books time and again to get at the information you need for talking and writing. But it is not enough to read only the textbook. At A-level you are expected to dig deeper. If you are studying the 1914-18 war, you would be expected to read a textbook on the causes of the war, the events on land, sea and air, and the peace treaties. You would also be guided to a book of war poetry, to biographies of some important personalities — Lloyd George (the British Prime Minister); the Kaiser; Clemenceau (The French Premier), and so on. You would need to dip into Winston Churchill's memoirs and read a novel such as *All Quiet on the Western Front*.

To guide your reading, the teacher will probably give you a book-list of textbooks, biographies and specialised books. You will be expected to choose these books in the school and public library. When you are set an essay, a book-list will be suggested. Perhaps this is the time to start your own library by buying paperback editions. Penguin and other paperback publishers have a wide range of books relevant to A-level work. You won't always be expected to read all of a book. You will be shown how to make brief notes on what you read, so you grasp and retain the essential points. Sometimes it's enough to read a chapter or two, and to 'de-gut' the chapter by making a note of the essential points.

Talking

Having done the reading, the talking begins. At A-level, teachers expect students to be able to discuss a topic, and you will be given training in this skill. First of all, however, some preliminary reading will be demanded: there's nothing worse than a half-baked discussion when people haven't prepared for it. Sometimes you may have to read an essay aloud to a group. One or two students can be asked to introduce a topic with a few minutes' talk. This is followed by debate and discussion. The teacher will guide this talk, so there's no rambling off the point. Sometimes you may have to defend a position, such as arguing that Napoleon's victories were achieved because of the weakness of France's enemies as much as by his own military brilliance.

At its best, history makes people think, formulate their opinions, and organise their ideas and information in support of a viewpoint. Viewed in this way, history can provide an intellectual training which will last you for life.

Writing

'Discuss' is the most over-used word in A-level exam papers. 'Britain lost the American colonies because of errors made in London. Discuss': such is a typical question. Thus the class talk-in is translated to paper. You will be trained in the special skills needed: organising information in your head or in note-headings, presenting a case, using the facts as evidence, and reaching a conclusion. And, as well as organising your ideas and knowledge, you will develop your own style of writing. You may also have to write an essay each week or fortnight on some aspect of the subject. You will be told the approximate length: the most important factor is not amassing information for its own sake but using it to support your argument. From time to time you will be set a timed essay to get you accustomed to writing it in 45 or so minutes, as in an examination.

As well as essays, there are other ways of writing about history. Some teachers carry on the project method used at CSE and O-level. Students choose a topic within a syllabus and complete an 'in-depth' study of it. Projects at A-level are not just fact-collections. Students are to assemble information, classify it, and present it in a coherent and logical way.

Using evidence

The historian's materials are evidence. A scholarly historian working in a university will read documents such as letters, memoirs, government reports, contemporary descriptions of an event. This evidence is found at places such as the Public Record Office, the British Museum, and local archive or document offices. At A-level, most of the source material or documents you will be asked to read are in printed form — in books. Reading what Mary, Queen of Scots actually wrote in her letters, or what the commissioners said in their horrifying reports on conditions in the mines in the 1830s, adds excitement and a sense of being there to history. You can get an extra feel for what happened centuries ago if you are able to read local documents about farming, houses, streets and buildings, conditions in the town workhouse and prison, and other places which you know by name or reputation. There should be a wealth of such material in your local library, assembled in a local collection of books, pamphlets, documents and pictures. Among topics studied for A-level are these taken at random: 'town growth in the 19th century', 'coal mining', 'the history of hospitals in the county', 'elections 1868-1910' and so on.

Although most teaching is centred on books, teachers introduce other methods too. There are many audio-visual aids available to stimulate your imagination. Films are one way of adding colour and personality to your reading, but do watch out for Hollywood inaccuracies. Films made of real events such as newsreels and documentary films about wars are invaluable. Television and radio must not be neglected. Apart from the rich provision of educational TV and radio available during the day, there's a constant stream of broadcasts from BBC and ITV on historical themes. A teacher will also use filmstrips, slides and other pictorial information.

Visits

A visit to the Imperial War Museum, the Science Museum in London, or a local country or town museum can bring history alive in a most amazing way. A visit to a battlefield of long ago, a ruined monastery, a canal or a railway will give you insights into history. You may not have to go far: a local museum or local archaeological site will give your imagination the same kind of stimulus. James Joyce in *Ulysses* wrote that, 'History is a nightmare from which I am trying to awake'. It can be a nightmare if it is seen as the boring process of taking or receiving notes for lesson after lesson. But, seen as a voyage of discovery into the past, and explored through books, visits and the use of the imagination, it is one of the most rewarding subjects to study.

The examination

At the end of the course comes the examination. This means sitting two or three three-hour papers. You have to write five or six essays in this time, or answer questions which ask for shorter replies. The question paper offers a wide selection because examiners know that students do not cover the whole of a very long period of history (sometimes 400 years) and therefore give them a wide choice.

If you study a special period such as the reign of Elizabeth I, which calls for knowledge of documents, the question paper takes a different form. You will have to write short answers about several documents, explaining and interpreting them. Some Boards have begun to experiment with multiple-choice questions at A-level (a statement is followed by several possible answers and you have to underline or tick the correct one) and some Boards accept project work.

The eight Boards all have rather different methods of examining. Towards the end of the two-year course your teacher will provide a detailed briefing on what kind of exams are set and how you should tackle them. Some old question papers will be answered in class and for homework, and there is usually a mock examination to give you practice in answering under exam conditions.

These are the qualities an examiner looks for in A-level candidates:

● accurate knowledge
● clear understanding of the subject or topic studied
● the ability to analyse historical information

- logical thinking
- skill in assessing evidence
- orderly presentation of facts and ideas
- the ability to write clear and accurate English.

Special papers

Some Boards set additional Special or Scholarship papers. These are not compulsory and are usually taken by candidates who are thinking of studying history at university. In the Cambridge Syndicate Special paper, for instance, two questions have to be answered in three hours: this gives plenty of time to write in depth about a particular subject and to show the power of judgement and critical skills required at this level.

A-level subject combinations and further courses

History at A-level is frequently combined with other arts subjects such as English, geography, religious studies, or a foreign or classical language. It also goes well with economics, business studies and social sciences. It is less usual to combine history with science subjects, although this could be very useful for primary teaching and for some paramedical careers. If you are very keen to take a broad A-level course and combine an arts subject with two sciences, then history would be a good choice on educational grounds. In this case, it is very important to check the career consequences of such a decision.

History is an excellent subject to use as a base for further and higher education. To gain entry to a degree course in modern history, ancient history or a similar subject at a university or polytechnic, it is not absolutely essential to have studied history at A-level, but it helps. It is also useful to have a modern foreign language at least to O-level. Being an academic, analytical and literary kind of subject, history is an admirable preparation for all arts courses. It is particularly useful for reading English, law, languages, sociology, theology and many other subjects at university. In recent years, some A-level courses have included demography (the study of population) and statistics, and this is very useful training for entry to business studies and economics courses. An A-level pass in history, therefore, is fully recognised as suitable for entry into any arts, social sciences and business studies courses at university, polytechnic or college of higher education.

Careers

There are few careers except teaching, museum and archive

work where history has a direct bearing.[1] However, you will find people with A-levels and degrees in history in many different jobs. It is widely recognised for entry to banking, journalism, the Civil Service, local government and trainee management posts in all kinds of commercial companies. The reason for this widespread acceptance of history as a good qualification is not because employers want you to know a string of facts, but because the study of history provides a good training in thinking, in arranging and sorting information and ideas, and in explaining things in clear written and spoken English.

Historical knowledge is a useful background for many problems encountered in work, everyday life, politics etc. For many people it is also a hobby and an interest which enriches their leisure time for the rest of their lives.

[1]See *History as a preparation for a career*, by J W Hunt, a pamphlet available free from the Historical Association, 59a Kennington Park Road, London SE11 4JH.

History of art
by Ann Powell

Introduction

History of art is an attractive course for students who are interested in all forms of art — painting, sculpture, architecture and design — and yet do not necessarily have a higher level of skill in painting or drawing. On the other hand, it is a subject which does attract students who are also taking A-level art because it offers additional insights into art seen throughout a long period of history, and so adds to your knowledge. In a nutshell, then, it means you look at the work of great artists, architects and designers — Michelangelo, Rembrandt, William Morris, Van Gogh, Picasso and many more — set against the times in which they lived.

As a subject, history of art is equivalent to any other arts subject such as history or English. The skills you need to study and do well in it are English skills — such as critical reading of books and the ability to express your ideas clearly in writing. You should also have some visual sensitivity although this will develop considerably during the course.

The history of art course is tempting to students who are likely to continue with the study of art for a Higher B Tech diploma or a degree in fine art or design. It is also very useful as a course at A-level for students who are thinking about taking

English, history or modern foreign languages courses at a university or polytechnic. Science and business studies students should also consider it as a possible option because it helps extend their knowledge of art and history beyond their own specialised areas of study. Don't think that history of art just means looking at pictures; it takes in the cultural history of western civilisation and therefore covers a wide range of fascinating topics.

The course of study

1 *Visual communication* One major theme of the course is visual communication. This means the way in which ideas and emotions can be expressed both visually as well as verbally. We are very familiar with this form of communication today because we are surrounded with images in newspapers, magazines, the cinema and television. But it was equally important in the past, and many artists were deeply involved in the problems of their day. They often moved in the same circles as writers, musicians, philosophers and politicians. In order to understand their work you need to understand the historical background. But conversely, knowledge of their work helps to bring alive the history of the period, giving you greater insight into the ideas and events of that time. This is why history of art is often offered as an option in a history degree.

2 *Art and the environment* Another important theme is art and the environment. All branches of the visual arts — painting, sculpture, architecture and design — are linked together. Changes in one art form often affect the others. You will find that studying the history of art will make you more aware and more critical of your environment — not only its architecture but all aspects of its design from the clothes you are wearing, the chair you are sitting on, and the typeface of the book you are reading.

3 *Art and artists* However, the main theme of study in art history is art and artists. You will be expected to have a very broad general knowledge of the history of western art from the classical period to the present day, and there are several excellent textbooks written specially for first-year students to help you. You will also be expected to have a much more detailed knowledge of at least one or two (London University Board) special periods. The time divisions of the special periods differ with each Examination Board, but they basically fall into six main areas and one will probably attract you more than the others:

1   *Classical art:* the art and architecture of ancient Greece and Rome from about 600 BC to about 300 AD. You will be mainly concerned with temple design such as the Parthenon of Athens and its sculptures.

2   *Medieval art:* the art and architecture of the Christian Church from its origins in the 4th century AD to the great Gothic cathedrals in France and England of the 12th, 13th and 14th centuries.

3   *Renaissance art* (and architecture) in both Italy and northern Europe in the 15th and 16th centuries: major artists of the period include Leonardo da Vinci, Michelangelo, Raphael, Titian, Van Eyck, Bosch, Bruegel, Dürer.

4   *Baroque and Rococo art* of the 17th and 18th centuries in Italy, France, Spain, England and the Netherlands: major artists of the period include Caravaggio, Poussin, Velazquez and Rembrandt in the 17th century, and Watteau, Tiepolo and Gainsborough in the 18th century. Major architects include Christopher Wren and Bernini.

5   *The 18th and 19th centuries:* Neoclassicism and the Gothic revival in architecture. William Morris and the arts and crafts movement.

6   *The origins of the modern movement, and the development of modern art, architecture and design:* this is the most popular but perhaps the most difficult option because you will be expected to discuss the philosophical and political ideas behind the various art movements of the late 19th and 20th centuries. The Impressionists (eg Monet) were not just painters of pretty pictures, but aimed at accurately recording modern life in a rapidly changing world which had been transformed by industrialisation. The next generation of artists, the so-called 'Post-Impressionists' (eg Van Gogh) were less objective and actively denounced the evils of modern urban life. In the 20th century modernist artists sought for honesty and truth in a world they believed was dominated by false values and this led to the rapid succession of art movements from Expressionism, Cubism, Futurism, Dada and Surrealism. At the same time, architects and designers, such as Frank Lloyd Wright, Walter Gropius and Le Corbusier faced up to the problem of redesigning the industrial city into a place which was fit both to live in and work.

This looks like a very long menu. But you will find that most schools and colleges will only be able to offer one or two of these periods. So you will have to find out what is available in your local area.

Coursework

Most classroom teaching in history of art revolves around slide lectures and discussions. There are textbooks, but you will find them useful only as an introduction to the subject and your reading will cover a wide range of subjects which at first sight may seem to have nothing to do with art. For example, English landscape painting and landscape gardening is intimately linked with both poetry and politics and has also influenced town planning.

Looking at things is as important as reading, and most schools and colleges try to organise relevant trips to local and national galleries and museums. You should also study the local architecture, not only the 'grand' buildings such as cathedrals, country houses and town halls, but also the ordinary everyday architecture of shopping precincts and housing estates.

Other useful sources of information include television and newspapers – the Sunday colour supplements often contain interesting articles on art, architecture and design. Homework will usually be preparing and writing essays based upon material derived from class, reading and your visits to museums and galleries.

The scope of the examination

History of art is offered as an A-level examination by six of the Examination Boards and you should examine their syllabuses carefully because each offers a different approach to the subject. None of the Boards expect an O-level pass and it is theoretically possible in some cases (such as the AEB) to complete the course in one year. The majority of the Boards, however, demand a written research project of about 5,000 words which has to be registered with the Board the year before the examination.

The AEB's examination does not include a written project and consists of two written three-hour papers. The first paper is on a special period chosen from six options:

1 Early Renaissance in Italy;
2 High and late Renaissance in Italy and Spain;
3 17th-century art in Europe;
4 18th- and early 19th-century art;
5 Neoclassicism, the Romantic movement and Realism;
6 Modern art and its origins.

The second paper is on general topics and includes four identified photographs. You are expected to answer short questions on them to show your skill at critical analysis.

In contrast, London University expects the student to write a research project and there are also two three-hour written examinations. Paper I is devoted to British art and there are six options of special periods ranging from the middle ages to the present day. Paper II is concerned with the art of the western world and offers five options of special periods ranging from the middle ages to the present day and it includes a compulsory photograph question.

A third alternative is offered by the Oxford Delegacy of Local Examinations which also demands a research project as well as two written examinations. One is a general paper and the other is on a very precise topic which can be chosen from a list which changes from year to year. In 1985 the topics are:

1 The interaction of Moorish and European art forms in Spain;
2 The English country house in the 18th century;
3 The Impressionist period;
4 The Bauhaus;
5 Art deco;
6 English sculpture 1920-70.

History of art is also offered by the Oxford and Cambridge Schools Examination Council, the JMB and the Northern Ireland General Certificate of Education Examination Board.

Combinations with other A-levels

Although an increasing number of students are now taking history of art at O-level, this is not essential and most students will not have studied history of art before A-level. An interest in history and in art is clearly necessary, and many students take these subjects or English literature or a foreign language with the history of art. If you wish to go on to study the history of art at degree level it is very useful to have at least one modern foreign language to O-level standard. Some students take A-level history of art, with art, design or craft subjects. This is quite acceptable although students should be careful not to concentrate their A-levels in too narrow a range.

History of art can also be combined with science subjects, which could be of great value for budding architects and industrial designers. Those who wish to train in conservation of paintings or other works of art would find chemistry extremely useful.

Further courses and careers
There are specialist degree courses in history of art, architecture and design. Some courses are purely theoretical; others are combined with studio work. At university or polytechnic, history of art can be combined with other arts subjects such as English, history, or a modern foreign language.

In art schools there are degree and diploma courses in a wide range of design fields, graphics, fashion, textile, photography and industrial design for which history of art forms an essential part of the training. (These art school courses will also require completion of a foundation course in art).

History of art is therefore an important qualification for any student thinking of a career in the visual arts as an artist, designer, or architect. You could even consider a career in art history itself although this may require further postgraduate training. This could mean teaching, working in a museum or gallery, publishing, library work, restoration, arts administration, conservation work, the antique trade or many others. History of art is also of great value to anyone thinking of a career which involves visual communication in areas such as advertising, public relations, theatrical design, display or fashion journalism.

Finally it could be a useful and enriching A-level for anyone who would enjoy studying it for its own sake and would like to appreciate more of the world of visual arts whichever career they embark on.

Philosophy
by David Isaac

Philosophy has been studied at universities for centuries. Only recently, it has been introduced at A-level (AEB and JMB). There is no O-level in the subject. Any combination of O-levels would be suitable for admission to an A-level philosophy course.

Philosophy is not an easy subject but it is not just for an intellectual élite, either. There may be something of a philosopher in all of us. Are you of a curious disposition, still asking the question 'why' when others who are more matter-of-fact or trusting are already satisfied with the answers given? Are you interested in moral, social or religious questions? If so then philosophy may be to your taste. You should first read something on the nature of the subject, such as E R Emmet, *Learning to Philosophise* (Penguin) or Bertrand Russell, *The Problems of Philosophy* (OUP) or L Stevenson, *Seven Theories of Human Nature* (OUP). You may well find that it is the intellectual food you have been looking for. Your appetite will be aroused and your interest could be life long.

Through the ages, philosophers have tended to ask the kinds of general, fundamental questions we would normally assume we know the answer to. However if we think more deeply about them we may realise we don't know the answers. For example: Am I free? Why should I be moral? What is virtue and justice? Is war ever just? Can religious beliefs be justified? How? Is reality as it appears to be? What can we know, and how? What is proof? How are language and thought related?

People generally start to study philosophy after they have studied other subjects over several years. As students of philosophy, they go on to re-consider all kinds of knowledge and to see other subjects in a new light. Philosophy has more to do with a way of looking at things and with an attitude of mind, with method and technique than it has to do with the facts or events in any one particular area of human experience. The study of philosophy will develop your capacity for analysis, reasoning and judgement; it will enable you to think more clearly, to break down and build up arguments and to be more critical and careful in your use of language. In many ways it will support and complement your work in other subjects.

Combinations

Philosophy cuts across the science/arts division and could combine well with other A-level subjects either in the arts or in the social, natural or pure sciences (such as with literature, politics and government, sociology, maths, and physics).

The course and the examination

Coursework includes the careful reading and analysis of prescribed texts from Plato to Russell and Sartre. These are likely to be concerned with moral philosophy or the theory of knowledge, and you will have to answer specific questions on passages selected from them. For the AEB exam, you also have to study 'themes'. At least three should be chosen from: "our perception of the external world"; "faith and the existence of God"; mind and body; scientific method; value judgements freedom, law and authority. For the JMB, you would study at least two out of the philosophies of mind, religion and politics, each with related 'contemporary problems'. (For this Board one of these two options may be examined by internal assessment of coursework.) Throughout your course, whichever syllabus is chosen, considerable emphasis will be put on essay writing and on discussion, which since the days of Socrates has always been important in philosophy.

And after
A course in philosophy is a useful background for entry into a number of vocational areas, such as public administration, teaching, management, computing and information technology. Indeed, any career where you need to be able to think logically and present ideas clearly would be an option. At university, it may be studied on its own or in combination with a range of other subjects in the arts or sciences. Most universities in the UK have welcomed the introduction of philosophy at A-level; some university departments have been involved in developing the syllabuses.

Bear in mind that philosophy is new at A-level: new not just to you but also to the teachers, to the Examination Boards and to the universities, as well as to everybody outside the educational system.

Religious studies
by A H B McClatchey

It is not divinity. It is no longer scripture. It is certainly not religious instruction. The subject is religious studies. The aim is to enable students to develop an understanding of religion, its place and significance in our life. One Examination Board sets out the matter in the following terms: 'to enable students to become aware of the existence of a religious interpretation of life, to make them sensitive to the issues involved and help them to arrive at their own interpretation'. Religious studies will also involve investigating religious language and ideas, appreciating religious feelings and responses and evaluating religious beliefs and practices. The syllabus will have been drawn up in such a way as to encourage an open and unrestricted treatment of the subject in school or college. The examination does not aim to assess the candidate's personal beliefs but to test his or her understanding of the reasons which lead to the position adopted. At the same time, a number of Boards include material which enables the pupil to study the importance of emotion in religious belief and commitment.

Recent changes

During recent years, the view of religious studies has developed considerably not only in aim but in content. Syllabuses have been extensively revised since the time when the scope was little more than the Old and New Testaments and the set books. Religious studies is no longer a matter of mapping the journeys of St Paul but now includes work on the Qur'an, ethics, Marx, humanism or missions to Africa. The very wide choice in the new syllabuses mirrors the changing attitude to religion which we find today in our own pluralist society. The religious studies teacher is concerned to help students to think about religion in a relevant context, to question and discuss the several issues selected for the examination. Most Examination Boards include, as one option, a paper on biblical studies and it may serve as a useful example of some of the new thinking in this area to quote from the introduction to one such paper: 'Though in a pluralist and cosmopolitan society the Bible is not the only literature that could be so used, yet its influence on western culture has been so formative and its assumptions so woven into our thought that study of it may still be one of the most effective ways of stimulating thinking about a religious interpretation of life.'

Many dimensions

The Bible provides many students with an excellent introduction to the extraordinary range of questions now included in religious studies. However religion has many dimensions. Three of the major ones are doctrine — Buddhism, for example, teaches the Four Noble Truths; mythology — expressing beliefs in story form, as in the Hindu epic, the Ramayana; and thirdly, ethics — nearly all religions prescribe principles and even codes of conduct, as in the ten commandments.

In addition, a religion is unlikely to be properly understood outside the context of its living practice. Ritual may play a great part. Students can expect to find here a whole new area open to them. It should introduce them to observation of other cultures than the one with which they are most familiar. The mass and what it means to the devout catholic, the worship in the synagogue or a mosque may show much more clearly than reading a book what the believer is doing when practising his religion. What the adherents of a religion say they are experiencing may, on occasion, be the key to a modern appreciation of an ancient religion. The impact of a religion on society may also reveal a great deal about its teaching in ways not always readily understood from books. Papal pronouncements about family planning are a case in point.

The practice of religion can also be better understood by studying some of the organisations and structures which have grown up in, for instance, Islam or Christianity. One recently proposed new paper in religious studies included the study of the following institutions: Methodism in England, the Sunni Sect, or the Ramakrishna Mission. One of the sections on Methodism set out the following: emphasis on laity, societies, class system, circuits, travelling preachers and conference, to give but one example of what practical investigation could lead to. Man can be seen to respond to the divine in many more sophisticated ways than asking a returned astronaut whether he saw God.

A-level courses
It is not necessary to have studied the subject at O-level before tackling A-level. The majority of Examination Boards offer predominantly Christian or biblical papers at O-level and the choice is now so great at A-level that for many students there is plenty of opportunity to approach it as though it were a new subject.

Religious studies has developed from the traditional form of examination on the Bible and some of the Boards still require two papers from the following:

1   Biblical studies;
2   Principles of Christian belief and action;
3   The origin and foundation of the Christian Church;
4   Christianity in a changing world.

Other Boards have a different approach but a quick look at one of the sections in this last paper, Christianity in a changing world, may be of help in considering a typical field of study and the depth of work required. The historical period covered is from the middle of the 19th century. Four questions are to be attempted, taken from any section of the paper which is made up of three sections:

A   Church and Society in Britain;
B   Christianity, science and biblical criticism;
C   The Church and world mission.

We find that section A covers not only Church and state, the Churches in politics and education, but also the Churches' attitudes to particular social questions: poverty, housing, industrial relations, war and peace, marriage, divorce and the family, race relations.

Looking at the syllabus

Prospective students are strongly recommended to inquire about the range of papers available and also what the papers themselves actually cover. A paper entitled 'some issues on religion and philosophy' includes a section which reads: the nature of man; man's place in the animal world; evolutionary philosophies; the physical basis of personality; heredity and environment; conditioning factors, including drugs, brain surgery, mass communication (including advertising); ideas of man's purpose and fulfilment in Marxism, Humanism, Existentialism, and Christian traditions; freedom and determinism; death.

A section in a paper (from another Board) called world faiths includes: the expansion of Buddhism in China and Japan, with special reference to the Pure Land School and to Zen; Buddhism today as illustrated in one eastern country (eg Thailand) and in the western interest in Tibetan Buddhism and Buddhist symbolism and art. Options from other Boards range from Rabbinic Judaism, the Talmud, Mishnah and Midrash to the significance of caste in Hinduism. These topics inevitably have a lot of surprises for those who may still be reacting against Sunday school of long ago. This makes it all the more important for inquiring students to bring themselves up-to-date about the syllabus and the options offered at the local sixth form or college. It is probably true that at least as much has been done in the field of religious studies as in the new maths or in the approach to teaching science.

Classwork

Such a wide syllabus must draw on a wide range of sources, and students are expected to read material outside the traditional textbooks on biblical studies. Books on major world religions, ethics and philosophy and also television programmes may be used. Religious studies is a subject which lends itself to class discussion covering all sorts of religious and ethical problems and the approaches to them of various religious ethnic or social groups. Visits may be made to places of worship of different religious traditions. Outside speakers may be invited to the school and students will be encouraged to consider current social, political and religious issues in the light of the established doctrines of Christianity and other religions.

Examinations

Most of the Boards set two papers of two and a half or three hours. Each paper will offer a choice of three or four essay subjects out of a range of questions.

Some Examination Boards set out their aims in general terms such as: 'primary aim is to encourage disciplined thought on the part of the candidates towards received tradition'. Hence the emphasis is on the religious significance of what is set. A further aim is to assess candidates' ability to think and argue intelligently about the subject.

Some Boards, however, set out the objectives of the examination relating to the individual papers, eg 'Examiners will look for evidence of wide reading and for the following abilities: to relate the material to contemporary problems of religion and ethics, to discuss and evaluate the points of view of the texts and the validity of writings about them'.

Subject combinations

Religious studies will combine well with almost any arts or social science subject including music and art. English literature, history and religious studies is a popular combination and students would find it useful to have a modern foreign language or Latin at O-level to leave open a wide choice of further courses at university, polytechnic or college of higher education. Those wishing to teach religious studies (or any other subject) should also have O-level mathematics. Religious studies could also be combined with science subjects such as mathematics or biology. This would be useful for those interested in philosophy, or paramedical careers (nursing etc) or those seeking a wide spread of A-level subjects on general educational grounds. For those aiming for more scientific careers, the combinations would have to be very carefully chosen with these careers in mind.

Careers and further courses

Students preparing for nursing, teaching or social work will find religious studies enables them to investigate, for instance, situation ethics, Freud, mysticism or the problems of the Third World. Religious studies can, of course, lead to entry for a degree in theology or to training for one of the many forms of accredited lay ministry in one of the Christian churches. Those who are going on to further education courses in English, history or sociology will find the subject a useful preparation.

Anyone who wants a career in serving the needs of others in, say, community or welfare services, hospital administration or local government will be made aware in religious studies of the vast range of human values, beliefs and cultural differences. Anyone hoping for a job with people can hardly do better than consider this subject in order to discover what people are like.

Religious studies is, in one sense, part of human geography, in another sense it observes what seems to transcend the human scene.

Chapter 10

Social sciences and business studies

Accounting
by Michael Talbot

Accounting as a subject at A-level is growing rapidly in popularity. Entries for the examinations are increasing by about 10% each year and more and more centres are preparing students for the examinations set by the Associated Examining Board (AEB), Joint Matriculation Board (JMB), Oxford, Welsh and now the Cambridge Board. Accountancy as a career has become more attractive, for it is seen as a means of getting into interesting — and profitable — jobs in the financial world, in banking, insurance and many other spheres of business activity.

The nature of accounting

To succeed at A-level in accounting, it is important to be numerate, but it is not essential to have passed O-level in mathematics. Students who take accounting have to be able to calculate and to list numbers because many answers to questions are expressed in money terms, just as is the case in real business situations. To take an example, the Designer-Jeans Boutique, after paying all expenses for the year ended 31 March, made a net profit before paying taxation of £10,000. This amount of £10,000 would have been determined by totalling the money received from customers (say £30,000), and deducting from this the costs to the owner of the boutique of the clothes sold, the rent and rates for the shop, wages to part-time sales assistants etc, a total of, say, £20,000. Not very difficult arithmetic, although it was necessary to be able to add and subtract amounts. The issue was concerned with the method of calculating the profit (or loss). From the accounting viewpoint, the main requirement was to find out the total turnover of a business (in this case, the total income from the clothes sold) and to subtract from this figure all the money paid out by the owner for the particular selling period.

A further step in this example could be to calculate the profit as a percentage of turnover ie £10,000/£30,000 x 100 = 33⅓%. Do you think 33⅓% is a good profit margin on the selling price of jeans? The question cannot be answered in this context without other information. For instance, to make a comparison, you need to know the average percentage return made by other shops selling a similar product. In any case, would it be preferable to make 33⅓% profit on turnover of

£30,000 or 50% on a turnover of, say, £18,000? What do you think?

From these simple examples it should be clear that there is more to accounting than merely manipulating numbers. Decision-making using a common-sense approach on the basis of quantitative information and techniques is a prime concern of managers in business rather than excellence at geometry, algebra, or mental arithmetic. In this way, therefore, accounting is allied with the business world rather than with mathematics.

In fact, at A-level, Examination Boards now allow the use of personal calculators in their examinations. There is little point in using limited examination time to ask candidates to add, multiply, and subtract figures when these basic functions can be completed in seconds with a calculator.

An understanding of accounting includes an awareness of its limitations. For example, the Designer-Jeans Boutique appears to have made £10,000 profit, but other factors may have to be taken into consideration. Did the total costs include an estimate of the fall in value of the shop fittings which one day will have to be replaced with new ones? Should the £10,000 be adjusted in some way to a lower figure if the cost of living has increased during the period in which the profit was made?

Relationship with other subjects

To an extent, students are specialising when they study accounting but no more so than if they study economics, government, law or business studies at A-level. Students of accounting are not necessarily intent on becoming accountants but they are indicating an interest in a career in business because they have chosen a subject which provides insights into the world of commerce and finance. And, while many trades and professions will continue to disappear, there is little doubt that the demand for people with a knowledge of accounting is unlikely to diminish. A knowledge of computing and data-processing will also become necessary. There are also behavioural and sociological aspects associated with accounting. An example of this would be the effects on staff of a proposal to introduce new machinery into a factory on the basis of cost information supplied by accountants. A final decision would depend on other factors such as union reactions and re-training.

Methods of study

Students are usually supplied with, or asked to buy, a single basic textbook selected by their teacher from the list of those recommended by the relevant Examination Board. A common teaching method is to divide a lesson into sections made up of different activities. A teacher will discuss or explain a topic in general, then demonstrate how to approach and solve a related problem. Students will then be asked to attempt a similar problem. At this stage teachers (subject to the number of students in the group) may give individual assistance and encouragement to students or may work through the solution to the problem with the whole group. Naturally, different teachers adopt different teaching methods, some being more informal than others. The core textbook enables the student to read ahead of the lessons and provides a range of exercises for classwork and homework.

Students who obtain high grades at A-level are not likely to have confined their reading to just one textbook. Additional books and articles in quality newspapers and financial journals, for example, cover topics in the syllabus in more depth, or provide another view.

Guidance on what to read will be provided by the teacher. There is an excellent range of textbooks on accounting but many are expensive, although most college and school libraries should have an adequate selection. Most public libraries will also have a collection of accountancy textbooks. Partly because accounting is a subject which for many years has been studied by correspondence courses, there are a number of self-help books or teach yourself books which can be useful for private study. These take various forms. In one, you are asked to study a short passage on a topic and then select the correct answer to a question from a list of, perhaps, four alternatives. According to the degree of accuracy of the answer selected, the student is directed to read another section of the book.

Another interesting approach is through case studies which provide details of a simulated business situation, such as estimated sales figures, costs and selling prices for a firm trying to decide whether to make canoes in wood or fibreglass. The student has to work through the data, and explain, with reasons, the course of action he or she would choose. These can also be used as basis for class discussion. Occasionally, you will watch television programmes which help to provide a broader framework to the subject.

However, the main route to success is by spending a lot of

time reading, solving quantitative problems, and writing concise and relevant essays. Essay writing is often difficult for students and should not be neglected. Many students over-estimate their ability at writing notes or essays and spend too much time studying solutions to questions which need numerical answers. This is understandable, but don't make the mistake of thinking that accounting is only concerned with numbers. In an examination 40% of the marks can be allocated to essay work and written comments about the solution to a numerical problem.

Links with O-level

To study and succeed in accounting at A-level is not dependent upon a student having taken the subject at O-level. But, some questions at A-level are based, for example, on a thorough knowledge of double-entry bookkeeping, a system of recording accounting information dealt with extensively in the O-level course. In practice, A-level courses tend to incorporate revision of O-level work by providing questions at greater depth in areas previously covered at O-level. A student who has already studied the subject to O-level obviously should have more time to concentrate on new ideas and concepts. As mentioned earlier, there are excellent textbooks available and private reading is very well rewarded at all levels of study. Students with no knowledge of the subject would be well advised to do some basic reading before beginning the A-level course.

The syllabus

Syllabuses for each of the Examination Boards are broadly similar. Differences occasionally occur when one Board or another introduces a new or revised syllabus. When you get a copy of a syllabus, look carefully to ensure that it is issued by the Board you intend to be examined by, and that it is the syllabus appropriate to the year that you plan to sit the examination.

Most of the emphasis at O-level is on bookkeeping and other aspects of financial accounting: the course is mainly concerned with recording information about what happens during a certain financial period. While this approach to the subject remains important at A-level, emphasis swings to analysing past trading figures and comparing them with those of similar firms. This helps to identify better practices for a business to follow in the future in order to improve profitability or to survive a liquidity crisis.

This interpretation of accounting statements is applicable to sole traders, partnerships and limited companies. Limited companies are, however, the more complex forms of business organisation and are governed by the requirements of the Companies Acts. Essay questions based on these Acts are a common feature of A-level examination papers.

Accounting systems serve to measure economic activity and thus provide information for decision-making by owners, lenders of money, and suppliers of goods for resale. However, accounting statements have limitations and these have to be understood by the A-level candidate, such as the difficulties of comparing the profit of a business for one year with that of an earlier year during a period of rising prices.

Most accounting syllabuses now include a study at an elementary level of various techniques used in business as a basis for planning business activity and profit forecasting. These techniques may be described in syllabuses under a general heading such as 'cost and management accounting' and itemised, for example, as the analysis of costs, standard costs and budgetary control. Many students find this the most interesting part of the syllabus and state their intention of continuing their study in this area at a higher and specialised level after they have taken A-level.

Assessment

There are generally two written papers, each of three hours and carrying equal marks. Compulsory questions are set on fundamental topics but there is an element of choice in other sections of the papers. The attainment of an A grade pass confirms that a candidate has shown an excellent knowledge of the subject, has the ability to think logically, handle figures with precision, write well, and to work at speed under the pressure of examination conditions.

Course and career implications

Many students, particularly those at colleges of further education, study A-level accounting along with related subjects such as statistics, law, government and politics, and economics. Their objective is normally a place at a university or polytechnic. Among the relevant degree courses at university is a BA in economics or in accountancy. Some universities and most polytechnics offer four-year sandwich degree courses whereby the first two years and the fourth year are spent in full-time study, with the third year devoted to work experience in industry or commerce. This placement with a firm for work experience is usually arranged with the help of the university or polytechnic staff and is very valuable experience. Other students choose to apply for a BTEC higher diploma or certificate course in business studies. These courses are available on a full-time, sandwich or part-time basis at many further education colleges or polytechnics.

For people who wish to specialise in accounting there are many ways to continue studying. These include full-time, part-time and correspondence courses. For example, the student with A-levels can enrol for a nine-month full-time foundation course at a polytechnic (or a three-year degree course in accounting and finance) before taking up a training period with a firm of chartered accountants. In this time he or she would study concurrently for professional examinations to become a qualified accountant.

However, it is not essential to have studied accounting in order to meet the entrance requirements of any of these courses in higher or further education. The advantages are that some prior knowledge of the subject has been obtained as a sound basis for later study, and a student has some factual basis for deciding whether to proceed or not with a contemplated course or range of subjects.

The study of accounting is an excellent preparation for many careers and professions and is valuable for people considering entry to the business world. Among relevant careers are insurance, banking, surveying, building society work, local government and even 'self-employed'. For these and many other jobs an understanding of accounting information, its value and its limitations will prove advantageous. An A-level in accounting is very useful if the student continues to study on a part-time basis for a professional qualification which includes accounting as a subject in its examination structure, for example the Institute of Bankers or the Institute of Cost and Management Accountants. Many employees are allowed day release or encouraged to attend evening classes to prepare for relevant examinations, and a student with A-level accountancy can gain exemption from some of the earlier examinations.

Business studies
by Peter Lambert

Studying business

i   The manager of a small publishing business is dissatisfied
    with the quality and cost of the warehouse and distribution
    services he uses, and is considering buying his own
    warehouse. Can he find the finance, and will the savings
    justify the initial outlay? The warehouse could be quite
    empty for much of the year and yet still be inadequate for
    peak periods.

ii A building site worker is very capable but antagonistic to
    poor supervision. He is highly involved in union affairs and
    well informed on safety matters. Would he make a good
    safety officer?

iii A ladder manufacturer makes do-it-yourself garden
    furniture with the waste wood which is unsuitable for
    ladders. Should they charge a price in line with the
    competition or just sufficient to cover costs?

These are some of the kinds of problems businesses may be
faced with, as well as other, smaller, but nevertheless
important day-to-day decisions. The success or failure of
business depends on the people who work in it, and the
decisions they make. Business managers have to combine a
variety of skills and resources to identify a customer's needs
and to produce and sell products or services which satisfy them.
Business studies looks at the objectives of people in business,
the environment they work in, the opportunities and problems
they face, and the methods by which they tackle them.

Business studies at A-level

Business studies at A-level is quite unlike any of the subjects
which are often grouped under this heading lower down the
school. It is not concerned with developing particular skills like
typewriting and bookkeeping, nor with providing the information content of commerce. Instead, it gives a broad view of an
organisation at work. This is frequently from the perspective of
management, but also from the different positions of workers,
shareholders, customers, interest groups, and government.

Among A-level subjects, business studies is unusual in that it
comprises studies in breadth rather than in depth. Elements of
a number of individual subjects (economics, accountancy,

history, sociology, etc) and skills (literacy, numeracy, judgement) are drawn together in an underlying theme of business problems and how they are solved.

A bridge is built between the academic and the practical, with ideas and theories being constantly applied to real business situations. The result is that A-level is both interesting and intellectually demanding. It is certainly not a soft option and will stretch the strongest candidate, while giving those who have not shone previously in more narrowly specialist subjects the opportunity to prove their all-round abilities.

Anyone for business?

Business studies at A-level is open to anyone. Few students will have had the opportunity to study business studies at O-level before entering on an A-level course, and it is certainly not a necessity.

People who have taken O-level business studies, economics or accounting may find their workload relieved in one or two areas, but the nature of the course and the approach is entirely different. A knowledge of mathematics (up to, say, O-level grade D) is useful because basic numeracy is one of the skills required, although maths within business studies is not difficult. One of the exciting aspects of the subject at A-level is that everyone starts equal on a new study. The most important requirement is willingness to work hard in tackling a new subject, to strive to overcome weak points, and to show initiative and perseverance in individual and group study.

Business studies is not simply for those who want to make money! Students have been known to show enterprise in setting up their own businesses, but the focus on objectives and decision-making relates equally to government services, charities, and even schools, as well as to profit-making ventures. Following a course in business studies will not make a businessman or woman of you, and fortune-seekers would probably be best advised to concentrate on their technological and inventive skills! But you will probably find a rich spin-off into many aspects of your life including your other A-level subjects. Not only will you be more aware of the way people work, but the understanding of decision-making will help to make you more effective in tackling problems large and small in many different contexts.

The subject will likely be of most interest to those who are keenly aware of the world around them. They may be interested in why a well-known shop has disappeared from the high street, or why the local council has decided to contract-out their refuse disposal services. You need not be a reader of the businessman's newspaper, *The Financial Times*. Most businessmen/women probably turn first to the sports or other columns of a newspaper! But, as you begin to understand business news, you will acquire an increasing interest in it, and this will enrich all classroom studies.

What is involved?

The practical nature of the subject and the problem-solving emphasis means that teachers use a wide range of teaching and study methods. There is, naturally, information to be acquired and principles to be understood, and these are constantly related to the business world. Sometimes a guest speaker is invited, or a company visit is arranged to focus on a particular topic. These excursions or visits require advance preparation and follow-up work. In the classroom, a large proportion of time is spent on business examples and case-studies which outline the development of a particular business or problem. Business games and role-playing exercises also help to illustrate aspects of the real world, and students work in groups, tackling problems managers have to face.

Typically, the whole range of topics for A-level is taught by one or two teachers. This ensures full integration of the various segments of the syllabus. Individual study normally involves reading and exercises from a wide range of books — some written specifically for the A-level course, others primarily for managers. Reading is also needed as preparation for classwork, and for periodic essays. The climax of the course may be a practical project (an examination requirement for the Cambridge Board) written up following a short period spent with a firm, studying some particular aspect of its operation. There may also be opportunities for practical experience within the school/college such as managing the tuck shop, vending machines, conferences, fêtes or magazine advertising. There may be a chance to take part in inter-school business games. These give a lot of fun, as well as providing a taste of board-level decision-making.

Syllabus and assessment

A-level business studies is offered by the Cambridge Syndicate and the Associated Examining Board (AEB). Each Board produces a detailed syllabus to show you exactly what is studied. The syllabuses are broadly similar, and both have an underlying theme of objectives and decision-making. They cover the following broad areas:

- forms of business organisation
- structures and decision-making processes
- objectives in business, and constraints affecting their attainment
- internal and external factors including economic, legal and social
- the collection, presentation and interpretation of business data
- an introduction to finance and accounting; financial management and budgeting
- the marketing function — market information and the marketing world
- product development
- production decisions including location, methods of production, stock control, cost information
- people in organisations — communication, motivation, collective bargaining, leadership and delegation .

Examinations under both Boards include short-answer questions, techniques, comprehension and essays, and candidates are tested across the whole syllabus range. However, the Cambridge Board also includes the practical project already mentioned and a case-study paper, in which a number of short questions are set on a brief account of a particular business and its problems. The AEB syllabus, however, includes a series of general topics to be considered from all points of view, which are examined within the essay paper.

An A-level in industrial studies has been introduced by the Oxford Board. This contains many of the organisational, strategic and social matters referred to above but also introduces the technology of the production process, and the choice of materials. The syllabus includes options such as foreign trade, technological development, management structures and techniques, and human relations in industry. Assessment is by means of two examinations (one dealing with the core syllabus, the other with the options), and an original case-study report prepared by the student on an aspect of manufacturing industry such as a local individual unit or a local group of firms.

Course and career implications

Business studies was introduced as an A-level more than ten years ago. Since then, it has been warmly welcomed by institutions of higher education and by the business world. It is a particularly useful subject to possess if you are seeking a job immediately after taking A-level, or after taking further qualifications. If you go into banking, accountancy, insurance and similar careers, business studies at A-level carries exemptions for the early part of some of these courses.

For people wishing to continue with further study at a higher level there is a wide range of business studies and management science courses at universities and polytechnics, as well as more specialist courses in economics, marketing, banking and finance etc. An A-level in business studies is not required for any of these courses but it is a useful starting point and is particularly helpful in giving an awareness of the field which will enable more informed course and career choices in the future. Equally, doing business studies at A-level does not commit you to this kind of subject and can be used simply to broaden the base of your subject combinations.

For instance, business studies with one or more of the maths A-levels, or a science at A-level, may be very useful to those thinking of scientific careers in industry. Business studies can also usefully be combined with economics or history as a base for social sciences or arts degrees. Some care is needed if a combination of business studies and economics at A-level is planned, because a few universities are not willing to accept the two as separate subjects for entry purposes. Within universities and polytechnics there are many courses which extend and develop the skills and knowledge acquired at A-level. After taking a higher education qualification, the range of possible careers opens up. Among them are marketing, finance, personnel, administration, as well as general management trainee schemes which lead to careers across the whole of the business world.

Probably the major advantage of doing business studies is the wider awareness it gives of the world in which you will ultimately find employment, and the impact it has on your own personal approach to decision-making. Among the skills it teaches are the setting of objectives, the identification of problems and constraints, the organisation of information and ideas, the evaluation of alternatives, planning, taking action, and reviewing results — all useful disciplines in any area but particularly when it comes to subject and career choices.

Communication studies and photography
by Alan Jamieson

Communication studies is a new A-level, offered at present by only one Examination Board, the AEB. But it is gaining in popularity, with almost 1,250 candidates each year.

The subject is concerned with many aspects of communication between people. It means the study of ideas, of information, and how people's opinions and attitudes are formed and influenced. It is all about written and spoken communication in many forms; it deals with print (in newspapers, books, magazines etc), with advertising, and with the influence of radio, television and other electronic methods of communicating with people. (It's *not* about transport – buses, trains and planes – nor about the technical aspects of telephone systems, postal services etc.)

Aims
The aims of this subject are set out in the AEB syllabus. These are briefly:

i   To give students an understanding of the importance of different systems of communication, which means, in addition to the print and electronic systems mentioned earlier, communication in families and in institutions such as schools, clubs, societies etc.

ii   To explore the processes by which people communicate with each other (listening, writing, speaking etc).

iii   To help students to understand how opinions are formed, how judgements are made, and how information can be presented and packaged in ways which influence people's attitudes.

Syllabus
As you might expect from reading the aims of the syllabus, the content of study is largely concerned with the different methods of communication, and their effectiveness. In the study of processes, for example, you would study, discuss and write about newspapers, books, radio and television, and also about all forms of advertising and information-processing. You would study how large organisations, companies and individuals set about the job of communicating with customers, clients, the general public and individuals.

Secondly, this subject is about the barriers which prevent communication. This means several things. One is the way in which people's emotional problems get in the way of communication; another is the barriers of language, not only foreign languages, but also the difficulties of explaining something in one's own native language.

A third element is how information is transmitted, and how people react to information. You would examine formal and informal methods of communication and assess their effectiveness. By this, we mean in committees, public meetings, speeches in parliament or from soapboxes and through the press, (the formal methods), and in conversation (informal methods). You would also study how society informs people by means of libraries, official statements, the use of broadcasts and so on, and how advertising assists business companies and large organisations. You would look at the ways by which all these forms of communication affect people, and how they bring about changes in the home, at work, in industry, in politics and in the arts.

Classwork

You would make a study of all these topics by reading, writing essays, and in discussions. You will find that your television watching, newspaper reading, advertisement scanning and everyday conversation take on a new perspective. You begin to think about how words are used in print and in talk. You talk yourself, write analyses of the different methods of communication, and begin to make your own judgements — which should then be examined in turn in class. There are plenty of books on methods of communication, and, of course, your reading takes in modern, current methods of communication — word processing, information storage and retrieval, the use of computers — in fact all the methods of electronic information-handling.

Practical skills

You do all this in class, guided by a teacher or lecturer. But you are also trained in effective communication yourself. You do a lot of practical work, using spoken, written and printed forms, as well as a range of visual material. You learn how to find out about and use different methods of information-handling. This means you use elementary methods of statistics, graphs and visual means of assembling and presenting information. You are taught the skills: how to make notes, write clear and concise accounts, prepare advertising copy, present material as if for radio and television, draft articles for newspapers, write film scripts, compose business reports, and use the telephone. And, finally, through discussion, you would talk about and analyse the the ways by which people are influenced through these methods of communication.

The examination
The AEB examination consists of two three-hour papers, plus a project (this carries 30% of the marks). Candidates choose their project title from a choice of six topic areas. The project could be the outline and contents of a television programme on a factual subject, a sound radio programme, an instruction manual on how to use a piece of equipment, a factual report as if for a newspaper (length about 4,000 words) on an event, a guidebook about an organisation or a service, and so on.

Going on
Communication studies doesn't necessarily lead into a directly relevant job or higher education course. In some centres, communication studies is offered as a general studies programme. Course and career implications are similar to general studies A-level. It is useful for a wide range of degree and diploma courses. Obviously it is linked to subjects such as English, languages, history. It would be useful for entry to jobs in libraries, business companies, radio and television, advertising, newspapers, printing. In the field of higher and further education, there are courses in various forms of communication — by graphical means, through electronics, in art and visual forms, and this subject would be very useful as an introduction. So it could be linked with arts A-levels or science A-levels, although if you intend to go to university, you would be well advised to take communication studies along with two traditional academic A-levels. With employers and admissions tutors at colleges and universities, you will have to be prepared to talk about the subject, because they may know very little about it.

Photography

Aims
Photography is offered at A-level by one Board, the AEB. The course isn't one simply in picture-taking and mounting

photographs. There's a lot more to it than that. The syllabus states clearly that the examinations (two papers) and the coursework (which is compulsory, with work to be submitted) are to test students' ability to use photography. This means not only showing how photographs reveal the world in which we live, but it is expected that students should also understand the technical and scientific aspects of their work.

The course

During the course of study, students learn the main practices of photography. This involves learning about colour, line, form and texture, and applying the medium to record people, objects, the living world and imagery. As well as studying the functions and uses of a camera, students learn how to process, print and enlarge from their own negatives. The practical examination which tests this work is fairly unique: there is one compulsory question and the exam is spread out over 18 hours.

The second part of the course of study is on the history of photography and the techniques. Here, you learn about early methods of photography in the 19th century and early 20th century, concentrating especially on technical developments and the impact of photography on newspapers, magazines and family life, and the recording of events both in war and in peacetime.

Photography is only one way of communicating information and ideas visually. During this part of the course, therefore, students compare the methods and results of photography with other visual media, such as painting, drawing, film, television and photomechanical reproduction. You would study the various ways, too, in which photography is used today in what is called 'mass media' — the means by which the general public is kept informed and entertained.

Photography is not only an artistic subject, it is also highly technical. You therefore have to know about optics — the science of visual perception. You study the workings of the human eye, how images are recorded, how colour is made up and recognised. In colour photography, you have to know about colour reproduction — the properties of transparencies, additive and subtractive synthesis. You go into detail on the functions of the modern miniature camera and its capabilities, lenses, range finder, twin lens reflex. You would use and appreciate the possibilities of a stand camera, double extension, filters and flash. An understanding of the science of light is, of course, very important in photography and you would therefore study the properties of natural and artificial light sources, lighting techniques and electronic flash. Processing procedures are another aspect of the technology and you would need to know all about sensitive materials and processing. In this way, then, the course at A-level blends history, art and science, and is remarkable in this respect.

Coursework

During the two years of the course, you would build up a folio or collection of your own photographs, as well as notes, essays and other written work which you will be required to complete. For the examination, you have to submit a large piece of paper mounted with monochrome photographs which you select yourself. In addition, you have to hand in six to twelve colour slides. Your work has to show that you can communicate your ideas through photographs. You work to a theme (the themes are part of the syllabus and your teachers will tell you all about them).

Equipment and costs

Students always ask the same question: 'Isn't A-level photography a very expensive course?'. The answer is that the centre (school or college) should not offer the course unless it has a properly equipped department. This means a range of cameras and equipment, and facilities for developing and printing. The school or college department should also provide some film — enough to be able to explore all the techniques. On the other hand, it would be unusual to take A-level photography if you didn't have a keen interest in the subject, and this usually means the student has access to or owns a camera. To be realistic, therefore, you will want to own your personal camera — not an expensive one, but capable of taking monochrome and colour transparencies. You certainly don't need an enlarger or dark room at home — the centre must provide these. You should expect to buy some film yourself, and because film is expensive these days, this should be borne in mind.

From what you have read so far, you will realise that A-level photography isn't just about taking pictures. A lot of reading has to be done, and before choosing this subject, you should look at books about the history of photography and its techniques in your school, college, or public library. You will also have to do a lot of writing, — notes, essays, descriptions — just like a subject such as history or English. Paper 2 of the A-level exam is a three-hour paper, with four questions to be answered, and this therefore means you need to know how to write essays.

The examination
As you have seen, there are three parts to the exam. Paper 1 called 'design and practice of the medium' carries 140 marks; paper 2 on 'history and techniques' carries 100 marks; and the coursework is marked out of 60, making 300 marks in all.

A-level and after
The course doesn't qualify you to be a professional photographer, but it is an excellent start for a career in journalism, or in any aspect of the communications industry — newspapers, publishing, advertising, printing and many more careers. An A-level pass in photography helps to get you on to courses of a vocational kind in polytechnics and further education colleges. It is not always acceptable, however, for entry to university courses, and you should check carefully with the admissions tutor of the university you have your eye on. The best advice to offer here is that if you are set for a university course and desperately want to take A-level photography, combine it with two mainstream A-levels — chemistry, physics, English, geography etc. A final word, people who take A-level in photography almost always speak enthusiastically about it, stressing how interesting and fascinating the course is, and they feel that what they have learned will be of great value to them in later jobs as well as giving them a lifetime's interest and enjoyment.

Economics
by Roger Opie

What is economics?
Economics is about scarcity and the distribution of resources. With £5 a week pocket money, would you prefer to buy chocolate and magazines, visit the ice-skating rink, or suffer the agonies of watching football at your local second division football club? Clearly your limited resources will force you to choose and to 'economise' because your £5 has put you in a position of 'scarcity'. You have an economic problem which on a different scale will be well known to a housewife with a limited housekeeping allowance who is forced to choose wisely

between necessities and luxuries. Similarly, a business manager has to make decisions about the goods he is producing; how many should be manufactured; what wages should be paid, what price will be asked. At a different level, the government has the task of raising money through taxation to provide for the needs of the nation such as defence, education, motorways and the Health Service. The common economic problem of allocating scarce resources is evident throughout the study of economics and has to be kept very much in mind by students at any level.

Sharing out money and resources

The study of economics can be broken down into macro-economics (which means the big or whole economy) and micro-economics, (meaning the small or component parts of the whole economy). Many teachers spend the first year of an A-level course covering micro topics before they turn to look at the overall performance of the economy in the second year of the programme. On the other hand, some teachers mix micro and macro elements to give an understanding of the inter-relationships between the two parts of the subject.

The A-level course

At the end of an A-level economics course it is expected that students will have an understanding of the structure of the UK economy, some awareness of current economic problems and a knowledge of their causes, and some understanding of the possible cures for these ills. At the beginning of an economics course, most students have not studied the subject before, and therefore you, like them, may be a little apprehensive about exposing yourself to a subject which attracts so much public attention and which seems to many to provide little or no salvation for the United Kingdom or indeed the world. Some students may have taken O-level economics, or business studies, or commerce, or a related subject. While these subjects cover some valuable background to A-level economics, they are by no means essential. Nor should it be assumed that at this level it is a mathematical subject. An O-level grade C or CSE grade 1 in mathematics may well be of help for the A-level course. However, for anyone considering the study of economics beyond A-level it may be useful to combine economics with A-level mathematics.

As economics is a social science, it tends to adopt a scientific approach to problems which involve human beings. Therefore, unlike the scientist in his laboratory, conditions cannot be held constant and controlled.

Syllabus

The Examination Boards which set A-level papers include much the same content in their individual syllabuses with some variations. A syllabus generally includes:

1 An explanation of the nature of economics and common economic problems.
2 Price determination – why and how consumers demand different products and how the producers attempt to meet their needs. This involves elementary graph work.
3 Business organisation – different types of business firms – how they are organised and financed – the Stock Exchange.
4 Population – the economic significance of population size; the age, sex and working structure of the population.
5 Regional policies – the problems of different areas and government policies to deal with them.
6 Trade unions – functions and problems, occupational and geographical mobility.
7 Market forces – different ways of organising industries eg monopoly, open competition and groups of producers combining together.
8 Costs of production and how firms attempt to maximise profits.
9 Large and small firms – the nation's main industries compared with smaller businesses.
10 National income – the measurement of national wealth and its significance.
11 Public finance – how the government raises and spends money – the budget.
12 Management of the economy – the theories of J M Keynes and other economists.
13 Inflation and deflation – causes, effects and remedies.
14 International trade – the balance of payments, the exchange rate, the European Economic Community.
15 Money and banking – the work of the banks; the role of interest rates and the effects of government monetary policies.
16 Investment and its importance for our economy.
17 Economic growth – how the standard of living is affected by the economic performance of a country.

It is advisable to obtain a copy of the economics syllabus at A-level set by the Examination Board used in your school or college. The syllabus tells you about the content of the course in some detail, and explains the methods of examination.

The examination

The A-level examination varies from one Board to another, but essentially there are now three recognised methods of testing:

1. An essay paper – the traditional three-hour paper which (usually) requires that five essays should be completed.
2. A data-response paper – a problem-solving paper which involves analysing statistics or other information.
3. A multi-choice paper – approximately 50 or 60 compulsory questions are set. There are several possible answers: you have to underline, tick or mark the correct one.

The customary breakdown of these papers in determining the final grade is: essay paper (40%), data-response paper (30%) and multi-choice paper (30%).

Methods of work

Much of the class time will be spent listening to a teacher, and taking notes of what is said. It is necessary to develop the skill of being able to write clear notes, and to check your understanding at regular intervals. Many topics in economics interlock and so you return to the main ideas time and again. However, a teacher may also use some of the following approaches.

1. Case-studies of specific industries and events.
2. Business games and simulation exercises – students work in imaginary firms under realistic conditions.
3. Visits to local industry, banks and large organisations to see how economic theory and practice are combined in practice.
4. Videos and films to illustrate certain concepts.
5. Outside speakers to present an insight into the real world.
6. Class discussion about syllabus topics or current economic issues.

Homework

The tasks will vary but will usually involve some background reading, essay writing and problem-solving. All A-level economics students should be prepared to read a good quality newspaper to keep up to date with the news, to read relevant magazines such as *The Economist*, to listen to and watch radio and television programmes that are relevant to the course. Students are often asked to keep a scrapbook of cuttings throughout the A-level course which provide contemporary examples to illustrate economic theories. Examiners like to see plenty of day-to-day examples in support of economic theory.

Reading
In addition to newspapers, magazines and textbooks, you will be encouraged to read widely. There are some very good paperback books on economic subjects. Penguin-Pelican produce several of these, including P Donaldson, *Guide to the British Economy*.

Some textbooks are listed below. This is not a complete list and every teacher will have their own special favourites.

Textbooks
G Staulake, *Introductory Economics* (Longman)
J Nobbs, *Advanced Level Economics* (McGraw Hill)
F Livesey, *A Textbook of Economics* (Polytech Publishers)

Topic Books
Heinemann publish an excellent series and the Manchester Economics Project (published by Ginn and Co) satellite texts are recommended. See also the Arnold Wheaton series on government, economics and commerce.

Combining economics with other A-level subjects
Economics at A-level can be combined with either arts or science options. However, it is strongly advised that all potential A-level economists should carefully consider the implications of their subject combinations for entry to higher education after 18, and for a later career choice.

Economics is often combined with arts subjects such as English, history, and geography. It also goes well with mathematics or statistics particularly for students who might want to study economics further after A-level.

A-level economics combined with maths and physics would be a very useful combination for most branches of engineering, particularly production engineering. It is also suitable for building and quantity surveying, and for general practice surveying. Combined with biology and chemistry, it would be useful for degree or diploma courses in agriculture, environmental sciences, agricultural economics and estate management. In both these cases it is important to realise that economics may be chosen instead of a third science subject. Three science subjects provide a wider range of subsequent scientific and technological courses and careers. So the wider insights and interests of combining economics with two science subjects must therefore be carefully considered against the narrower range of science options thus afforded.

On to university and polytechnic

A pass at A-level in economics is a useful entry aid qualification for many degree and diploma courses. If you want to go on and study economics as a subject at university or a polytechnic, it is not absolutely essential to have studied the subject to A-level, although a large proportion of students starting on economics degree courses have done so. For entry to a degree course in economics, a pass at O-level in maths or statistics is essential. A-level maths is desirable for people who wish to study the whole range of economics subjects, particularly econometrics. Other university courses for which economics is a good qualification are social sciences, geography, business studies, politics and government, history, accountancy, law, sociology and agriculture. For those students going on to courses in polytechnics and colleges of higher education in arts, sciences or commercial subjects, economics is an excellent introduction. It gives insight and an understanding which are very useful for students on a range of degree or diploma courses in, for example, computer studies, business studies, catering, building and many other practical and commercial subjects.

Jobs after A-level

For people taking jobs after A-level, economics is useful for careers in banking, insurance, accountancy, retail management, surveying and many other careers in the financial and business world. It is also a very useful background to have if you are looking for jobs in local government or the Civil Service. Employers say that A-level economics gives a student a broad knowledge of the commercial and government world, so that they have a head start over other entrants to these jobs and careers. Economics gives, too, a broad base of knowledge to help people who are studying on day release for the examinations of professional bodies such as accountancy and banking. It may also give exemption from some parts of these exams. A CRAC book in the *Connections* series on economics gives a clear insight into careers in economics.

The last word
For students who have a keen interest in current affairs, a desire to become more closely acquainted with the problems facing the country, a willingness to keep themselves informed by reading newspapers, news magazines and journals, and by watching quality television programmes related to the subject, and who have the inclination to sit, argue and discuss relevant topics, economics will probably be a most stimulating and rewarding A-level subject.

Government and politics (including British constitution)
by R W Dade

What is the subject about?
For most young people of 15 or 16, government and politics at A-level will be an unfamiliar subject. For this reason the largest part of this section will be concerned with the content of the course.

Different Examination Boards vary slightly in emphasis, but the core of each syllabus is a consideration of how we in Britain govern ourselves. To this end, the following areas would be studied although not necessarily in this order. After each heading a very sketchy, if a little irreverent, section has been added to give an indication of some of the issues involved.

1   Fundamental concepts are related to the British constitution, the sovereignty of parliament, etc. Is it true that parliament can quite legally pass a law that all men be henceforth known as women? Should a law be obeyed even if your conscience says it is wrong?

2   Political parties: their finance, composition, policies. Do the trade unions run the Labour party and does big business control the Conservatives? What should be the relationship between the party conference and the party's MPs?

3   The electoral system: the way in which we vote for MPs. How did it happen that the Labour party received fewer votes but won more seats in February 1974 than the Tories? Should we hold elections at fixed intervals?

4   The House of Commons: why might a man hear a bell in a restaurant, leave his meal in a hurry, come into contact with a Whip, and then put a top hat on his head, in order to prevent a sheaf of papers being wrapped up with green ribbon and sent to a house with pink leather seats? Is the House of Commons declining or gaining in influence?

5   The House of Lords: is it true that the only member of the communist party in parliament is to be found in the House of Lords? Should the House of Lords be abolished?

6   The monarchy: which of the following is the monarch legally unable to do:
i   Declare war on any country?
ii   Let everyone out of prison?
iii   Marry a Catholic?
iv   Make your politics teacher a lord?
Is the monarchy an integral part of British democracy?

7   The government (that part of our political systems that puts laws into effect): is the prime minister as powerful as a president? Do programmes such as 'Men from the Ministry' and 'Yes, Minister' fairly depict the jobs of ministers and civil servants?

8   The judiciary (courts), police and civil rights: why is it that 98% of all criminal cases are tried by magistrates who, when appointed, have little or no legal training? Can (and should) a police officer detain a suspect for questioning?

9   Pressure groups: how do such bodies as the AA, the Child Poverty Action Group, and the Lord's Day Observance Society, among other groups, contribute to our political system? Are pressure groups selfish?

10   Local government: why bother to have local government when only one in three electors troubles to vote at local elections? Should rates be abolished?

The A-level syllabus
These topics form the core of any government and politics syllabus, but for many Boards there is a second section where there is a choice of subjects. Although the options offered depend on the Examination Board, the following topics may also be available:

1   British political history since the Second War: a fascinating background to current affairs dealing with such subjects as unemployment, housing, Ulster, race relations, education and the EEC.

2   A study of one or more other countries' political systems

including Russia, France, USA, Germany, China, the Irish Republic. Is it true that you can vote for anyone in Russia . . . so long as he or she is a communist? How powerful is the USA's president compared with the leader of the communist party in Russia?

3 Political theory and political sociology: who was Karl Marx, and how many horns grew out of his head? What are socialists, Conservatives, Liberals, Nazis, Fascists, anarchists, anarcho-syndicalists?

4 Public administration: a closer look at the institutions of British government and current issues in the news about those institutions. Do all nationalised industries make losses, and would it be better to sell them back to private ownership?

Sometimes, government and politics is taken as a single paper as part of another A-level. For instance, in the A-level course, economic and public affairs (Cambridge), it is possible to study politics (the structure and working of British government) with one of the following:

● economics
● English economic and social history 1815-1973
● world affairs since 1945.

Subject combinations

The subject, because it is self-contained, may be taken by pupils who also study subjects as diverse as art and chemistry, but it may be of particular interest to those who have chosen to study economics, sociology, modern history and law. Generally speaking, the type of pupil who should find government and politics an interesting A-level subject will be the one who wants to make sense of current affairs.

Anyone who enjoys debating controversial issues in the news, and who wants to learn the facts with which to back up a point of view will enjoy the subject. Although no pre-packaged answers to the many complex questions of politics will be offered, the student of government and politics will, at the very least, be equipped with sufficient information to reject the more nonsensical interpretations of current affairs.

Classwork

Much of the course can be taught in the same way as any other classroom subject. A teacher will, for part of the time, be telling pupils things (factual information, how to answer particular essays, and so on) that will be written down in note form. However, as with many other sixth-form subjects, pupils themselves may be expected to read out their essays. Additionally, discussion work is a vital and lively classroom activity. Sometimes research into the subject can be undertaken in class. Clippings and/or notes can be taken from newspapers and political weeklies, such as *The Economist,* and from publications produced by government departments, pressure groups and political parties. An outside speaker may come to give a talk in the classroom, although it may be more convenient to visit the headquarters of various political institutions and listen to representatives on their own ground. TV programmes recorded on video-cassettes and cassettes with filmstrips may also be used as aids to learning.

Homework
Homework would consist of writing essays based on information gleaned from textbooks and various other sources, listening to radio and TV programmes, reading newspapers and political journals. There may also be opportunities to write projects as a means of covering certain sections of the course, as well as compiling a folder of press cuttings for reference purposes.

Textbooks
Harvey and Bather, *The British Constitution,* Macmillan, 1977.
Pears *Cyclopaedia* (annual): section on recent events.
R K Mosley: *British Government and Politics* (annual).
F Randall: *British Government and Politics,* M & E Handbooks, 1979.
C A Leeds, *Government and Political Studies,* in two volumes, National Extension College, 1978.
Sked and Cook, *Post-War Britain,* Pelican, 1979.
Padfield, *British Constitution Made Simple,* W H Allen.
Conservative Research Department, *Five Years' Work, Politics Today,* 1984
Jock Bruce Gardyne, *Mrs Thatcher's First Administration,* Macmillan, 1984.
D Coates, *Labour in Power,* Longman, 1980.
D Madgwick, *Britain Since 1945,* Hutchinson, 1982.
Philip Norton, *The British Policy,* Longman, 1984.
D Coates and G Johnston, *Socialist Arguments,* Oxford, 1982.
   Although the above is by no means an exhaustive list, it is a fair guide to the sort of reading material that students could expect to encounter.

What about O-level?
Since some of the factual material covered by the A-level course is inevitably to be found in the O-level syllabus, there is a small initial advantage in having done an O-level before tackling A-level.

However, taking O-level is certainly not necessary. Many pupils have not taken any kind of course in politics before embarking on A-level, let alone an O-level in the subject. In any case, much of the subject matter at A-level would be new even for someone who had studied the subject at O-level.

The syllabus
To find out exactly what is involved in the course that you will be taking, find out which Board's examination you will be sitting, and then obtain a copy of the syllabus from the Board, or your school, college, or local centre.

How you are assessed — examinations
Examination Boards differ slightly in their method of assessing pupils, and so you should consult the syllabus for the precise details. However, an exam involving two three-hour papers consisting wholly or mainly of essay questions would be a fair guide as to what to expect. In addition to essays, there could be compulsory questions requiring paragraph answers.

Compared with O-level, the questions tend to be much more searching and testing, and are frequently phrased in a less straightforward manner. It is important, therefore, to learn how to interpret the meanings of questions. Past papers in the subject are easily obtained from school, college, or Board.

The good A-level candidate is the one who writes well-structured essays clearly organised with logical arguments founded on factual evidence, using recent examples wherever possible. The examiner will not necessarily penalise the expression of strongly held political viewpoints, so long as the student shows he has been thorough in considering and dismissing with reasoned argument, opposing points of view. A sterile detachment from any political commitment is certainly not demanded.

Implications for careers and higher education
In higher education, many degree courses will have a strong politics content although clearly prospectuses should be consulted for precise details. Courses where politics could figure strongly, apart from a degree in politics itself, would be

sociology, social studies, modern history, international relations, law, economics, public administration, PPE (politics, philosophy and economics).

Many courses offered at polytechnics and colleges of higher education (eg higher diploma courses in business studies) could have a government section. Examinations for professional bodies such as local and central government will naturally have a strong politics content.

Apart from its value as a help in acquiring further qualifications, A-level itself should equip a young person with the skills and knowledge necessary to participate in community affairs, and in trade unions and professional associations. Furthermore, it should provide vital information for employment in such fields as journalism, social work, secretarial work, local and central government.

Psychology
by Peter Sanders

Introduction
In the first edition of this book, Denis Gahagan wrote: 'Psychology at A-level is one of the most exciting additions to have been made to the curriculum in recent years.' It is now 13 years since its introduction as a pilot scheme by the AEB, seven years since its debut as a national exam and we now have two A-level syllabuses (not to mention two ordinary/alternative syllabuses as well). Psychology is now firmly established as an A-level subject in a growing number of schools and colleges. In 1983, for instance, there were over 3,200 candidates.

Psychology is a subject in which ideas can change fairly rapidly, so in an attempt to keep up to date the AEB is in the process of revising the current syllabus. Unfortunately, the changes are not finalised yet so the information given here will refer only to the current syllabuses offered by the AEB and JMB.

What is psychology?
If, at a party, you are introduced to someone who is studying psychology, what are your immediate thoughts about this person, and the subject they are studying? Maybe you think that they are learning how to help mentally disturbed people, or learning how to judge personality by observing behaviour? On both counts you would be mistaken, certainly at A-level

238

and degree level. Although some psychologists practise as clinical psychologists most do not, and few psychologists would claim to be able to judge someone's personality simply by observing their behaviour.

The study of psychology involves a scientific approach to normal behaviour and states. Trying to evolve explanations for such everyday questions as how drivers can react so quickly to jaywalking pedestrians; how we remember long shopping lists yet forget postcodes; why children make mistakes when solving problems, and why we obey orders that we may not agree with. In the study of psychology a wide range of scientific methods are employed, from observation in natural environments to laboratory experiments, and it is this scientific basis which unites all those who study the various topics within psychology.

It is always difficult (sometimes it seems impossible) to apply the rigorous methods of science to human behaviour, but it is precisely this challenge which attracts people to the study of psychology, and why we find it so stimulating and exciting.

Psychology at A-level
The major aims of psychology at A-level are, assuming no previous knowledge of the subject, (i) to acquaint students with some of the major methods and approaches adopted by psychologists in their study of human behaviour, (ii) to introduce them to a wide range of topics of enduring and current interest for psychological theory and research, and (iii) to equip them with a number of skills sufficient to enable them to carry out their own psychological investigations.

As an A-level student, you will be expected to pursue learning through reading introductory textbooks, class teaching and discussion, and essay writing either as a class activity or as homework. You will be exposed to information and views which often do not tally with each other and are sometimes downright contradictory. This sense of conflict and debate is at the heart of psychology and you will be expected to weigh up the various points of view and their evidence, and then join in the debate with your own contribution.

You may be surprised to find that you will also be spending a proportion of your time – maybe a couple of hours each week – doing practical work. This is, for many students, where psychology comes into its own and the subject matter comes alive (often literally!). Practical work in A-level psychology is limited only by (i) the strictures of scientific method, (ii) ethical considerations such as not harming humans or other sentient beings, and (iii) your imagination. Students are usually guided through the various methods of observation, survey, case-study and experimental method employed by psychologists in a series of class practicals organised by the teacher. Examples of practicals are relating a vocabulary test to a reading test, examining stereotypes; maze learning, using insects. Although there is no requirement in either syllabus, many students also complete a project or some other self-generated practical work.

Which O-levels?

Both the AEB and JMB offer psychology at A/O level and although these syllabuses offer some preparation for the A-level, both A-level syllabuses are designed for students with no previous experience of psychology. The practical work involves some simple statistical procedures in order to analyse the data collected by observation, survey or experiment. It is not absolutely necessary to have O-level or CSE mathematics, though you may find they help. Many students who have little confidence in their maths ability tackle the statistical components of the A-level with ease.

There are many introductory textbooks available, though many are written for an American market. Two British books written specifically for A-level psychology students are Radford, J and Govier, E (eds) *A Textbook of Psychology,* Sheldon Press, 1980, and Dobson, C, Hardy, M, Heyes, S, Humphreys, A and Humphreys, P, *Understanding Psychology,* Weidenfeld and Nicholson, 1981. Another book which many A-level students find helpful is the *Handbook for Psychology Students,* available from the Association for the Teaching of Psychology, c/o the British Psychological Society.

Syllabus content and assessment

The two syllabus schemes are organised quite differently but cover roughly the same subject areas within psychology. The form of exam differs considerably between the two Boards, particularly the method of examination of the practical work component.

i AEB syllabus and exam

The syllabus is divided into three sections which correspond to the three papers in the examination:

Paper 1 material is intended to be covered in the first year of an

A-level course and comprises four sections:

Section A: Scope and methods of psychology (the aims of psychology and the different subject areas within it).
Section B: Cognitive processes (concerned with thinking such as memory, problem solving, perception, language).
Section C: Biological basis of behaviour (the role of the nervous system, human and animal behaviour as part of evolution).
Section D: Socialisation (the effect on both adult and infant humans of living in a society).

Paper 2 material is intended to be covered in the second year of A-level study and offers the student the option of pursuing one of two broad areas of psychology in more detail. Students must choose between:

Option 1: Comparative and experimental psychology. This extends the student's coverage of the issues contained in sections B and C of paper 1. Memory, perception, attention, language, problem-solving, the nervous system and its involvement in emotion, sleep and language, and the study of other species are all given a more detailed coverage.
Option 2: Social and developmental psychology. This option extends the material partly covered in section D of paper 1 such as theories of child development and introduces the subjects of social influence processes, eg conformity and obedience, attitude formation and change including prejudice; and the study of interpersonal interaction and behaviour in groups.

The examination consists of three papers, two written papers each requiring students to answer four essay-type questions, and the oral examination (paper 3) which covers the practical work. The candidate must have performed and written-up ten pieces of practical work which she takes to the oral exam. The examiner will spend around 30 minutes discussing the student's work with the student. The two written papers carry 40% of the total marks each and the practical write-ups and oral exam jointly carry the remaining 20%.

ii JMB syllabus and exam
The syllabus is divided into five main areas which are examined by two written papers. Any area may be examined on either or both written papers.

1 *Biological basis of behaviour.* This includes the structure and function of the nervous system, visual and auditory systems, and localisation of functions in the brain.

2 *Cognitive and linguistic development.* This covers the development of the human infant's perception, intelligence, thinking and language abilities, looking at the relative contributions of heredity and environmental factors.

3 *Development of social behaviour.* This area covers the evolutionary context of social behaviour, the role of parent-child interactions and play, moral development, and the effects of roles, peer groups and adolescence.

4 *Acquisition of knowledge and skills.* This section looks at the learning of skills (eg reading, kicking a ball), and the role of attention, perception, memory and individual characteristics of the learners.

5 *The design of investigations and the statistical analysis of data.* Here the student is given guidelines as to what practical work is acceptable and desirable. This part of the syllabus is examined by teacher-assessed practical work and one compulsory data-type question on each of the written papers.

The two written papers carry 40% of the total marks each, with the teacher-assessed practical work contributing the remaining 20%.

Subject combinations

A-level psychology can be combined with any other science, social science or arts A-level depending upon the career interests of the student. Those interested in paramedical or other scientific careers should make sure that they have chosen enough pure sciences as their other A-levels for their intended career. For anyone intending to study psychology beyond A-level, it would be useful to have maths and at least one other suitable subject, such as biology, at O-level.

Further courses and careers

Psychology would be a useful (but not essential) background for entry to degree courses in psychology, social sciences, and for such vocational training as teaching, speech therapy, occupational therapy, nursing, social work, etc. Psychology would also be useful for degree or higher diploma courses in business studies and management science, particularly for the options in personnel work, industrial relations, advertising, marketing, public relations and tourism. There are very few jobs where sooner or later you will not be dealing with people. An A-level in psychology would be no guarantee of success with managing, helping or persuading people, but would be an interesting background! Psychology has an increasingly important application in retail management, market research, secretarial work, police work and sales. Further qualifications for these jobs can be obtained through day-release or part-time study. Further information on courses and careers in psychology may be obtained from the British Psychological Society, St Andrews House, 48 Princess Road East, Leicester LE1 2DR.

Law
by Roger Garland

The study of law

If you were to ask most people 'what is law?' they would reply in terms of the police and the control of behaviour and possibly mention divorce and employment laws. In fact the study of law is a study of every aspect of our lives because it is law which provides the formal framework which guides and protects society. Rules of law are used by the state to make sure that we have such a framework and those rules are used to help solve arguments between people, to provide punishment for those who break the rules and compensation for those who are injured. Even the simplest thing we do can be subject to law but we do not think about it because it is accepted as part of the fabric of our lives. Everyone can understand that buying an expensive item such as a house or car involves law but the same rules apply when you buy an ice-cream or a record.

At A-level it is intended that you should obtain an insight into the way which some areas of our lives are governed by rules. You will also look at the ideas which lie behind the rules and at the people and organisations who have the job of applying these rules to settle disputes. The study of law will appeal to all who have an interest in people and their daily lives and wish to see how attempts have been made to resolve a whole variety of social and economic problems by the intervention of law. Each Examination Board offers particular areas of rules to examine but all require some knowledge of the court system and of the basic vocabulary of the law.

Because few students will have had any contact with law, it is necessary to start by obtaining a basic descriptive knowledge of the rules, but at the end of the course you will be expected to be able to comment critically on the material you have studied. One distinctive feature of examinations in law is the problem question where a fictitious situation is described and you have to analyse the situation by identifying the legal issues involved

243

and then explain which rules could be relevant. You must discuss whether some rules might not apply (because of particular factors, which you have identified) and then suggest what you consider would be the most likely result if the fictitious situation had been dealt with by a court of law.

Even at A-level the student of law is expected to be alive to the fact that in many situations it is not possible to be absolutely sure which answer is correct because all that can be done is to speculate on the most appropriate solution to the problem, if your analysis and view of the situation is acceptable. The essence of studying law is the development of an awareness of those situations in which it is impossible to be certain while at the same time developing a confidence in your studies so that you can identify relevant rules, concepts and principles.

If you have any interest in social, ethical or moral questions then law is a fascinating subject. The simple question 'Is it wrong to tell lies?' receives a different answer depending upon the particular context in which it is asked and it is fascinating to examine the historical, social, political and economic reasons which have led to different conclusions. These conclusions, however, have practical implications in our everyday lives because we need to know when we can or cannot rely on promises and statements made to us by others in buying and selling things, to give just one example. Another question, which raises practical social and moral issues to which the law has had to provide a variety of answers, is 'How far can I say what I like?'. If you study law you will discover that many of our everyday actions and expectations are ruled by an unspoken understanding of law. You will gain an insight into the problem of giving practical solutions to difficult social problems. You will begin to understand why it is so difficult to avoid acting unlawfully! If you are considering law as an option you can gain some idea of its significance simply by listening to radio, watching television and reading papers and magazines. Every day someone somewhere wants to make new laws, get rid of old laws, or reform existing laws because law is the means by which society formally seeks to change itself and its direction. A country's laws and its attitudes to the law are a mirror of the country itself.

Classwork

To do well in law requires you to do a lot of reading of textbooks and also of the original materials of the law. You will need to look at parts of Acts of Parliament, Statutory Instruments and Law Reports (the reports of decisions given by judges). You do need some feel for language because you need to appreciate how words can have different meanings in different contexts which have an impact on the solution to a problem. For example, in one case in 1930, a man, who had been found drunk on his bicycle was charged by the police with being 'drunk in charge of a carriage'. The man argued that his bike was not a carriage and quoted the old music hall song 'Daisy Bell' to prove it: 'It won't be a stylish marriage, I can't afford a carriage, but you'll look sweet upon the seat of a bicycle made for two'. He also pointed out that bikes were not subject to the toll charges for carriages under a variety of Turnpike Acts. However, the judge said that the man was guilty because under the Licensing Acts a bike was a carriage because it was parliament's intention to prevent injury to persons caused by drunks in charge of carriages and as the bike could cause such injury it was a carriage 'for the purpose of the Acts'. The man was fined heavily though he was not sent to prison because it was his first such offence.

You will probably be given lectures on each of the main areas of the syllabus which will be followed up by discussion of the problems in those areas with sample problem and essay questions being given for discussion. You should be given a lot of practice in writing answers because the technique of answering law questions, whether essays or problems, is important. You should also visit courts and tribunals in your area.

It is not necessary to have studied law at O-level. Indeed, the O-level syllabus tends to be very wide and is essentially descriptive. If you have done O-level law it will help in the first four or five weeks of the A-level course but it is certainly not a requirement to have done it.

Examinations

At the moment four Boards (AEB, JMB, Oxford, WJEC) offer A-level law. London will be offering the subject for examination from 1986. All have a two-paper format with a general paper 1 and specific paper 2. In paper 1 the commonly prescribed general matters concern the role of judges, the nature of legislation and case law, courts and tribunals, the legal profession and its services and an introduction to basic legal concepts such as corporate personality, ownership, possession, tort and contract. The Oxford syllabus is much more defined in paper 1 as it concentrates on the legal system. In paper 2 the Boards differ. The London paper 2 requires a more general coverage than the other Boards but all of them require consideration of specifically defined areas of substantive law. The areas of contract and criminal law figure with several Boards but the areas of civil liberties and police powers are also popular with the Boards. Employment features in the Welsh Board's list of optional areas and can be covered in the new London syllabus. The most distinctive paper 2 syllabus is that of the AEB which sets prescribed texts for analysis and examination. The best thing is to obtain a copy of the syllabus from the Board or your school, college or local centre and to obtain copies of examination papers. There is a wide choice so it is best to be well informed.

All the Boards use examinations only for assessment with no elements of teacher or other continuous assessment. Marking is done by a team of examiners at each Board and the only general comment is that there have been fewer A grades in recent years but if you study law that could change!

Further courses and careers

Law is not an essential subject for any degree course but is particularly useful if you intend to study business studies, the social sciences, and of course law itself. Law was not always accepted for matriculation purposes by the JMB universities, but now that JMB is offering an A-level in the subject, that view has changed. If you wish to study for a law degree at a particular university or polytechnic you would be wise to check with the admissions staff about their attitude to A-level law. This does vary and in the past some of the more traditional university law departments have preferred students to start law fresh at university level.

If you intend to follow a career where the law is of importance, such as accountancy, social work, local government, the Civil Service, insurance, banking and building society work, then A-level law is an extremely useful foundation to your later professional studies because it will have offered you a valuable perspective and true understanding of the relationship between rules and the underlying principles.

Sociology
by Tony Marks

The nature of sociology

Sociology is a subject which attempts to look at what people in society do from an objective, some would say scientific, point of view. This is the case with a number of social sciences such as psychology, economics and social anthropology. On investigation, the distinctions between the disciplines are often blurred. Sociology for the most part is concerned with the analysis of advanced industrial societies like our own. The commonplace as well as the unusual, the everyday, unobjectionable social processes and social problems are, in principle at any rate, of equal interest to sociologists. In particular, sociologists examine the social structure and look at the recurrent and persistent patterns of social behaviour in complex societies.

The contrast between natural and sociological explanations is a common focus. Students may find themselves confronting questions such as: Is there a maternal instinct? Is intelligence inherited? Is it human nature for there to be leaders and led? Are racial differences a product of biology or society?

There is no one set of generally preferred answers to these and other questions. What is valued by examiners and others is an ability to assess evidence and promote a case. Students are not tested on how they would like the world to be — social scientists have no greater moral correctness than anyone else — but on their grasp of a sociological understanding of societies. While students who may have strong political or religious affiliations are sometimes attracted to sociology, they are just as likely to be required to confront inconvenient facts as other students. Such students are just as welcome as any others and can offer a different perspective in class discussion.

Although originally more concerned with complex societies, increasing attention is now being focused on the analysis of underdeveloped or Third World societies and their relationships with the richer societies of western countries and socialist societies. This orientation is evident in the AEB syllabus and is perhaps most obvious in the Cambridge Examination Board's scheme.

Different Examination Boards and their requirements

The Associated Examining Board has the bulk of A-level

candidates in sociology. The other Examination Boards with A-level schemes in sociology are the Joint Matriculation Board, the Oxford Delegacy of Local Examinations, the University of London Examination Board and the University of Cambridge Local Examinations Syndicate.

Since its inception in the middle of the sixties, GCE A-level sociology has grown very rapidly to the point where approximately 18,000 candidate entries were received in 1983.

The A-level syllabus

All the A-level schemes devote considerable attention to the problems of theory and method. The nature of human beings and their relationships with society are central concerns, together with a discussion on how far these processes can be revealed by different methods of investigation. A recurrent theme in sociology at this level is the lack of agreement between sociologists on a number of fundamental issues. This does not mean there is no sociology as such. In sociology as in the study of history or literature or indeed most subjects, the student is confronted by many different, sometimes contradictory, assumptions of writers in the field; these differences are highlighted rather than swept under the carpet to promote a spurious unity. Consideration of these issues is more prominent in sociology than in many A-level subjects.

Syllabus demands do vary, but not dramatically, and students are advised to contact the various Boards in order to obtain syllabuses, chief examiners' reports and perhaps most useful, previous examination papers. It would also be useful to read *Sociology — the choice at A-level* edited by G Whitty and D Gleeson. Students and teachers might also benefit from looking at copies of the *Social Science Teacher*.

Coursework

Some branches of sociology are heavily reliant on a variety of social statistics. Candidates are not, however, required to have a detailed knowledge of statistical techniques appropriate to social investigation. An ability to comprehend tables, graphs and other stimulus material is nevertheless important. Students who do possess a relatively sophisticated grasp of statistical procedures may well find this an advantage.

The most important capacity needed by a student of A-level sociology is the ability to read a good deal. There is no single textbook which dominates even one of the syllabuses. Successful students need to be familiar with a variety of material and it is helpful if this includes a quality newspaper and journals such as *New Society* as well as specifically sociological writings. Class discussion will also form an important part of the course at most schools and colleges.

Unlike many A-level students, a substantial number of sociology students have little or no previous experience of the discipline. Some will, of course, have studied sociology at O-level or a CSE social studies course for example. While the study of sociology and related subjects at lower levels in the education hierarchy can be helpful, it is by no means essential. Sociology students are unlikely to be involved in orthodox laboratory work but could find themselves in a laboratory situation or in other, natural social research situations. This might be in school or college, or be outside educational institutions altogether, and might include their own homes. Guest speakers, visits and various audio-visual devices feature quite often in teaching programmes. It is clear, however, that a good deal of studying — reading for the most part — is a high priority for most students.

Examinations

Assessment varies between the Boards but they all have a mixture of traditional essay questions and/or more structured essays and/or the interpretation of stimulus material of various kinds. No nationally available courses permit the presentation of a research project or coursework as part of the assessment.

Subject combinations

Sociology can be taken with a range of other A-levels. It is often combined with English or history or geography or economics. It may blend well with a foreign language, particularly as many language courses now cover the social system and social institutions in the country concerned. Sociology may also be taken as a third A-level with two other science subjects. While this has to be balanced against the narrowing of scientific options it has obvious relevance to paramedical and social services and management careers. Anyone wishing to study sociology beyond A-level would be in a better position with an O-level pass in mathematics or statistics in order to widen their choice of sociology degree courses and to extend that choice to include the other social sciences such as economics, politics, social administration etc.

It is not essential to have studied sociology at A-level to get into a degree course in the subject. Most courses take people with all sorts of A-level backgrounds, which, considering the nature of the subject, can only enhance their interests.

Further courses and careers

In its relatively short career as an A-level subject, sociology has gained wide acceptance as a qualification for admission to various higher education courses and to professional careers. Peter Neville has spelt out many of the details in the *Social Science Teacher*.[1] His conclusion '. . . A-level sociology now appears to be accepted as one of Britain's major GCE subjects. It has a high potentiality for higher education not only within the arts and social sciences but as a third A-level on many science and engineering courses . . .' is sufficient for our purposes. Apart from its general usefulness, sociology is perhaps especially valuable for students who are seeking a career in what some have called 'people processing'. Education, some hospital careers, commerce and local government are among the areas where sociology qualifications are especially relevant. Indeed, the professional training of many in the caring professions such as teaching and social work often has the study of sociology as a major component. There is little doubt that independently of any vocational relevance, the study of sociology, which challenges taken-for-granted assumptions about social life, is sometimes disturbing and often challenging and exciting.

[1]See: the *Social Science Teacher* Volume 10 No 2, December 1980.

Section 3
Appendices

Appendix A

List of contributors

Keith Barber, (BSc), is head of department of Environmental Studies at Impington Village College, Cambridge. He has been editor of *Environmental Education* and is currently Chairman of the National Association for Environmental Education.

Nova Beer is head of drama at Westminster College, Oxford. She was formerly drama adviser for Sussex, and spent several years as an examiner in English and drama. She is currently chief examiner for A-level theatre studies for the AEB.

Michael Brimicombe, MA, DPhil, head of physics and electronics at Cedars Upper School, Leighton Buzzard. Summer school tutor for the Open University (quantum mechanics). Probably the only teacher who has taught both A-level electronics syllabuses. Spent several years writing and revising electronics syllabuses at O-, A/O- and A-level. Author of an A-level electronics textbook and has developed a simple microprocessor system for use in schools. He is chief examiner for one of the Boards.

Peter Bryan, MA, is secretary to the Collegiate Board, Cambridgeshire Education Committee, and a senior examiner in A-level geography for the University of Cambridge Local Examinations Syndicate.

Judith Christian-Carter, BEd, MPhil, AIHE, is head of home economics and textiles at Theale Green School, Reading, and formerly president of the National Association of Teachers of Home Economics. She has written many articles on home economics and nutrition and has lectured extensively to teachers, as well as advising on and writing educational materials. She is at present chief examiner for O-level food and nutrition.

R W Dade, BA, BPhil, is head of economics and government at the Broxbourne School, Hertfordshire.

Robin Derbyshire, MA, is head of modern languages and deputy headmaster at the Ingatestone Anglo-European School in Essex. He is assessor in German for one Examination Board, and reviser in German for another Board.

Keith Dixon is head of craft, design and technology at Impington Village College in Cambridgeshire.

Roger Garland, LLB, LLM, is principal lecturer in law and senior course tutor in the department of business and legal studies at North Staffordshire Polytechnic. He has been a chief examiner at A-level for constitutional law, and is at present chief examiner in A-level law. He is a member of the Schools Council Social Sciences Committee and chairman of the Association of Law Teachers.

John Garner, BSc Tech, Manchester, FIHT, is senior lecturer in surveying in the University of Leeds and chief examiner for O-level and A-level surveying for one of the Boards. He is co-author of a textbook on surveying and has published several articles for professional journals.

Denis Henry, MA, was director of studies and head of classics at Stonyhurst College, Lancashire. He wrote on various aspects of classics, taught in secondary and adult education and was an examiner at A-level for many years.

Elisabeth Henry, MA, has been deputy head of St Mary's Sixth-Form College, Blackburn, Lancashire. She is a contributor to academic journals, and a book reviewer for *The Times Educational Supplement*, as well as a co-author of several books, especially on the tragedies of Seneca. She is presently writing a study of Virgil, arising from a Fellowship held at the British School in Rome.

Peter Holmes, MSc, FSS, FIS, AFIMA, is the director of the Schools Council Project on Statistical Education based at the University of Sheffield. He is the editor of *Teaching Statistics*, and is chief examiner in A-level statistics for one of the Boards.

David Isaac, BA (Oxon), MA (Warwick), MPhil (London), teaches European thought and literature at the Cambridgeshire College of Arts and Technology.

Alan Jamieson, MA, MEd, FBIM, taught history in secondary schools, a college of education and for the Open University, and was an examiner at A-level in history for two of the Boards. As a director of CRAC, he organises conferences and courses on a wide range of subjects concerned with careers education, educational change, and university and college entrance, and has written several books on history, the teaching of history (including *Practical History Teaching)* and on careers.

Deryk Kelly, BSc, is the leader of the engineering science project team within the department of education at Loughborough University of Technology. He is actively concerned with the development and examining of engineering science and was responsible for the production of a set of students' texts and guides on the subject. He is chairman of the Physics Advisory Committee of one of the Examining Boards. He taught physics and applied science for several years in schools, and was science co-ordinator in the Schools Council's Project Technology team.

Norman Laing, NDD, ATD, taught in secondary schools and further education colleges, and is now head of the department of art, food and fashion at Tresham College, Northants, and is chairman of examiners in art at A-level for one of the Examination Boards. He is a practising artist and designer.

Peter Lambert BSc, General Inspector, Business Studies, Birmingham Education Department. Formerly, co-ordinator of the CRAC Insight Programme. As head of business studies at Reigate Grammar School and an examiner for the Cambridge Board, he spent two years developing a new syllabus, examination and teaching materials in business studies for the International Baccalaureate and is now chief examiner for business studies for the IB.

Tony Marks, BA, is head of the division of sociology in the department of teaching studies at the Polytechnic of North London. He has taught sociology at A-level, and was chief examiner for sociology at A-level for the AEB. He is currently chief examiner for the Cambridge Local Syndicate, and for the Mode II/III examinations under AEB. He is co-editor of a textbook used on A-level courses, and has written several articles on various aspects of sociology.

A H B McClatchey, MA, formerly assistant secretary at the Oxford University Appointments Board and secretary, Dublin University Appointments Committee, gained industrial experience with Shell, Pfizer and Rank-Xerox. He is now Rector of Hartlebury, in Worcestershire, and is an examiner at A-level for one of the Boards, as well as being a member of the Schools Council's Examination Committee in religious studies.

Alan Mills, BSc, MSc, MBCS, is a senior lecturer in the school of mathematics and computing at Leeds Polytechnic, and a chief examiner of A-level computer science for one of the Boards.

Mary Munro, MA, Dip. Inf. Sci., is principal officer for guidance with Cambridgeshire Careers Service. Formerly a mathematics lecturer at the Cambridgeshire College of Arts and Technology, she has also worked on various mathematical and computer projects. She has written extensively on careers, careers information and educational choice.

David Nelson, MA, CertEd, FIMA, formerly head of mathematics at Devizes School, Wiltshire and Ampleforth College, and is now a lecturer in the department of education, University of Manchester. For ten years he was a senior examiner in A-level pure mathematics for the Cambridge Board. He is a member of the Teaching Committee of the Mathematical Association and his publications include *Adventures with Your Computer*.

Roger Opie, MA, is now deputy headmaster of St Mary Redcliffe School, Bristol. He formerly taught at Henbury School as head of economics and as head of the upper school, and is chairman of the West of England Branch of the Economics Association. Recently, he has written a new book in CRAC's *Connections* series on *Economics*.

Mary Peach, BSc, PhD, formerly head of biology and senior mistress, James Allen's Girls' School, Dulwich, is chief examiner in A-level biology for one of the Boards.

Rex Pope, BA, MLitt, is senior lecturer in social and economic history at Preston Polytechnic, and chief examiner for A-level economic history for one of the Boards. He has contributed articles and reviews to several professional journals.

Ann Powell, MA, PhD, is senior lecturer in the history of art at Ealing College of Higher Education, London; chief examiner in the history of art at A-level for one of the Boards, and the author of *The Origins of Western Art*.

John Raffan, BSc, MA, taught chemistry and other sciences at Bootham School, York, Manchester Grammar School, Cambridge Grammar School for Boys and was head of science at The Netherhall School, Cambridge. He is now a lecturer in the Cambridge University department of education, fellow and tutor of Hughes Hall and a director of studies for Clare and Christ's Colleges. He is an examiner at A-level for two Boards (reviser for one), co-author of *Chemistry for Modern Courses*, chairman and member of several committees involved with various aspects of education, and director of in-service courses for teachers.

Peter Sanders is senior lecturer in social sciences at Wigan College of Technology, chief examiner for JMB A/O-level psychology, and senior visiting examiner for

AEB A-level psychology. He is also currently the chairperson of the Association for the Teaching of Psychology.

Jack Sanderson, MCIOB, is lecturer in building in the department of construction management in the University of Reading, chief examiner for building construction, A-level, for the AEB.

Tom Shipp, BSc, MIGeol, FGS, is head of chemistry at Workington Grammar School, Cumbria, chairman of the Geology Subject Committee of the Joint Matriculation Board, and part-time tutor in earth science for the Open University, as well as general secretary of the Cumberland Geological Society.

Michael Talbot, MCom, ACIS, is head of the department of business and management studies at Wirral Metropolitan College, and a former chief examiner in accounting at A-level for one of the Boards. After commercial experience, he taught accounting at all levels at a college of further education and at a polytechnic.

Mike Torbe, BA, taught in schools in Bristol and at a college of education in Sheffield. He is now teacher-adviser in English with Coventry Education Department, and chairman of publications for the National Association for the Teaching of English (NATE). He has written several books and articles on various aspects of education and the teaching of English.

John Turner, LRAM, was principal lecturer and head of the music department at Shoreditch College of Education, Surrey. He served on secondment as director of the special music course at Pimlico School, London. Previously he was head of department at two north London schools where he taught music to all levels. He began his teaching career as Captain, RAEC, and was principal lecturer in music at the College of the Rhine Army. He has been a member of the University of London Advisory Panel for music examinations at O- and A-levels. He has recently become increasingly involved as an examiner and adjudicator.

Frank Vigon, MA, was deputy head of Goyt Bank School, Stockport, and treasurer and research director of the General Studies Association. He has written and lectured extensively on the teaching of general studies.

Roger Wakely, MA, teaches physics at The Haberdashers' Aske's School, Elstree, Hertfordshire. He is also involved in Project Technology, and is head of careers.

Some of the Examination Boards have asked that chief examiners or examiners should not be linked to the Board: this is the reason for the phrase that a contributor is 'chief examiner of one of the Boards'.

■■■■■■■■■**Appendix C**■■■■■■■

Examination Boards for the General Certificate of Education at A-level

*Associated Examining Board
Wellington House
Station Road
Aldershot
Hants GU11 1BQ

Joint Matriculation Board
Manchester M15 6EU

*Oxford and Cambridge Schools
Examination Board
Elsfield Way
Oxford OX2 8EP
and
10 Trumpington Street
Cambridge CB1 1QB

*Oxford Delegacy of Local
Examinations
Ewert Place
Summertown
Oxford OX2 7BZ

†Southern Universities Joint Board
for School Examinations
Cotham Road
Bristol BS6 6DD

*†University of Cambridge
Local Examinations Syndicate
Syndicate Buildings
1 Hills Road
Cambridge CB1 2EU

*University Entrance and
School Examinations Council
University of London
66-72 Gower Street
London WC1 6EE

Welsh Joint Education Committee
245 Western Avenue
Cardiff CF5 2YX

*These boards have arrangements for examining pupils living abroad
†These boards are now linked

Examination subjects for the General Certificate of Education at A-level

Every effort has been made to provide a complete list of subjects offered by the GCE Boards in 1985, but it is not possible to give here the actual titles of all syllabuses. Further details are to be found in the Boards' annually published regulations and syllabuses. The list does not cover special syllabuses for individual schools or groups of schools.

Other foreign languages may be available on request.

Some Boards offer more than one syllabus in some subjects.

Key		
	AEB	Associated Examining Board
	C	University of Cambridge Local Examinations Syndicate
	L	London University Entrance and School Examinations Council
	O/C	Oxford and Cambridge Schools Examination Board
	JMB	Joint Matriculation Board
	O	Oxford Delegacy of Local Examinations
	S	Southern Universities Joint Board for School Examinations
	W	Welsh Joint Education Committee

Subjects					Boards			
Accounting	AEB	C			JMB	O		W
Accounts, principles of					JMB			W
Ancient history			L	O/C	JMB	O		W
Ancient history and literature					JMB			
Archaeology		C			JMB			
Art	AEB	C	L	O/C	JMB	O	S	W
Art and crafts	AEB							
Art and design								W
Art, history of	AEB		L	O/C	JMB	O		
Biology	AEB	C	L	O/C	JMB	O	S	W
Botany		C	L	O/C		O		W
British constitution								W
British economic and social history			L					
British government and politics					JMB			
Building construction	AEB							
Business studies	AEB	C						
Ceramics						O		
Chemistry	AEB	C	L	O/C	JMB	O	S	W
Classical civilisation			L			S		
Classical studies								W
Communication Studies	AEB							
Computer science	AEB	C	L					W
Computer studies					JMB	O		W
Constitutional law	AEB							
Craft (design and practice)					JMB			

Subject	AEB	C	L	O/C	JMB	O	S	W
Design					JMB			
Design and craft (wood)	AEB							W
Design and craft (metal)	AEB							W
Design, communication and implementation	AEB							
Design/craft/technology			L			O		W
Domestic science	AEB				JMB			
Drama (see theatre studies)								
Dress	AEB		L					
Economic and political studies				O/C				
Economic and public affairs		C						
Economic and social history			L			O	S	W
Economic geography	AEB					O		
Economic history	AEB							
Economics	AEB	C	L	O/C	JMB	O	S	W
Electronics	AEB	C						
Embroidery	AEB							
Engineering						O		
Engineering design, elements of		C						
Engineering drawing	AEB		L			O		W
Engineering science	AEB		L		JMB			
English	AEB	C	L					W
English literature	AEB		L	O/C	JMB	O	S	
Environmental biology					JMB			
Environmental studies	AEB		L					
Environmental science					JMB			
Fashion and fabrics					JMB			
French	AEB	C	L	O/C	JMB	O	S	W
General studies	AEB	C	L		JMB	O		
Geography	AEB	C	L	O/C	JMB	O	S	W
Geology	AEB	C	L	O/C	JMB	O		W
Geometrical and building drawing		C						
Geometrical and engineering drawing					JMB			
Geometrical and mechanical drawing		C						
Geometrical drawing (building)	AEB							
German	AEB	C	L	O/C	JMB	O	S	W
Government and politics	AEB		L					
Graphic communication	AEB							
Greek		C	L	O/C	JMB	O	S	W
History	AEB	C	L	O/C	JMB	O	S	W
Home economics		C	L					W
Home economics/dress and fabrics						O		
Home economics/food and nutrition						O		
Home, family and society					JMB			
Horticultural science						O		
Human biology	AEB							
Industrial Studies						O		
Italian	AEB	C	L	O/C	JMB			W

Subject	AEB	C	L	O/C	JMB	O	S	W
Latin	AEB	C	L	O/C	JMB	O	S	W
Latin with Roman history				O/C				
Law	AEB				JMB	O		W
Logic			L					
Mathematics	AEB	C	L	O/C	JMB	O	S	W
Mathematics, applied	AEB				JMB		S	W
Mathematics, further		C	L	O/C	JMB	O		
Mathematics, higher			L					
Mathematics, pure	AEB	C	L		JMB	O	S	W
Mathematics, pure and applied	AEB							
Mathematics, pure with computations	AEB							
Mathematics, pure with statistics	AEB		L		JMB		S	
Mechanics, applied				O/C				
Metalwork		C			JMB	O		
Modern European languages (other than French, German, Italian, Russian and Spanish)			L					
Modern languages, other approved					JMB			W
Music	AEB	C	L	O/C	JMB	O	S	W
Needlework and dressmaking		C						
Oriental and African languages			L					
Philosophy	AEB				JMB			
Photography	AEB							
Physical science	AEB	C			JMB			
Physics	AEB	C	L	O/C	JMB	O	S	W
Physics and mathematics						O		
Political studies				O/C		O		
Politics and government		C						
Psychology	AEB				JMB			
Public and Social administration	AEB							
Religious studies	AEB	C	L	O/C	JMB	O	S	W
Russian	AEB	C	L	O/C	JMB	O		W
Social biology		C						
Sociology	AEB	C	L		JMB	O		W
Spanish	AEB	C	L	O/C	JMB	O	S	W
Statistics	AEB				JMB			
Surveying	AEB							
Textiles and dress			L					
Theatre studies	AEB							
Welsh								W
Woodwork		C			JMB	O		
Zoology		C	L	O/C		O		W

Book list
How to find out more

More information can be obtained from your subject teachers, careers teachers, and local careers officers, and from the publications listed below which should be in your school library, your local public library or in the careers office.

Careers reference books

Occupations 85: Available from Careers and Occupational Information Centre (COIC), Manpower Services Commission, Moorfoot, Sheffield S1 4PQ.

Working In: Available from MSC at moderate prices, this series of booklets prepared by COIC deals with a wide variety of professions and occupations.

Equal Opportunities: A Careers Guide, 7th Edition, by Ruth Miller and Anna Alston 1984.

Careers Encylopaedia, 11th Edition, published by Cassell, 1984, 35 Red Lion Square, London WC1R 4SG.

AGCAS Careers Booklets: 70 titles prepared by the Association of Graduate Careers Advisory Services and available from Central Services Unit (for university and polytechnic careers and appointment services), Crawford House, Precinct Centre, Oxford Road, Manchester M13 9EP.

Common Cores at Advanced Level, a report by GCE Boards, 1983.

Students' books

Decisions at 15/16+: A guide to opportunities for study, by M Smith, Careers Research and Advisory Centre (CRAC), Bateman Street, Cambridge CB2 1LZ.

Your Choice at 17+, by M Smith and P Marsh, CRAC, new edition, 1981.

Beyond School, by M Smith and P Marsh, CRAC, 1984.

CRAC-Daily Telegraph Careers Guides 1 Into Industry, CRAC.

                                                 2 Into the Professions, CRAC, 1980.

Jobs and Careers After A-levels, by Mary Munro, CRAC, 1983.

Higher and further education

The Compendium of University Entrance Requirements: Published annually by the Association of Commonwealth Universities for the Committee of Vice-Chancellors and Principals, 29 Tavistock Square, London WC1H 9EZ. Available from Lund Humphries and Co Ltd, The Country Press, Drummond Road, Bradford BD8 8DH.

Which Degree: Published by V N U Publications, 55 Frith Street, London WC1.

How to Apply for Admission to a University, UCCA, PO Box 28, Cheltenham, Glos GL50 1HY.

Degree Course Guides: A selection of 42 subject guides which analyse all the major subjects in depth (ie law, computer sciences, oriental studies, etc). Available from the Careers Research and Advisory Centre (CRAC), Bateman Street, Cambridge CB2 1LZ.

Polytechnic Courses Handbook: Published for the Committee of Directors of Polytechnics by Lund Humphries. Provides comparative descriptions of all full-time and sandwich courses in polytechnics and advises on how to apply. Copies obtainable from CDP Secretariat, 309 Regent Street, London W1R 7PE.

The Handbook of Degree and Advanced Courses in Institutes, Colleges of Higher Education, Colleges of Education, Polytechnics, University Departments of Education, 1984: Published for the National Association of Teachers in Further and Higher Education by Lund Humphries, The Country Press, Drummond Road, Bradford BD8 8DH.

Your Choice of Degree and Diploma, by Alan Jamieson, CRAC, 1985.
Sandwich Courses, 1984-5, CRAC, 1984.
Directory of Further Education, CRAC, 1984-5.
A Year Off, CRAC, 1983.
The Job Book, CRAC, 1984.
Student Eye, CRAC, 1983.
CRAC Connection Series, Links between school subjects courses and jobs:
    Economics, by Roger Opie;
    Biology, by Dr Alan Lansdown;
    Law, by Esmor Jones;
    Physics, by Richard Braun.